D A V I D   A .   F R I E R

❧

CONFLICT OF INTEREST
IN THE
EISENHOWER
ADMINISTRATION

❧

IOWA STATE UNIVERSITY PRESS / AMES

PROFESSOR DAVID A. FRIER is presently serving as a member of the Department of Political Science at Western Illinois University where he teaches both graduate and undergraduate courses dealing with American institutions. This book, which is an outgrowth of Professor Frier's intense interest in the field of governmental ethics, followed several years of study of administrative conflict of interest in the national government of the United States. The author holds the Doctor of Philosophy degree from Southern Illinois University.

© 1969 The Iowa State University Press
Ames, Iowa, U.S.A. All rights reserved

Composed and printed by
The Iowa State University Press

Standard Book Number: 8138-0535-X
Library of Congress Catalog Card Number: 69-18485

TO MY FATHER AND TO THE MEMORY OF MY MOTHER

ACKNOWLEDGMENTS

DAVID A. FRIER is presently serving as a member of the Department of Political Science at Western Illinois University, Macomb, Illinois, where he teaches both graduate and undergraduate courses dealing with American institutions. This book, which is an outgrowth of Professor Frier's intense interest in the field of governmental ethics, followed several years of study of administrative conflict of interest in the national government of the United States. The author holds the Doctor of Philosophy degree from Southern Illinois University.

THE IOWA STATE UNIVERSITY PRESS

AMES, IOWA 50010

frequent condition throughout the period of writing, they could always be counted on to provide a ready smile and a word of encouragement. Lastly, I would like to thank Miss Ruby Kerley, social studies librarian at Southern Illinois University, who spent countless hours over the past few years in helping me to locate the material used in this work. Whatever errors remain, of course, are mine alone.

DAVID A. FRIER

FLICT OF INTEREST
HE EISENHOWER
MINISTRATION

DAVID A. FRIER

)NTENTS

ecurring motif in General Eisen-
ver's 1952 presidential campaign
s his promise to conduct a moral
sade against "wastefulness, ar-
ance, and corruption" in the
eral Government. Given the no-
ety of the mink coat and deep
ezer scandals of the Truman Ad-
iistration, it was perhaps inevita-
that a Republican presidential
irant would come out squarely
inst such corruption.

rier's book, however, estab-
es that Eisenhower's great moral
sade was, in fact, a mockery
l shows that the standards of
priety enunciated by the candi-
e Eisenhower were quite differ-
from those applied by him as
sident. From the campaign slush
d of vice presidential candidate
hard Nixon to the vicuna coat
d oriental rug of Presidential As-
ant Sherman Adams, the story
s much the same. It was the ac-
unt of an administration charac-
ized by mighty moral pronounce-
nts, but vacillating responses to
crucial ethical problems it en-
untered. It was also the story of
"great crusader" whose insen-
ivity to the flagrant violations of
own moral credo is difficult to
concile with his evident sincerity.

▶

CONFLICT OF INTEREST IN THE EISENHOWER ADMINISTRATION

Throughout his book, the author also sharply castigates the American news media for its coverage of the conflict of interest disputes. "The press," Frier writes, "controlled largely by the more conservatively oriented interests, was not nearly so incensed by improprieties under the Republican Eisenhower as it had been by similar events under the Democrat Truman. This was true despite the fact that the Eisenhower Administration encountered more, serious conflict of interest disputes than existed under the administration whose 'mess' it had promised to clean up."

Frier feels that Eisenhower should shoulder most of the responsibility for the moral deterioration of his crusade in as much as the former President failed to provide either the men, the direction, or the example so necessary to establish that high degree of morality he sought for his administration.

Chapter 1

ENTER THE DEVIL

The choice of a prince's ministers is a matter of no little importance; they are either good or not according to the prudence of the prince. The first impression that one gets of a ruler and of his brains is from seeing the men that he has about him. When they are competent and faithful one can always consider him wise, as he has been able to recognize their ability and keep them faithful. But when they are the reverse, one can always form an unfavorable opinion of him, because the first mistake that he makes is in making this choice.

MACHIAVELLI/The Prince

FOR A CENTURY and three-quarters public officials, scholars, newsmen, and a host of others in the United States have attempted to define a vague, nebulous thing called "conflict of interest." Interestingly, *The Dictionary of American Politics, Black's Law Dictionary,* and *The Encyclopedia of Social Sciences* fail to list the phrase among their many thousands of entries. However, Bayless Manning, Professor of Law at Yale University and author of the most definitive work on federal conflict of interests laws, states simply that a conflict of interest exists when a government employee's public responsibility clashes, or appears to clash, with his private economic affairs.[1] No administration in American history has been completely free of this phenomenon, and some, notably those of Grant and Harding, were riddled with such notorious cases as the Credit Mobilier and Teapot Dome. Certainly, it appears true, as Charles Evans Hughes once remarked, that "guilt is personal and knows no party."[2]

In its narrowest and perhaps crudest sense, conflict of interest

[1] Bayless Manning, *Federal Conflict of Interest Law* (Cambridge: Harvard University Press, 1964), p. 3. See also The Association of the Bar of the City of New York, *Conflict of Interest and Federal Service* (Cambridge: Harvard University Press, 1960), p. 3.

[2] Quoted from Jules Abels, *The Truman Scandals* (Chicago: Henry Regnery Company, 1956), p. 307.

3

refers to a set of circumstances in which a public official uses his
government position, either overtly or covertly, in such a way as to
achieve personal monetary gain. In its broadest sense, it refers to
any situation in which an official's public responsibility and private
interests conflict and does not suggest that the clash has been resolved to the advantage of the private rather than the governmental
interest. Indeed, most of the presidential and congressional efforts
to deal with this phenomenon over the years have been directed
toward the elimination of these situations of temptation. On a very
elementary level, for example, a federal law or agency rule prohibiting an Internal Revenue agent from reviewing his own tax
returns eliminates temptation and, simultaneously, the possibility
of dishonest behavior. Moreover, such restrictions remove those
situations which so often appear to involve conflict of interest and
which tend to destroy the citizen's respect for the public service.[3]

Once, in discussing his code of ethical conduct, President John
F. Kennedy remarked that "even though a technical conflict of interest . . . may not exist, it is desirable to avoid the appearance of
such a conflict from a public confidence point of view."[4] Chief
Justice Earl Warren, speaking for a majority of the Court in the
famous Dixon-Yates case, argued in even stronger terms that the
conflict of interest law is "directed not only at dishonor, but also
at conduct that tempts dishonor. . . . To this extent, therefore,
the statute is more concerned with what might have happened in
a given situation than with what actually happened." He concluded that the conflict of interest law "attempts to prevent honest
government agents from succumbing to temptation by making it
illegal for them to enter into relationships which are fraught with
temptation."[5]

Historically, Congress has passed precious few laws in this
area, and those which it has passed have been, according to Professor Manning, "archaic, inconsistent, overlapping, ineffective to
achieve their purposes, and obstructive to the government's efforts
to recruit able personnel."[6] About the only general laws which are
applicable—none actually uses the phrase "conflict of interest"—are
those which prohibit a public official from dealing in his public
capacity with a private firm in which he has a financial interest,
from accepting compensation from a private source for services
rendered before a government agency, from acting as an agent for
a private concern in a proceeding against the United States, and

[3] Manning, *Federal Conflict of Interest Law*, p. 3.
[4] Quoted from George C. Wilson, "McClelland To Press Korth Conflict Probe," *Aviation Week and Space Technology*, October 21, 1963, pp. 26–27.
[5] United States v. Mississippi Valley Generating Company, 364 U.S. 520 (1961). See also Rankin v. United States, 98 Ct. Cl. 357 (1943).
[6] Manning, *Federal Conflict of Interest Law*, p. 6.

from accepting payment for assisting a party in obtaining a government contract. Even these statutes are virtually unused because, commonly, the offending official has been allowed to resign without formal charges being brought against him.[7]

This dearth of formal law often proves disquieting to many Americans, long conditioned to accept the notion that any evil can be eliminated by statute—to borrow a phrase from H. L. Mencken, that it is possible to "pass a law and save a soul." In part, however, this can be explained by the fact that conflict of interest is a phenomenon so subtle as to be beyond resolution by statute. Alexis de Tocqueville once observed that "there is no country in which everything can be provided by the laws, or in which political institutions can prove a substitute for common sense and public morality."[8] Apparently, President Johnson concurs in such a view, for in May, 1965, he suggested that the solution to the conflict of interest problem might lie largely in what he termed "the area of judgment, propriety, and good taste."[9]

When one speaks of conflict of interest today, then, he usually is not concerned with such notorious scandals as the Teapot Dome and Credit Mobilier. The officials involved in these affairs were scoundrels, pure and simple, and they were every bit as aware of this fact as were the investigating officials. Moreover, there has always been ample federal law to deal effectively with public servants who steal and bribe. Thus, what conflict of interest has come to mean, and what is primarily of interest to this study, is that vast, gray area which lies just short of illegal activity, which is often not governed by statute but more often by the less precise standards of personal ethics and morality. Indeed, rather than by federal statute, conflict of interest today is much more likely to be judged by the Kantian categorical imperative: "I am never to act otherwise than so that I could also will that my maxim should become a universal law."[10]

A cursory examination of the Truman, Eisenhower, Kennedy, and Johnson Administrations reveals that public officials have come to be subject to a rather strict code of conduct completely outside the framework of formal statutes. This code, developed

[7] For a general understanding of conflict of interest one should examine the following seven statutes: 18 *U.S.C.* 434; 18 *U.S.C.* 281; 18 *U.S.C.* 1914; 18 *U.S.C.* 283; 18 *U.S.C.* 284; 18 *U.S.C.* 99; 18 *U.S.C.* 216. See also Chapter Two, Bar of New York, *Conflict of Interest and Federal Service,* pp. 27–71; "Our Archaic Laws on Conflict of Interest," *New Republic,* September 12, 1955, p. 8; "Why Men Hate To Leave Home," *Business Week,* August 10, 1959, p. 36.

[8] Alexis de Tocqueville, *Democracy in America* (New York: J. & H. G. Langley, 1843), p. 126.

[9] Charles Mohr, "Johnson Orders Top Aides To File Finance Reports," *New York Times,* May 10, 1965.

[10] Immanuel Kant, *Fundamental Principles of the Metaphysic of Morals* (New York: The Library of Liberal Arts, 1949), p. 19.

gradually through years of trial and error and, though largely unwritten, generally has been sufficient to prevent a public official from using his office in any manner which would bring personal reward, from accepting gratuities of any kind from interested parties, from fraternizing excessively with any member of a regulated industry, from soliciting business on official government stationary, and from participating in government contract negotiations with private firms in which he has even a remote interest. In fact, any public official with the slightest degree of political sophistication should realize that when he persists in these activities, or any of a dozen or more similar peccadillos, and is "found out" by enterprising reporters or congressional investigatory committees, he will most certainly be forced to leave government service.

Officials so accused seldom leave their administration under a cloud of scandal, as was the case, for example, with President Truman's Assistant Attorney General T. Lamar Caudle. Indeed, offending officials may leave with a polite "thank you" note in hand, such as that received by President Kennedy's Secretary of the Navy Fred Korth, or they may depart with bands playing, planes flying, and a new medal for service, as was the case with President Eisenhower's Secretary of the Air Force Harold Talbott.[11] But leave they do. And, predictably, in the future, whether new Administrations be Democratic or Republican, liberal or conservative, such a standard of behavior will still be applicable—and, unhappily, probably be violated. Perhaps the great Roman Emperor Julius Caesar provided the guideline for the contemporary bureaucrat some two thousand years ago when asked why he divorced his beautiful wife Pompeia. "Because the members of my family should be free from suspicion as well as from guilt," he answered.[12]

There is little doubt that Dwight Eisenhower's first presidential campaign victory was attributable in no small measure to his campaign promise to rid the nation of conflict of interest scandals such as had occurred during the Truman Administration. "Ladies and gentlemen," candidate Eisenhower told a Knoxville, Tennessee, audience shortly before the election, "the purpose of those associated with me in this crusade—and my purpose—are simple and simply stated. We want to substitute good government for bad

[11] Secretary of the Air Force Talbott's conflict of interest difficulties are examined in Chapter 6 and Secretary of the Navy Korth's in Chapter 16.

[12] Caesar, it will be recalled, had divorced his wife Pompeia after her would-be suitor Clodius was discovered in the ruler's house. Since Clodius had gained his entrance by subterfuge—he disguised himself as a singing girl—there was reason to believe that the beautiful Pompeia was completely innocent. It is a matter of record that Caesar refused to testify against Clodius when he was tried for sacrilege. "Why, then did you divorce your wife?" the prosecutor asked. The great ruler answered, *"Quonium meos tam suspicione quam crimine indicio carere oportere."* U.S., *Congressional Record,* 85th Cong., 2d Sess., 1958, 104: 11248.

government."[13] Given the notoriety of the mink coat and deep freezer scandals during the previous Democratic Administration, the Republican Presidential hopeful could hardly be faulted for coming out squarely against corruption in government. The appeal is seductive, for everyone is against corruption in government, just as all profess hostility to sin. When Ohio's Michael V. DiSalle, for example, was asked whether corruption would be an issue in the 1952 campaign for the United States Senate, he replied, "I suppose so, but I don't know who's going to take the affirmative."[14]

The moral and ethical shortcomings of various officials in the Truman Administration, coupled with such things as the point-shaving scandals in college basketball and an alarming increase in the crime rate so forcefully brought to the public's attention by Senator Kefauver's crime hearings, had suddenly turned America's attention, once again, to the question of corruption in government. As author William Lee Miller so aptly pointed out in his splendid little volume, *Piety Along the Potomac,* Americans have long exhibited something of a perverse attraction to the notion that the country is going to hell in a handbasket, that its very moral fiber is gradually being weakened by greedy and dishonest bureaucrats in Washington, D.C.[15] And the American news media, so long suffering under twenty years of Democratic rule, was perfectly willing to provide the scapegoat in President Truman and his "scandal a day" Administration. Indeed, as late as 1956 *Time* magazine was still reporting that "the instances of wrongdoing in the Truman Administration . . . came as a flow of names in a record of corruption that threatened to poison the entire U.S. government."[16]

It must be readily admitted, of course, that revelations concerning officials in such agencies as the Reconstruction Finance Corporation and the Bureau of Internal Revenue gave the public more than a little cause for alarm. It was discovered, for example, that President Truman's military aide, Brigadier General Harry Vaughan, once accepted a $520 deep freezer in return for his helping David Bennett, president of a Chicago perfume manufacturing concern, skirt World War II travel restrictions. (The General termed the gift simply "an expression of friendship.") Similarly, Reconstruction Finance Corporation loan examiner E. Merl Young's wife Lauretta, a White House stenographer under Truman, received a $9,540 mink coat from a lawyer who represented several firms which had applied for RFC loans. Young eventually resigned

[13] U.S., *Congressional Record*, 83d Cong., 1st Sess., 1953, 99 (Part 3): 3094.
[15] William Lee Miller, *Piety Along the Potomac* (Boston: Houghton Mifflin Company, 1964), pp. 30–31.
[16] The Corruption Issue: A Pandora's Box," *Time*, September 24, 1956, p. 15.

his $4,500 government post in order to accept an $18,000 position with Lustron Corporation, a manufacturer of prefabricated metal houses and a firm which had been the recipient of some $37,500,000 in RFC loans. Even the Chairman of the Democratic party, William Boyle, was forced to resign after it became known that he had been instrumental in exacting over $600,000 in RFC loans for the American Lithofold Corporation.[17]

The controversies which Republicans generally came to refer to as the "Truman tax scandals" were, if anything, even more infamous than those in the Reconstruction Finance Corporation. John J. Williams, Republican Senator from Delaware, long regarded as an unrelenting foe of corruption in public service, was the first to uncover evidence which suggested that many of the Internal Revenue offices across the nation were riddled with, and in some instances headed by, corrupt officials. In one of the more extreme cases the Senator found that an $800,000 tax claim had been settled for a mere $1,000. Before the controversy died, the Commissioner of Internal Revenue had been charged with failure to pay some $116,000 in income taxes, the assistant commissioner had been indicted on the same charge, and the Secretary of the Treasury, John Snyder, had removed a number of Internal Revenue collectors, the most famous being St. Louis collector James Finnegan, and some 200 lesser employees.

In justice to President Truman, it should be noted that he did not condone these instances of improper conduct in his Administration, although he was reported to have called Senator Fulbright's report on the RFC irregularities "asinine" and the Arkansas Senator himself "an overeducated s.o.b." However, in an oft-quoted speech of March 29, 1952, President Truman told 5300 Democrats at a $100-a-plate Jefferson-Jackson Day dinner in Washington, D.C., "I hate corruption everywhere, but I hate it most of all in a Democratic officeholder, because it is a betrayal of all that the Democratic party stands for."[18] Moreover, it is a matter of record that he removed his Assistant Attorney General in charge of tax collection,

---

[17] A book which deals specifically with the "scandals" in the Truman Administration is Jules Abels' *The Truman Scandals*. Although the author is rather violently anti-Truman (for example, he asserts categorically that the instances of corruption in the Truman Administration were more numerous and more serious than those in the Grant and Harding Administrations), the book does catalog most of the indiscretions which occurred in the Truman official family. A better book, though it, too, uses a rather journalistic and sensational approach, is Blair Bolles's *How To Get Rich in Washington* (New York: W. W. Norton & Co., Inc., 1952). For a much shorter account of this subject see Alfred Steinberg, *The Man From Missouri* (New York: G. P. Putnam's Sons, 1962), pp. 404–8. For an exhaustive listing of the official improprieties during the Truman years see Fletcher Knebel and Jack Wilson, "The Scandalous Years," *Look*, May 22, 1951, pp. 31–37.

[18] William T. Lawrence, "Truman Announces He Will Not Run Again," *New York Times*, March 30, 1952.

T. Lamar Caudle (who, along with White House Appointments Secretary Matthew Connelly, was later convicted of tax fraud conspiracy), in order to expedite the investigation of the Bureau of Internal Revenue.

When this failed, President Truman retained New York attorney Newbold Morris, a Republican and a vigorous reformer, to conduct an extensive investigation of the Bureau. What followed, however, appeared to be taken from an old Mack Sennett movie. Morris began his investigation with a flourish by investigating his immediate superior, Attorney General J. Howard McGrath. And McGrath, who from the outset had regarded the Morris appointment as a reflection on his conduct in office, ultimately dismissed the New York investigator. President Truman then dismissed his Attorney General and thus brought an end to a rather dismal scenario. However, "what remained firmly in the public's mind," according to Truman biographer Alfred Steinberg, "was the fact that Morris had come to Washington to do a job and had been fired."[19] Thus it was that "mink coats and deep freezers" became the symbol of Democratic decadence in the Republican crusade to "clean up the mess in Washington."

Being against corruption certainly is a well-worked and frequently successful political strategy. However, when the General styled his campaign for the Presidency as a veritable crusade to return morality to the Federal Government, it seemed not unfair to have expected that, once in office, he would have demanded a most exacting standard of behavior from officials within his Administration. Certainly one would have hoped, indeed expected, that the ethical standards which would govern the conduct of these officials would have been well above the minimal ones established by the scanty conflict of interest statutes. Yet, it is the principal argument of this study that Eisenhower failed—failed not only to impose this rigorous code of ethical behavior upon the captains of industry who served on his so-called "team," but failed even to set the proper tone for an ethically strong Administration by providing it with a personal example of impeccable behavior. However crude the expression, the undeniable fact is that the pecuniary gains derived by officials forced to leave the Eisenhower crusade were meager when compared to the thousands of dollars worth of tax-free gifts which the President accepted for his Gettysburg farm.[20]

Moreover, it seems indisputable that the Eisenhower Administration was afflicted with a good many more conflict of interest disputes than was the Administration whose mess the General had

[19] Steinberg, *The Man From Missouri*, p. 407.
[20] For the most complete list of the gifts accepted by President Eisenhower see U.S., *Congressional Record*, 85th Cong., 2d Sess., 1958, 104 (Part 9), pp. 11246–57.

promised to clean up. The incidents under Eisenhower were, in addition, of a much more serious nature than those under Truman, inasmuch as they seldom involved relatively minor indiscretions of relatively lower ranking officials and secretaries, as had often been the case in the Truman Administration. To the contrary, the Eisenhower scandals involved officials such as the vice-presidential candidate, the national chairman of the Republican party, an assistant to the President, a member of the subcabinet, an Assistant Secretary of Defense, the top two officials in the General Services Administration, and three members of powerful regulatory commissions. "This record," editorialized the *Trenton Times Advertiser,* "silences every criticism of the hanky-panky of the Truman Administration."[21]

A recurring motif in this study, though certainly a secondary one, is concerned with the fact that the American news media, controlled largely by the more conservatively oriented interests, proved to be not nearly so incensed by improprieties under the Republican Eisenhower as they had been by similar events under the Democrat Truman. *Time,* which styles itself the nation's leading news magazine, displayed perhaps the greatest propensity to treat the various cases of corruption under Eisenhower with what Ralph McGill termed "the soothing syrup cure, the once-over-lightly hair singe, or the well-reasoned excuse and boys-will-be-boys touch."[22] Indeed, its coverage of the Eisenhower years would seem to validate Bernard Fall's remark that "if *Time* magazine had existed in the time of Galileo, it would have come out with the straight poop on a flat world."[23]

[21] Quoted from "The Failure To Lead on Moral Issues," *Democratic Digest,* April, 1960, p. 8.

[22] McGill's comments, which originally appeared in the *Atlanta Constitution,* were reprinted in Ralph McGill, "There Was a One-Party Press in the Talbott Scandal," *Democratic Digest,* October, 1955, pp. 16–17.

[23] *Daily Egyptian* [Southern Illinois University], January 19, 1966, p. 4. The September 24, 1956, issue of *Time* was a case in point. One article, "The Corruption Issue: A Pandora's Box," supposedly addressed itself to the charges of Republican corruption which had been raised by various campaigning Democrats, especially former President Harry Truman and Presidential nominee Adlai Stevenson. However, the article disposed of the six Eisenhower aides who had been accused of wrongdoing in slightly over seven column inches and promptly proceeded to devote over twenty column inches to an account of some two dozen scandals of the Truman Administration. The names of the Democratic officials were, without exception, set off in bold face type, whereas the names of the Republican officials were, without exception, in regular print. The article concluded with the remark that "Adlai Stevenson . . . must have suffered a considerable lapse of memory when he opened up his Pandora's box on the corruption issue." *Time,* September 24, 1956, pp. 14–15.

Chapter 2

THE INCORRUPTIBLE MR. ADAMS

If anyone ever comes to any part of this Government claiming
some privilege . . . on the basis that he has any connection with
the White House he is to be thrown out instantly. . . . I can't
believe that anybody on my staff would ever be guilty of an in-
discretion. But if ever anything came to my attention of that
kind . . . that individual would be gone.

DWIGHT EISENHOWER

IT WAS JUNE, 1958, and already Washington had begun its long
annual swelter in the heat and humidity of a southern summer.
It was steamy within the White House, too, but not altogether for
reasons of climate. Presidential Assistant Sherman Adams had been
under intermittent attack for nearly six months, when at last President Dwight Eisenhower came to the defense of his trusted aide. His
usual sincere self, the President told the newsmen who had assembled for his press conference of the eighteenth, "Anyone who knows
Sherman Adams has never had any doubt of his personal integrity
and honesty. No one has believed that he could be bought." And
as his statement reached its dramatic peak: "I personally like Governor Adams. I admire his abilities. I respect him beause of his
personal and official integrity. I need him."[1]

Reading his prepared statement from a packet of small cards,
the solemn President conceded that Governor Adams had indeed
been "imprudent" when he accepted favors from the Boston textile
magnate, Bernard Goldfine.[2] Nevertheless, he insisted, "a gift is
not necessarily a bribe. One is an evil, the other is a tangible expression of friendship." The propriety or impropriety of the situation, he argued, must be determined by an examination of the
circumstances under which the gift was accepted. "Among these
circumstances," he said, "are the character and reputation of the

[1] For the text of the President's press conference see *The New York Times,*
June 19, 1958.
[2] "The Administration," *Time,* June 30, 1958, p. 9.

11

individual, the record of his subsequent actions, and the evidence of intent or lack of intent to exert influence." Then came the President's plaintive pleading "I need him," which in the light of the events which had preceded it, was perhaps the President's most sincere and authentic remark. But better to examine the record and allow each reader to judge for himself.

L'affaire Adams began, not in the heat of a Washington summer, but in the bleakness of its winter. At the presidential press conference of February 26, 1958, Clark R. Mollenhoff of the *Des Moines Register and Tribune* asked President Eisenhower if he thought it proper that Sherman Adams had contacted the Acting Chairman of the Civil Aeronautics Board on behalf of a private litigant. He pointed out to the President that several congressmen had contended that the intervention was clearly in violation of CAB rules. "Well, again you are bringing up a thing I have not heard of," the President responded. And in the next few sentences, he proceeded to prove, beyond the shadow of a doubt, that he knew nothing about the incident. "Any time that [cases before the Civil Aeronautics Board] have anything to do with foreign routes that CAB has authorized, or refuses to authorize, then the President himself is required to make the final judgment," Eisenhower continued. "My staff would want to get any additional information that I need. So, I would assume it is so on that case."[3]

Actually, the case to which the columnist referred had nothing to do with foreign air routes, and anyone who had read the newspapers of the previous few days, as, no doubt, every member of the Washington press corps in attendance had, knew quite well that it did not. Mollenhoff referred to two letters from Sherman Adams to Murray Chotiner, acting counsel for North American Airlines, in which the Presidential Assistant suggested a way to delay the CAB's revocation proceeding against North American, an airline, incidentally, which operated exclusively as a nonscheduled domestic carrier. It is also interesting to note that Chotiner was the former campaign manager for Vice President Nixon, and two years before, had himself been the subject of an investigation by the Senate Permanent Investigations Subcommittee on charges of "influence peddling" in the granting of government contracts.[4]

The two Adams letters, uncovered in a public hearing by the Special Subcommittee on Legislative Oversight some two weeks earlier,[5] were first mentioned in a front page story in *The New*

[3] For the text of the President's press conference see *The New York Times*, February 27, 1958.

[4] U.S., Congress, Senate, Permanent Subcommittee on Investigations of the Committee on Government Operations, *Textile Procurement in the Military Services*, Report No. 1166, 85th Cong., 1st Sess., 1957, pp. 25–26.

[5] U.S., Congress, House, Special Subcommittee on Legislative Oversight, *Hearings, Investigation of Regulatory Commissions and Agencies*, Part 2, 85th Cong., 2d Sess., 1958, p. 525.

York Times on February 14,[6] and four days later the same paper featured a thorough discussion of their contents.[7] In the first of his two letters to Chotiner, Adams told his friend, "I went over carefully the North American case with the Acting Chairman of the Civil Aeronautics Board [Herman B. Denny]." Adams than advised Chotiner to appeal any adverse ruling of the CAB to the United States Circuit Court [*sic*] because Federal law prohibited any interference with an airline's operation before a final decision was given by this Court. Such an appeal, he speculated, might delay any adverse order by the CAB by "as much as two years." At least, he told Chotiner, "the Acting Chairman [of the CAB] pointed out that this was so in a somewhat similar case." In his second letter, Adams said only, "I have read your letters of June 30 and July 1. I am looking into the matter and shall try to keep you advised." The letters, which were marked "personal and confidential," began "Dear Murray" and were signed "Sherm."[8]

The February 19 edition of *The New York Times* had, moreover, carried Chotiner's explanation of the correspondence between Adams and himself. It was, to say the least, a unique interpretation of the whole affair. "Historically the Republican party has been the champion of the small business man, individual initiative in the free enterprise system," the California lawyer said. "In my opinion, the CAB appointees of the President were violating these precepts of the party, and I felt it imperative to call the President's attention through Adams, who was his chief of staff."[9] Yet, it was obvious that the real question had been completely ignored. As the Special Subcommittee on Legislative Oversight's former Chief Counsel Bernard Schwartz so succinctly expressed it, "Are we to assume that it is customary for the chief assistant to the President to go over a case with the head of an independent agency at the request of a lawyer for a private firm?"[10] Editorially, the *Washington Post* observed that "if the letters mean what they appear to mean, Mr. Adams perpetrated a gross impropriety by intervening with a quasi-judicial agency in an affair that should not have concerned the White House."[11]

Yet, despite the newspaper coverage, it was not difficult to see why the President knew nothing of Adams' intervention in the CAB proceeding. Ironically, the same edition of *The New York*

---

[6] Jay Walz, "Schwartz Says Mack Got $2,650 in Miami T.V. Case," *New York Times,* February 14, 1958.

[7] Walz, "Schwartz Cites Adams Letters on Airline Case," *New York Times,* February 18, 1958.

[8] House Special Subcommittee on Legislative Oversight, *Regulatory Commission Hearings,* Part 2, 1958, p. 525.

[9] Jay Walz, "Two Tell of Asking a Friend To Aid in TV Case," *New York Times,* February 19, 1958.

[10] Walz, *New York Times,* February 18, 1958.

[11] *Washington Post,* February 20, 1958.

Times which first revealed the existence of the two Adams letters also reported that the official White House plane, The Columbine III, had taken Eisenhower and a small group of close friends to George Humphrey's Thomasville, Georgia, plantation for a ten-day golfing and quail hunting vacation. There the most significant problem facing the President, it seemed, was the unseasonably cold Georgia weather. "It looks as though we will just sit around the fireplace for a few days and hope for better weather to come," Humphrey had said. "Certainly there will be no hunting for birds this afternoon." Press Secretary James Hagerty told reporters he assumed the President and guests would play bridge that evening.[12]

As the President's press conference "explanation" of Adams' CAB intervention ended, reporter Mollenhoff jumped to his feet in an attempt to clear up the confusion. "Mr. President, on that line . . ." he began. Then Eisenhower, with a display of cold anger, cut the newsman off abruptly. "I don't want anything more about that," he said.[13] Eisenhower's irritation caused most observers to assume that the President had not been doing his homework, i.e., that he had chosen to play bridge at Humphrey's Milestone plantation rather than read the newspapers and periodicals. However, *The New Republic's* T.R.B., who was growing "increasingly perplexed" by the manner in which *Time* magazine failed to report the many indiscretions of the Eisenhower Administration, had a somewhat different view. "We wonder," he asked facetiously, "does Ike read [only] *Time?*"[14]

Specifically, T.R.B. pointed out that the February 17 issue of *Time,* which carried a column on Bernard Schwartz entitled "The Unlovable Counsel" and which reported that the "doomsday rumble" of Schwartz' voice was reminiscent of Senator Joseph McCarthy, contained no reference to the Adams letters.[15] The February 24 issue, which contained a second column on Schwartz entitled "Lo, The Investigator" and which accused the "cocky law professor" of "flinging his innuendoes high wide and handsome," again contained no reference to the Adams letters.[16] Finally, the March 3 issue was a complete black-out, with no reference to either Schwartz or the Adams letters. Apparently, *Time* did not think that it was particularly newsworthy that the President's most trusted aide had been accused of meddling in the business of a powerful, and supposedly independent, regulatory commission.

Eisenhower's response to Mollenhoff's question simply revealed once again what the members of the Washington press corps had

[12] Felix Belair, Jr., "Eisenhower Flies to Frigid Georgia for Ten-Day Rest," *New York Times*, February 14, 1958.
[13] *New York Times*, February 27, 1958.
[14] T.R.B., "Washington Wire," *New Republic*, March 10, 1958, p. 2.
[15] "The Unlovable Counsel," *Time*, February 17, 1958, p. 26.
[16] "Lo, The Investigator," *Time*, February 24, 1958, p. 15.

long suspected. The President of the United States was less than well informed about the men and activities within his own Administration. Indeed, his innocence about happenings in his own house provoked a rash of jokes, most of which poked fun at his well-known disdain for newspaper reading. They ranged from one liberal writer's reference to the President as the "Kansas Hindenburg"[17] to such quips as, "Eisenhower's refusal to read newspapers stemmed from the fact that it made his lips tired." Whether humorous or vicious, the jesting did dramatize the problems of administrative control raised by the President's all-to-frequent unfamiliarity with the activities of his subordinates, problems brought caustically but properly into perspective by *The New Republic's* T.R.B. when he observed, "Eisenhower's ignorance shows the range of Adams' opportunity to operate."[18]

Less than four months after Eisenhower's rebuff of reporter Mollenhoff, Sherman Adams' name was once again on the front pages of the newspapers.[19] On June 10, 1958, an investigator for the House Special Subcommittee on Legislative Oversight, Francis X. McLaughlin, introduced evidence in a public hearing which indicated that New England industrialist Bernard Goldfine, a man who, according to one acquaintance, "collected public officials,"[20] had paid some $1,642.28 in hotel bills for Adams between November, 1955, and May, 1958. Specifically, McLaughlin produced photostatic copies of eleven of Adams' bills from the Sheraton-Plaza in Boston which contained such notations as "charge complete bill to Bernard Goldfine" and "entire bill to be charged to Mr. Goldfine." More importantly, however, the House investigator testified that John Fox, former publisher of the *Boston Post,* and several unspecified employees of the Federal Trade Commission had charged that Goldfine received preferred treatment before at least two of the regulatory commissions as a result of his close association with the Presidential Assistant.[21]

Roger Robb, attorney for Bernard Goldfine, told reporters outside the hearings room, however, that the subcommittee had simply allowed "wild accusations" to be bandied about in open session. It did "exactly what we said it was going to do," he said. It conducted a "smear session." Still, he conceded that Goldfine had paid Adams' hotel bills at the Sheraton-Plaza, but pointed out that the Stratmore Woolen Mill, one of the three Goldfine com-

[17] Margaret Halsey, "Beware the Tender Trap," *New Republic,* January 13, 1958, p. 9.
[18] T.R.B. "Correspondence," *New Republic,* April 7, 1958, p. 24.
[19] William M. Blair, "Adams' Bills Paid By Industrialist," *New York Times,* June 11, 1958.
[20] *New York Times,* June 12, 1958.
[21] House Special Subcommittee on Legislative Oversight, *Regulatory Commission Hearings,* Part 9, 1958, pp. 3484–89.

panies which had become embroiled in a controversy with the Federal Trade Commission in 1955, maintained a permanent suite there. He discounted completely the implication that his client had expected to receive political favors from the Presidential Assistant in return for his generosity. Bernard Goldfine and Sherman Adams had been "intimate friends" of some twenty years, he said.[22]

Adams, who was on a fishing trip to New Hampshire, was not immediately available for comment. Presidential Press Secretary James Hagerty indicated that he would have "no comment" until he had had an opportunity to talk with the absent angler. However, when Adams' return to Washington was delayed by inclement weather, Hagerty decided to issue a statement to the press. "Insinuations made yesterday that Mr. Goldfine received any preferred treatment from Federal agencies because of his friendship with Governor Adams will be quickly disposed of and proved completely false," he told the assembled reporters. When asked specifically about President Eisenhower's view on the Adams affair, Hagerty asserted that "he feels the same as I do—that the matter will be quickly disposed of and proved false." This Presidential view, formulated even before consultation by the President with his assistant, would change ever so slightly over the next few weeks.[23]

Upon his return, and following a conference with the President, Adams decided to break his self-imposed silence. Shortly after 4:00 on the afternoon of June 12, Hagerty released the text of a letter which Adams had sent to subcommittee chairman Oren Harris.[24] Reporters scrambled for copies of the document as television cameras scanned the crowded White House press room. The letter left many of the more experienced members of the Washington press corps stunned. After terming the insinuations that Goldfine had received preferred treatment before the Federal Trade and Securities and Exchange Commissions "unwarranted and unfair," Adams readily conceded that he had, in fact, allowed the textile magnate to perform a variety of favors for him. His defense, if indeed it could be called a defense, was that his interventions with the regulatory commissions were not intended as repayment for these favors.[25]

First, Adams admitted that Goldfine had paid his hotel bills at the Sheraton-Plaza. But, he told Harris, he had been under the impression that Goldfine maintained the apartment on a "continuing basis." Adams failed to mention, of course, that the photostatic copies of his hotel bills, already incorporated into the public record

[22] Blair, *New York Times*, June 11, 1958.
[23] Blair, "White House Sees Adams Maligned," *New York Times*, June 12, 1958.
[24] For the text of the letter see *The New York Times*, June 13, 1958.
[25] T.R.B., "Innocence Abroad," *New Republic*, June 23, 1958, p. 2.

as a result of the hearings, indicated quite clearly that he had been placed in a number of different suites during his stays at the Boston hotel. Apparently, the Presidential Assistant was under the impression that the Boston industrialist maintained there a "roving" as well as a "continuing" suite. He did, however, contribute one additional bit of information which the House investigators had missed. He and his wife had also been guests of Mr. and Mrs. Goldfine at the Mayflower Hotel in Plymouth, Massachusetts, the previous year, he told the chairman. Moreover, he said, they had been guests at the Goldfine home in Chestnut Hill on numerous occasions.

Second, Adams conceded that he made inquiries with two of the regulatory commissions on behalf of Bernard Goldfine. Late in 1953, he said, he called the chairman of the Federal Trade Commission, Edward F. Howrey, about a complaint Goldfine had received from the commission's wool division. In a subsequent memorandum from Howrey, Adams was informed that Einiger Mills had filed a complaint against the Goldfine-owned Northfield Mill for inaccurate labeling of fabrics.[26] Specifically, it charged that fabric labeled "90% wool, 10% vicuña" contained a substantial amount of nylon fibers. After an investigation by the wool division confirmed the Einiger charges, Northfield was ordered to correct the labels to show the nylon content of the fabric, as it was required to do under the Wool Products Labeling Act.

At the time the Howrey memorandum was written, however, Northfield had failed to comply fully with the commission's directive. "Mr. Hannah [head of the Division of Wool and Fur Labeling] advised me," the memorandum concluded ,"that if Northfield will give adequate assurances that all their labeling will be corrected, the case can be closed on what we call a voluntary cooperative basis." A second call to Howrey's office, this one from Adams' secretary some four weeks later, revealed that Northfield had agreed to comply "in every respect" with the requirements of the Wool Labeling Act and that the Federal Trade Commission considered the case closed. Howrey's memorandum was then sent to Adams' central files and the whole thing was reportedly forgotten.

But the affair did not stay forgotten for long, principally because the Goldfine mills continued to violate provisions of the Wool Labeling Act. In the spring of 1955, the Boston textile magnate had a second request for the Presidential Assistant. This time he wanted his friend to arrange an appointment with Howrey so that he might discuss the various commission charges against his firms. Adams told Representative Harris in his letter that he had, in fact,

[26] For the text of Howrey's memorandum to Adams see *The New York Times,* June 13, 1958.

arranged just such a meeting. "This I did and it was all that I did," he insisted. "I made no representations to Mr. Howrey, nor did I ask that he or the commission do or refrain from doing anything." It was only later, he said, that he learned that the mislabeling activities of the Goldfine mills had been of such a serious nature as to elicit a cease and desist order from the commission. "Mr. Goldfine never informed me of this proceeding, or asked me to take any action with respect to it," Adams told Chairman Harris.

Finally, Adams admitted that in 1956 he had asked the President's Special Counsel, Gerald Morgan, to determine why the Securities and Exchange Commission was investigating Goldfine's East Boston Company. In response to Adams' request, Morgan called the General Counsel of the regulatory commission, discussed the details of the East Boston controversy with him, and subsequently relayed them to the Presidential Assistant. The essentials of the case were, incidentally, that the Securities and Exchange Commission had taken legal action against the East Boston Company and its subsidiary, The Boston Port Development Corporation, for their failure to file the required annual financial reports. The alleged violations ranged over an eight-year period. "Morgan informs me that he did not disclose that it was I who had requested the information," Adams told Chairman Harris, "and further [informs me] that he made no representations nor did he ask the General Counsel to do or refrain from doing anything. When I received the information, I did nothing further."[27]

It is certainly not difficult to understand the incredulity which gripped the members of the Washington press corps. Whatever else they had thought of the Presidential Assistant—his personal idiosyncracies, for example, had earned him such nicknames as "Frosty" and "Rasputin"—they had generally accepted without question the fact that he was intellectually competent, politically shrewd, and above all, a dedicated public official of impeccable integrity. All of them knew, for example, that the man described by *Business Week* as the "hardrock moralist and conscience of the Administration"[28] even insisted that he be billed for personal telephone and postage expenses at the White House. Thus, they assumed that the Governor was both too smart and too honest ever to place himself in a position which would give even the appearance that he had peddled political influence for personal gain. Yet, it appeared that he had done just that. The keeper of the Republican conscience had been caught *flagrante delicto* in some highly questionable activities.

[27] House Special Subcommittee on Legislative Oversight, *Regulatory Commission Hearings*, Part 9, 1958, pp. 3591–93.
[28] "Favors Were a Mistake," *Business Week*, June 21, 1958, p. 34.

Obviously, the hero had feet of clay and, quite possibly, he had a head of clay as well. "Adams, for all his toughness and for all his experience, had at the very least made a political blunder so colossal and so boneheaded it would not be expected of a small-town alderman," commented *Newsweek*.[29] T.R.B. concluded that the Presidential Assistant was, pure and simple, not particularly bright. He had suspected as much, he said, after Adams had "pooh-poohed Sputnik as a kind of Democratic basketball and tried to sneer it out of the skies." After this latest revelation, however, he was convinced. "The man who had been running America was stupid," he proclaimed. "Only a provincial, a small-town yokel, a hick, could lack imagination enough to see the awful peril of his own exposed position, or sophistication enough to know about Caesar's wife."[30]

Surprisingly enough, the views of both Eisenhower and Hagerty remained fixed despite the many concessions made by Adams. Shortly after the release of Adams' letter to Harris, for example, reporters asked Hagerty if the President thought Adams' imprudence would jeopardize his usefulness to the Administration. "Not at all," he replied. However, Hagerty declined a reporter's request that he differentiate clearly between the Adams case and the seemingly similar ones which had occurred during the Truman Administration. Yet, while admitting that he was not particularly well informed about the improprieties under the previous Administration—itself an amazing confession for any Republican to make in light of the 1952 campaign—he did suggest that the difference probably lay in the fact that Adams and Goldfine were "old friends."[31]

The following day a White House reporter, one who had obviously done a bit of research in the preceding twenty-four hours, pointed out to Hagerty that a number of officials in the Truman Administration, including the President's military aide Major General Harry Vaughn, had accepted home deep freezers as gifts. He also revealed that the General had argued, in a statement issued through President Truman's press secretary, ironically enough, that the freezer in question did not involve influence peddling because it had come from "a dear old personal friend." Then, quite pointedly, the newsman asked Hagerty if he saw any dissimilarity in the Adams and Vaughn cases. "Certainly," the press secretary replied. What, exactly, was the distinction, the newsman asked. "If you don't know the difference, I do," Hagerty answered lamely.[32]

---

[29] "The Adams Case," *Newsweek*, June 23, 1958, p. 23.

[30] T.R.B., *New Republic*, June 23, 1958, p. 2.

[31] William M. Blair, "Adams Concedes Calling Agencies; Denies Pressure," *New York Times*, June 13, 1958.

[32] Blair, "Hagerty Refuses Reply on Reports of Gifts to Adams," *New York Times*, June 14, 1958. See also T.R.B., *New Republic*, June 23, 1958, p. 2.

The Adams letter to Chairman Harris, which purportedly
"laid the facts out on the ground," failed to end the controversy,[33]
in part because new discoveries by the press and the subcommittee
quickly outstripped the admissions which the Presidential Assistant
had made. Indeed, less than twenty-four hours after Adams had
admitted that Goldfine had paid his Boston and Plymouth hotel
bills, the newspapers reported that Adams had also accepted expensive gifts from the Boston millionaire. Included among the gifts
which the Assistant had purportedly accepted from Goldfine were
a $700 vicuña coat and a $2,400 oriental rug. Although the White
House refused either to confirm or deny the stories, Hagerty did
tell the assembled newsmen, for the third time in as many days,
"the President has complete confidence in Governor Adams."
Moreover, he said, the rumors that Eisenhower had asked for
Adams' resignation were definitely not true.[34]

Less than seventy-two hours after the vicuña coat–oriental rug
revelations, the subcommittee's attorney, Francis X. McLaughlin,
testified that he had discovered that Goldfine had paid one of
Adams' hotel bills at the Waldorf-Astoria in 1954. The bill, which
amounted to $267.05, included valet service, one long distance
phone call, and several local calls. It will be recalled that Adams
had previously justified his acceptance of the Boston hotel suite on
the grounds that he thought that Goldfine maintained the apartment on a "continuing basis." Inasmuch as the Presidential Assistant and his family had stayed in a number of different suites at the
Boston hotel, his explanation had, from the very outset, been
greeted with a good deal of skepticism. When it was discovered
that Goldfine had also paid Adams' bill at the Waldorf-Astoria,
where no permanently rented suite had ever been suggested, the
Governor's position became obviously untenable.[35]

Another witness before the subcommittee, attorney Charles F.
Canavan of the Federal Trade Commission, testified that he had
once recommended that criminal proceedings be instituted against
Goldfine, his son, and three of their mills for repeated violations
of the Wool Labeling Act. A Canavan memorandum, dated March
13, 1956, charged specifically that "the acts of the respondents . . .
were premeditated, and the violations . . . willful. In addition,
the magnitude of their deception, and the unjust enrichment of
the proposed defendants seems to justify a penalty greater than
merely a future restraint." However, Canavan's recommendations
were rejected by his superior, Harvey H. Hannah, in favor of a
cease and desist order.[36]

[33] Blair, *New York Times*, June 13, 1958.
[34] Blair, *New York Times*, June 14, 1958.
[35] House Special Subcommittee on Legislative Oversight, *Regulatory Commission Hearings,* Part 9, 1958, pp. 3595–97.
[36] *Ibid.,* p. 3658.

Such an order, Hannah argued in a memorandum drafted at the time of the controversy, "will undoubtedly suffice to protect the public interest at the present time." Hannah also felt, and certainly not without justification, that the allegations contained in the Canavan memorandum would be extremely difficult to prove, "beyond a reasonable doubt," in a regular criminal proceeding.[37] Hannah insisted, however, that he had never advised the Chairman of the Federal Trade Commission that the Northfield case could be closed on a "voluntary cooperative basis," as Howrey had maintained in his memorandum to Adams. "I didn't discuss with [Howrey] any way of trying to close the case or anything like that," he testified under oath to the members of the subcommittee. "That is [Howrey's] statement, not mine."[38]

But perhaps the most startling disclosure of this period, and one which proved to be particularly embarrassing to the Eisenhower Administration, concerned Goldfine's meeting with Chairman Howrey in the spring of 1955. At the conclusion of the conference, Goldfine told Howrey's secretary, in a tone clearly designed for other personnel to hear, to "get Sherman Adams on the phone." In the course of his brief conversation with the Presidential Assistant, the textile manufacturer said, "Sherm, I'm over at the Federal Trade Commission. I have been well received over here." There was little question, of course, but that the call was intended to let everyone know that he was on a first-name basis with Eisenhower's chief of staff. Hannah, for example, told the members of the subcommittee that he thought that Goldfine had made the telephone call solely because "he wanted us to know that he knew Adams."[39]

Suggestions for Adams' ouster increased significantly after these new disclosures. Peter Mack, Jr., Democratic Congressman from Illinois, called for Adams to resign, "not tomorrow, but right at this hour."[40] The Presidential Assistant was obviously in trouble. Finally, on June 16, Adams announced that he would appear voluntarily before the Subcommittee on Legislative Oversight. He would answer "every one" of the questions posed, he said.[41] The significance of his decision can well be judged by the fact that in his nearly six years as Presidential Assistant he had never appeared before any legislative committee, although he had had several opportunities to do so. Each time he had been invited to appear he had refused on the grounds that his intimate relation with President Eisenhower cloaked him with executive privilege. And despite the periodic grumblings by Congress, it displayed little disposition

[37] Ibid., p. 3676.
[38] Ibid., p. 3632.
[39] Ibid., p. 3634. See also "The Nation," Time, June 23, 1958, p. 11.
[40] Blair, New York Times, June 14, 1958.
[41] Blair, "Adams To Testify," New York Times, June 17, 1958.

to bring the matter before the courts by attempting to subpoena the refractory Assistant.[42]

Promptly at 10:00 on the morning of June 17, and accompanied only by his wife and the President's Special Counsel Gerald Morgan, Adams stepped into the caucus room of the Old House Office Building. He paused briefly to glance at the 600 spectators who were packed three and four deep, and marched swiftly past assembled newsmen to take his seat at the witness table. As Chairman Harris told the extraordinarily large crowd that he would "insist on co-operation," the Presidential Assistant placed a cough drop in his mouth, removed a paper clip from a stack of notes, and carefully arranged the papers before him. For the first time in his career, the President's *alter ego* was face to face with a congressional investigatory committee.[43]

Adams' testimony was interesting and, at least at first glance, convincing. In his introductory remarks he conceded, for example, that he may have erred in his behavior but insisted that "if there were any mistakes made, they were mistakes of judgment and not of intent."[44] Later he stated categorically that "no call of mine, no appointment that I have ever requested to be made, or any inquiry that has been made by me . . . has ever been intended to be made to affect the decision of any official in the Government of the United States."[45] He had, to be sure, contacted various regulatory agencies on behalf of his friend Goldfine. "But is there any member of this committee who has not made a phone call for a constituent," he asked most pointedly, either ignoring or unaware of the difference between his role and that of a member of Congress. He was convinced, he said, that his calls to the agencies had not given Goldfine any favors or benefits "that he could not have received had he gone directly to the agency involved and he and I had been complete strangers."[46]

Congressmen John J. Flynt of Georgia and John E. Moss of California made concerted efforts, with little success, to force the Presidential Assistant to concede to the obvious, i.e., that his telephone calls carried an influence second only to that of the President of the United States. "Do you realize that a member of a regulatory body might attach a great deal more significance to a call from

---

[42] Edward S. Corwin, one of the foremost authorities on constitutional law, has stated, "I know of no instance in which a head of a department has testified before a congressional committee in response to a subpoena, nor been held for contempt for refusal to testify." Edward S. Corwin, *The President: Office and Power, 1787–1957* (New York: New York University Press, 1957), p. 113.

[43] "The Administration," *Time*, June 30, 1958, p. 10. See also House Special Subcommittee on Legislative Oversight, *Regulatory Commission Hearings*, Part 10, 1958, p. 3712.

[44] *Ibid.*, p. 3714.

[45] *Ibid.*, p. 3715.

[46] *Ibid.*, p. 3717.

you than they would from a party litigant, from a party under investigation, from a counsel for such a party, from a member of this or the other body of Congress?" Flynt asked. "I think that poses a very appropriate question," Adams responded.[47] "When you call personally . . . isn't it your opinion that a reasonable person would conclude that you would perhaps have more influence . . . than the average member of Congress or the average official in the lower echelons in the administration?" Moss asked. "There have been times when I have had some doubt about that," Adams replied. "I don't want to be facetious, Mr. Moss. . . . I think [your question] is well taken."[48]

Robert W. Lishman, Chief Counsel for the subcommittee, insisted, moreover, that commission rules and Federal statute prohibited disclosure of much of the information Adams had sought to obtain. Rule 1.115 of the Federal Trade Commission provides that "it has always been and now is strict Commission policy not to publish or divulge the name of an applicant or a complaining party."[49] Title 15, Section 50 of the *United States Code* provides that "any officer or employee of the commission who shall make public any information obtained by the commission without its authority, unless directed by a court, shall be guilty of a misdemeanor."[50] Thus, Lishman argued, the identification of Einiger Mills as the complainant, in Howrey's memorandum to Adams, was clearly in violation of established commission practice and Federal law.

When confronted with such evidence, Adams simply pleaded ignorance. "I had no knowledge of the rules," he told the members of the subcommittee, "and I had no knowledge, certainly, of the fact that the information which I received was not perfectly proper. . . . Had I known that, quite obviously my decision might well have been different."[51] Later, however, the White House would contend that the Howrey memorandum contained no confidential information.

On June 18, Hagerty informed reporters that an investigation had revealed that several weeks before the controversial memorandum was written, Einiger Mills had declared openly that it was the complainant and had, moreover, notified Northfield Mills of that fact. Thus, he contended that the confidential status of the complainant no longer existed.[52]

Adams freely admitted that he had accepted both a vicuña coat and an oriental rug from Goldfine. However, he managed to

[47] *Ibid.,* p. 3723.
[48] *Ibid.,* p. 3726.
[49] U.S., *Federal Trade Commission Rules,* Number 1.115.
[50] 15 *U.S.C.* 50.
[51] House Special Subcommittee on Legislative Oversight, *Regulatory Commission Hearings,* Part 10, 1958, p. 3724.
[52] *New York Times,* June 19, 1958.

ignore completely the implications involved. The material for the coat, he pointed out, cost only sixty-nine dollars at the Goldfine mill, or substantially less than the $700 figure which had gained currency in the newspaper accounts. Apparently by the Adams rationale it was perfectly proper to accept a cheap vicuña coat but not an expensive one. Interestingly enough, only a few years earlier an official in the Truman Administration told a congressional committee that it was perfectly all right to accept a twelve-pound ham as a gift, but not a larger one. The oriental rug, Adams said, was simply a loan from Goldfine. In 1954, according to Adams' testimony, his industrialist friend decided that his old rug was too "shabby" to adorn the floor of a Presidential Assistant and asked if he could "send down" a new one. "But it is his property," Adams insisted. "He has always considered it such."[53] Later, however, an enterprising reporter uncovered an article in the December 28, 1954, issue of the *Washington Star* which quoted Mrs. Adams as saying that she had recently "purchased" an immense oriental rug.[54]

But it was Chairman Harris who wrung the most significant concessions from the Presidential Assistant. Considering the fact that the Arkansas Congressman had appeared to be less than enthusiastic about a vigorous investigation of the regulatory agencies only a few months earlier, his adroit questioning came as something of a surprise to many observers of the congressional scene. Perhaps, as *Newsweek* observed, Harris "was not unmindful of the great publicity windfall the Adams case had brought him."[55] But regardless of the motivation, in response to the chairman's questioning, Adams quickly conceded that appointments to the regulatory commissions were "cleared" through him and that he had, in fact, "recommended" Howrey's appointment to the Federal Trade Commission. Then Harris administered the *coup de grâce*. "Have you in your position, found it necessary to ask any Commissioners of these agencies to hand in their resignations?" For perhaps thirty seconds the Presidential Assistant sat in complete silence, as if stunned by the question. Then he turned to confer with counsel Morgan. Finally Adams replied, "If you insist on the question, I should have to answer it in the affirmative."[56]

The chairman pressed on. "In view of these incidents and the long-time relationship that existed between you and Mr. Goldfine

[53] House Special Subcommittee on Legislative Oversight, *Regulatory Commission Hearings*, Part 10, 1958, pp. 3716–17.
[54] T.R.B., "Consider the Facts," *New Republic,* June 30, 1958, p. 2. See also *Washington Star*, December 28, 1954.
[55] "Two Men in the White House: The Heat's On," *Newsweek,* June 30, 1958, p. 17.
[56] House Special Subcommittee on Legislative Oversight, *Regulatory Commission Hearings*, Part 10, 1958, p. 3736. See also *Newsweek*, June 30, 1958, p. 17.

and the position you occupy, do you think, Governor Adams, that in these instances that you overstepped the bounds of propriety?" Reporters noticed that the Assistant's hands trembled. He clasped them together and, finally, cupped them firmly over his chin. Much of the color had drained from his naturally ruddy face.[57] "Mr. Chairman, that is a fair question," he began. "Now, Mr. Chairman, I have no excuses to offer. I did not come up here to make apology to you or this committee. But there again, if there were any errors here . . . they were errors perhaps of inexperience," he continued. "Nevertheless, I think, to repeat, that there are lessons to be learned. . . . If I had the decisions now before me to make I believe I would have acted a little more prudently."[58] Harris then announced that the subcommittee would adojurn. But, for Adams, the ordeal had just begun.

It was an ordeal which had been repeated, with only minor variations, throughout the earlier Eisenhower years. From the campaign slush fund of Vice-Presidential candidate Richard Nixon to the vicuña coat and oriental rug of Presidential Assistant Sherman Adams, the story was much the same. It was a story of an Administration characterized by moral pronouncements and amoral responses to many of the crucial ethical problems of the fifties. It was also the story of a great crusader, whose sincerity seemed beyond doubt, but whose insensitivity to the flagrant violations of his own moral credo seemed at times beyond belief. Chronologically, of course, the Adams affair was toward the end in a series of conflict of interest cases. But it exemplified, perhaps better than any of the others, the gap between the verbiage and the performance of the Eisenhower years. Adams' fate shall be left to a later chapter. And so, to begin at the beginning.

[57] *Time,* June 30, 1958, p. 12.
[58] House Special Subcommittee on Legislative Oversight, *Regulatory Commission Hearings,* Part 10, 1958, p. 3738.

Chapter 3

THE POOR RICHARD SHOW

I had recognized from the time I became a member of the Committee on Un-American Activities, and particularly after my participation in the Hiss case, that it [was] essential for me to maintain a standard of conduct which would not give my political opponents any solid grounds for attack.

RICHARD NIXON

As THE Supreme Commander of Allied Expeditionary Forces from 1943 to 1945 and as the Supreme Commander of the North Atlantic Treaty Organization forces from 1950 to 1952, Dwight Eisenhower led the great crusades against Fascism and Communism in Western Europe.[1] In 1952 the General returned to the United States to launch yet another crusade, this one against a Democratic Administration which he charged was guilty of "wastefulness, arrogance, and corruption in high places." In accepting the Republican Presidential nomination in Chicago that year, Eisenhower told the assembled delegates, "You have summoned me on behalf of millions of your fellow Americans to lead a great crusade. . . . Mindful of its burden and of its decisive importance, I accept your summons, I will lead this crusade."[2]

However, the crusade against the deep freezers and mink coats of the Truman Administration began in a less than inspirational manner. Indeed, the General's initial campaign efforts were such as to provoke the *New York World Telegram and Sun*, a fiercely pro-Eisenhower Scripps-Howard newspaper, to lament editorially that Eisenhower's campaign was "running like a dry creek." If he had any thoughts of winning the Presidency, the editorial con-

[1] Dwight D. Eisenhower, *Crusade in Europe* (Garden City, New York: Doubleday and Company, Inc., 1948). See also Dwight D. Eisenhower, *The White House Years: Mandate For Change, 1953–1956* (Garden City, New York: Doubleday and Company, Inc., 1963), pp. 3–25.

[2] For the text of Eisenhower's acceptance speech see *The New York Times*, July 12, 1952.

tinued, he would have "to come out swinging."[3] Apparently the widely quoted editorial had its impact upon Republicans, for a little more than a week after its publication Eisenhower's Executive Assistant, Arthur H. Vandenberg, announced that shortly after Labor Day Eisenhower would launch a "two fisted attack" on the "mess in Washington." The General "will pull no punches," Vandenberg promised.[4]

As Vandenberg predicted, early in September a new militancy appeared in Eisenhower's campaign speeches. Their dominant motif, especially those delivered in his swing through the South, was "corruption," or as the General preferred, "the mess in Washington."[5] A "mess," he told a Tampa audience, had been defined in one dictionary as "a confused, inharmonious, disagreeable mixture of things; a medley, a hodgepodge, hence a situation resulting from blundering or from misunderstanding; a state of confusion, embarrassment, a muddle, a botch." Then looking up from his prepared text, he told the assembled throng, "Ladies and Gentlemen, that's the meaning I have of it."[6]

Earlier, he told an Atlanta audience, "This mess is not a one-agency mess or a one-bureau mess or a one-department mess—it is a top-to-bottom mess."[7] With a harshness seemingly out of character for the General, he heaped ridicule and scorn upon the officials in the Truman Administration, the very officials who had been responsible for his own mercurial military rise. "This mess," he concluded, "is the inevitable and sure-fire result of an Administration by too many men who are too small for their jobs, too big for their breeches, and too long in power."[8]

But Eisenhower's most vitriolic attack on the Democratic Administration came a week later in Indianapolis, Indiana. Speaking to an audience composed largely of staunch midwestern Republicans, the Presidential nominee remarked parenthetically that as late as 1950 he had no thought of entering politics. "But no American can stand to one side while his country becomes the prey of fearmongers, quack doctors and barefaced looters," he said. "An American doesn't twiddle his thumbs while his garden is wrecked by a crowd of vandals and his house invaded by a gang of robbers.

[3] *New York World Telegram and Sun*, August 25, 1952, p. 15.
[4] Leo Egan, "General To Expose Washington Mess," *New York Times*, September 2, 1952.
[5] It is interesting to note that when Emmet John Hughes joined the Eisenhower campaign staff in mid-September of 1952, he flatly refused to incorporate the word "crusade" or the phrase "mess in Washington" into any of the campaign speeches he wrote. Such terms were, he argued, "petty, self-righteous, and extravagant." Emmet John Hughes, *The Ordeal of Power* (New York: Atheneum, 1963), p. 30.
[6] For the text of the Tampa speech see *The New York Times*, September 4, 1952.
[7] For the text of the Atlanta speech see *ibid.*, September 3, 1952.
[8] *Ibid.*

He goes into action . . . by getting into politics—fast and hard."[9] With allowances for the typical excesses of campaign oratory, such remarks are questionable in taste and hardly in keeping with the basic tenets of a moral crusade. Nonetheless, they were character- istic of the style and tone of Eisenhower's post-Labor Day cam- paign.

Early September also found the GOP Vice Presidential can- didate, Richard Nixon, vigorously attacking the demon corruption, as well as the customary companion demons of communism, con- trols, and Korea. In a September 3 speech in the textile town of Sanford, Maine, Nixon asserted that for every scandal uncovered in the Truman Administration "there are ten which haven't yet been uncovered" and promised the throngs of well-wishers who had gathered into the War Memorial Gymnasium that "the Administra- tion has not heard the last of charges of corruption."[10] Ironically, neither had Nixon. Within two weeks, the Democrats would level almost identical charges against the Republicans and their Vice Presidential candidate.

Nonetheless, there was little doubt that the Republicans had hit a responsive chord in their attacks on the so-called mess in Washington. Eisenhower's September 2 speech in Miami, for ex- ample, was liberally laced with enthusiastic shouts from his listen- ers of "yahoo" and "pour it on."[11] It has long been thought, of course, that there is little risk and much potential gain to be de- rived for American politicians who are solidly on the side of motherhood, the flag, and free enterprise and just as solidly against corruption. As William Costello pointed out in his "unauthorized" biography of Richard Nixon, "being against corruption, anybody's corruption, has all the orthodoxy and fire of damning war from a bomb shelter."[12] Such were the political portents and realities of the Eisenhower crusade for morality in government.

By mid-September it was clear that Eisenhower's promise to clean up the mess in Washington was being received with increas- ing enthusiasm throughout the United States. The Gallup Poll reported fifty-one percent of the American voters committed to vote Republican, forty-two percent committed to vote Democratic, and seven percent undecided. Of special significance, moreover, was the fact that this Republican advantage was fully seven percent stronger than the one enjoyed by Thomas Dewey at a similar stage in the 1948 Presidential race.[13] Though restrained by a wariness

[9] For the text of the Indianapolis speech see *ibid.*, September 10, 1952.
[10] John Fenton, "Uncovered Graft Charged by Nixon," *New York Times*, September 4, 1952.
[11] W. H. Lawrence, "Eisenhower Hailed in Tour of South," *New York Times*, September 3, 1952.
[12] William Costello, *The Facts About Nixon: An Unauthorized Biography* (New York: The Viking Press, 1960), p. 103.
[13] "Ike's Dilemma," *Newsweek*, September 29, 1952, p. 24.

wrought by twenty years outside the White House, the lean and hungry GOP was beginning to savor the scent of victory.

But on the morning of September 18, the *New York Post* charged in a lead story that a "millionaires club" composed of a number of prosperous California businessmen had paid GOP Vice Presidential candidate Richard Nixon some $16,000 to $17,000 since he was elected to the United States Senate in 1950. The disburser of the fund, Pasadena corporation attorney and investment banker Dana C. Smith, conceded that the *Post* story was "essentially" correct but emphasized that the fund had not been paid directly to the Senator and that it had been used exclusively for such things as stamps, phone calls, trips, and Christmas cards. None of it, he said, had gone for the Senator's "personal use."[14]

The *Post* story quoted Smith as saying that Nixon's salary was "pitifully inadequate" to do "the kind of job he wanted to do and that we wanted him to do." The job that Smith and his associates wanted the junior Senator to perform, it seemed, was "a selling job to the American people in behalf of private enterprise and integrity in government." "Dick is the outstanding salesman for free enterprise in the Senate," Smith said. "[Senator] Knowland is almost unknown. [Governor] Warren has too much the social point of view for the people behind Dick. We couldn't go for Warren, but Dick did just what we wanted him to do."[15] Apparently private enterprise, as understood by the millionaires club, meant opposition to public housing, opposition to labor legislation, protection for tax loopholes for the oil industry, abolition of rent controls, etc. Certainly, Nixon's voting record, both as a Representative and as a Senator, had not varied appreciably from this view of private enterprise.[16]

Yet, despite the fact that the story raised a rather serious question of propriety about a Vice Presidential candidate, it received, at least for the first forty-eight hours, about as little newspaper coverage as had the fund itself in the two years of its existence. A survey conducted by Jean Begeman in *The New Republic,* for instance, revealed that of the some seventy representative newspapers he examined, only seven had chosen to print the story on the first day (only three of these on the front page) and many had suppressed it on the second day as well.[17]

Among the factors contributing to the journalistic silence, no doubt, was the unusual handling of the story by the Associated Press. Although it was authorized to reprint any part of the *Post*'s

[14] Quoted from the *St. Louis Post-Dispatch,* September 18, 1952.
[15] *Ibid.*
[16] "Richard Nixon's Secret Income," *New Republic,* September 29, 1952, p. 11.
[17] Jean Begeman, "Nixon: How the Press Suppressed the News," *New Republic,* October 6, 1952, p. 11. See also "Not Much News in Los Angeles," *New Republic,* September 29, 1952, p. 8.

story, for some reason it chose to ignore it until 5:00 P.M., or some seven hours after the story broke. Even then the AP elected to transmit the Democratic National Chairman's attack on the fund and Nixon's defense of it without ever having carried a detailed summary of the *Post*'s exposé. Although the United Press transmitted an excellent account of the fund, many of the nation's newspapers subscribed only to the AP wire service, and some of those which subscribed to both the AP and UP waited in vain for an AP confirmation of the story.[18]

Still, some of the newspapers which carried an account of the Nixon fund elected to ignore the United Press version and instead to run Peter Edson's syndicated column, which also dealt with the fund and which, coincidentally, had been scheduled for release the same day. Interestingly, the Edson column was anything but unfriendly to Nixon. Indeed, the candidate's explanation and justification of the fund played a more prominent role in the article than did the disclosure itself. The *New York Post* charged that the handling of the story by the Scripps-Howard correspondent reflected a "lack of enthusiasm for the news that must have infected most editors who saw his copy."[19]

However, the newspaper response to the story might also be explained by the fact that it involved a Republican rather than a Democrat. James Wechsler, liberal editor of the *New York Post,* editorialized, "We can only voice the obvious suggestion that the story might have been greeted with more immediate and general press enthusiasm if a Democratic nominee had been involved."[20] In view of the great number of newspaper endorsements of the Eisenhower-Nixon ticket, such an attitude was not particularly farfetched. During the week of the fund disclosure, for example, the periodical *Editor & Publisher* released a poll which showed that 690 daily newspapers, with a circulation of 27.2 million, had endorsed the Republican ticket, whereas only 140 dailies, with a circulation of 3.2 million, had favored the Democrats.[21]

Nixon, who was whistle-stopping through the Central Valley in California when the *Post* story hit the streets, initially refused to make any comment on the charges. In retrospect, it seems clear that he underestimated the damage which these revelations might inflict upon the Republican campaign to "clean up the mess in Washington." "The *Post* did not worry me," Nixon said. "It was to be expected. The *Post* was still the most partisan Democratic paper in the country."[22] On the afternoon of the eighteenth Nixon

[18] *St. Louis Post-Dispatch,* September 24, 1952.
[19] *Ibid.*
[20] *Ibid.*
[21] Begeman, *New Republic,* October 6, 1952, p. 13.
[22] Richard Nixon, *Six Crises* (New York: Pocket Books, Inc., 1962), p. 85.

released a rather routine memorandum to the press in which he confirmed that he had been the recipient of such a fund but insisted that it had been used only for "political expenses which I believed should not be charged to the Federal Government."[23]

The following morning in Marysville, California, however, the Vice Presidential candidate broke his self-imposed silence. Just as the "Nixon Special" began to pull out of the station, a clear voice called out for Nixon to "tell them about the $16,000." Nixon was literally enraged by the comment and shouted for the engineer to "hold the train." Pointing directly at the man who had called out, Nixon told the crowd that "the Communists, the left-wingers, have been fighting me with every smear. . . . They started it yesterday . . . [when] they tried to say that I had taken money, $16,000. . . . What I was doing was saving you money. . . . What else, what would you rather have me do?"[24]

Throughout the next day, the twentieth, Nixon campaigned across Oregon and, at some of his stops, was heckled unmercifully. At Eugene, Nixon was confronted by a particularly hostile group of young people, thought to be college students, carrying placards which read "Will the Veep's Salary Be Enough," "No Mink Coats For Nixon—Just Cold Cash," and "Sh-h-h Anyone Who Mentions $16,000 is a Communist." Nixon chose to answer the placard which made reference to the mink coat. "That's right, there are no mink coats for Nixon and no mink coats for Pat Nixon, his wife," he said. "I'm proud of the fact that Pat Nixon wears a good Republican cloth coat, and she's going to continue to."[25] Later that day in Portland demonstrators threw pennies into the Nixon limousine.[26]

The seriousness of the fund revelations became even more apparent when *The New York Times* released a study of one hundred representative newspapers which revealed that editorial opinion was running almost two-to-one against the Vice Presidential candidate. Indeed, two of the nation's leading newspapers, the *Washington Post* and the *New York Herald Tribune*, had specifically called for Nixon's resignation. The *Tribune*'s disenchantment with Nixon was particularly significant inasmuch as the paper was regarded in many quarters as the voice of the Republican party. "The proper course of Senator Nixon in the circumstances," editorialized the *Tribune*, "is to make a formal offer of withdrawal from the ticket." Thus, within forty-eight hours it had become increasingly

[23] Gladwin Hill, "Nixon Affirms Getting Fund of $16,000 From Backers," *New York Times*, September 19, 1952.
[24] "What Senator Nixon Said," *U.S. News and World Report*, October 3, 1952, p. 6.
[25] Lawrence Davies, "Nixon Not Quitting," *New York Times*, September 21, 1952.
[26] Nixon, *Six Crises*, p. 97.

clear that criticism of the fund was a good deal more than a smear
perpetrated by the crooks and the Communists.[27]

News of the Nixon fund reached the Eisenhower campaign
train, the "Look Ahead Neighbor," in the Midwest, where the Republican Presidential standard bearer was, ironically, denouncing
corruption in the Truman Administration with his customary
fervor. Indeed, on the very day that the *Post* broke its story,
Eisenhower used the Third Chapter, Sixth Verse of Ecclesiastes—"a
time to keep and a time to cast away"—as the text of his political
address in Des Moines, Iowa. Specifically, Eisenhower called upon
the American people to "cast away" the "incompetent fumblers,
mossbacks, cronies, crooks and the disloyal in the executive department."[28] The following day Democratic National Chairman
Stephen A. Mitchell suggested that Eisenhower might well accept
his own advice and cast away his running mate. And to add to the
Republican embarrassment, Mitchell reminded Eisenhower that
early in his campaign he had said that he would "rather not be
elected President than to be elected by the help of those who have
lost their sense of public morals."[29]

Eisenhower himself was reported to have received information
of the fund with a good deal of incredulity and suspected that the
liberally oriented *Post* had probably overplayed the fund's significance in order to place his running mate in a bad light. Certainly
such an attitude was not without justification since the *Post*'s editor,
James Wechsler, and its leading political columnist, Murray Kempton, had evidenced something less than enthusiasm over the Eisenhower-Nixon ticket from the very outset. Still, columnists reported
that Eisenhower was unable to suppress the fact that he was upset
about the fund and, apparently, was even fearful that the disclosure
may have dealt his moral crusade a fatal blow. *Newsweek* reported,
for example, that his delivery of a political speech in Omaha,
Nebraska, that first night after the disclosure was "fumbling and
halting" and "his mind seemed miles away."[30]

Initially, however, Eisenhower adopted the same tack as had
Nixon, i.e., he said nothing. Indeed, he refused to break this silence
until 10:00 Friday morning, or some twenty-four hours after the
Post story had appeared, and then only with a rather terse and
tentative news release to the effect that "I believe Dick Nixon to
be an honest man" and "intend to talk with him at the earliest
time we can reach each other by telephone."[31] And in Kansas
City that same evening Eisenhower told the audience, "knowing
Dick Nixon as I do, I believe that when the facts are known to all

[27] *New York Times,* September 21, 1952.
[28] *Ibid.,* September 19, 1952.
[29] *Ibid.*
[30] *Newsweek,* September 29, 1952, p. 24.
[31] "Republicans," *Time,* September 29, 1952, p. 11.

of us they will show that Dick Nixon would not compromise with what is right."[32] It was painfully obvious to Nixon and his staff, however, that the Presidential candidate had stopped considerably short of an unqualified endorsement of his running mate in both of his public statements.

On the twentieth Eisenhower called in all the reporters on the train for an off-the-record talk about the Nixon affair. Just prior to this meeting, a private poll had indicated that an overwhelming majority of newsmen on the "Look Ahead Neighbor" were of the opinion that Nixon would have to be dumped from the ticket. "I don't care if you fellows are forty to two against me," Eisenhower said. "I'm taking my time on this. Nothing's decided, contrary to your idea that this is all a setup for a whitewash of Nixon. Nixon has got to be clean as a hound's tooth." Nixon himself was reported to have learned of the General's "hound's tooth" remark with "faint incredulity."[33] "I must admit," he said, "that it made me feel like the little boy caught with jam on his face."[34] But it also made him increasingly aware that his situation was desperate and, possibly, even hopeless.

Eisenhower's inability to reach a decision on the fate of his running mate was certainly not a unique phenomenon. There was substantial evidence to suggest that procrastination in time of crisis was the Eisenhower *modus operandi*. Apparently Eisenhower had long operated under the assumption that if one maintained a discreet silence long enough most of the alternatives in a given situation would be eliminated and a decision, if indeed any formal decision had to be made, would be virtually automatic. This was exactly what happened in the Nixon controversy. "Events—not for the last time—were to outrace an Eisenhower decision," said his chief speech writer Emmet John Hughes. "Suddenly and dramatically, Nixon, from Los Angeles, was telecasting his apologia to the nation."[35]

The Nixon telecast was at once horribly corny and immensely successful. The more sophisticated viewers generally regarded the Vice Presidential candidate's *ad hominem* approach as simply atrocious. An article in *Variety*, for example, asserted that the performance was "in the best tradition of the American soap opera. It was a slick production . . . parlaying all the schmaltz and human interest of the 'Just Plain Bill'—'Our Gal Sunday' genre of weepers."[36] On a more serious level, Walter Lippmann, who had supported the Eisenhower candidacy, argued that "this thing in

[32] James Reston, "Eisenhower Defends Nixon," *New York Times*, September 20, 1952.
[33] Costello, *The Facts About Nixon*, pp. 104–5.
[34] Nixon, *Six Crises*, p. 98.
[35] Hughes, *The Ordeal of Power*, p. 39.
[36] "Just Plain Dick," *Variety*, October 1, 1952, p. 101.

which I found myself participating was, with all the magnification of modern electronics, simply mob law. . . . How can a television audience be asked, or allowed, to judge the matter before General Eisenhower finished his inquiry and reached his decision?"[37]

The fact was, however, that the group which was most offended by the Vice Presidential candidate's emotional appeal was undoubtedly a minority and was probably largely committed to vote for Governor Stevenson anyway. Indeed, this group had become disenchanted with Nixon years before over what it regarded as his intemperate charges against Jerry Voorhis and Helen Gahagan Douglas in previous congressional campaigns. In determining the content of his telecast Nixon had, in the vernacular, chosen to hunt where the ducks were, i.e., he made his pitch to that vast television audience which had long shown a preference for the "I Love Lucy" show over the more erudite forms of television fare. In fact, Nixon's aides initially wanted to purchase the thirty minutes following the "I Love Lucy" show on Monday night so that he might be assured a large, ready-made audience. In the end, however, they had to settle for the slot following the Milton Berle show on Tuesday so that Nixon would have ample time to prepare.[38]

In his telecast Nixon attempted to project the image of an innocent man wrongfully accused. "My fellow Americans," he began, "I come before you tonight as a candidate for the Vice Presidency whose honesty and integrity have been questioned." And in the next thirty minutes Nixon literally ran the gamut of human emotions. First, he stressed the fact that unlike the Democratic Presidential candidate who, he said, had "inherited a fortune from his father," the Nixon family "was one of modest circumstances and most of my early life was spent in a [grocery] store." Actually the speech was so replete with reference to the candidate's financial difficulties (e.g., "I don't happen to be a rich man"; "I worked my way through college"; "We live rather modestly"; "We have no stocks and bonds of any type"; "Pat doesn't have a mink coat"; "We had a rather difficult time after we were married"; etc.) that some observers referred to the telecast facetiously as the "Poor Richard Show."[39]

Nixon also made passing reference to his military experiences in the South Pacific during World War II where "the bombs were falling" and which, he guessed, "entitled [him] to a couple of battle stars." And as if this were not sufficient to assure his image as a

[37] Walter Lippmann, "Mob Law in the Nixon Affair," *St. Louis Post-Dispatch*, September 25, 1952.
[38] Earl Mazo, *Richard Nixon: A Political and Personal Portrait* (New York: Harper and Brothers, 1959), p. 122.
[39] Richard Nixon, "My Side of the Story," *Vital Speeches*, October 15, 1952, pp. 11–15.

THE POOR RICHARD SHOW

patriotic American, he remarked parenthetically that "every cent" of the family savings during this period had gone into government bonds.[40] Still, it would have been difficult to fault the candidate for his flag waving exercise had he not suggested, or at least implied, that many of those who had criticized him about his political fund had done so because of his relentless fight against "the crooks and the Communists and those that defend them." He asserted, for example, that he knew "that this is not the last of the smears." But he also pointed out, none too subtly, that "some of the same columnists, some of the same radio commentators who are attacking me now and misrepresenting my position were violently opposing me at the time I was after Alger Hiss."[41]

Borrowing a page from the 1944 Presidential campaign in which Roosevelt accused some Republicans of stooping to attack his little Scotch terrier Fala, Nixon admitted that he had, in fact, accepted as a gift from a political admirer a little black cocker spaniel pup named Checkers.[42] "The kids love the dog," he said, "and I just want to say this right now, that regardless of what they say about it, we're gonna keep it."[43] Of course, it has never been too hazardous to come out strongly for dogs, and Nixon's defense of the canines proved to be no exception. In the weeks following the telecast, Nixon was literally flooded with dog collars, blankets, a dog kennel, and at least a year's supply of dog food.[44] Later the "Tail Waggers Club" of Washington, D.C., made Checkers a life member, and as was generally the case "where dogs do things like performing rescues," the fifty dollar contribution by the owner was waived.[45] It was quite obvious that to a good many Americans anyone who loved dogs could not be all bad.

In the last analysis, however, Nixon's references to his humble origin, his military exploits, and his love for animals did not constitute the most criticized aspects of his telecast. Whereas one might well question their good taste or pertinence, the very accuracy of some of the candidate's other remarks was subject to debate. He insisted, for example, that "it was not a secret fund" despite the fact that the general public, and most of the professional politicians, had no knowledge of it whatsoever. Even Eisenhower and his staff were unaware of its existence. The day after the story broke, for example, an official on the Nixon train told reporters that "it may be assumed that General Eisenhower was not aware of the existence of the trust fund."[46] And Arthur Krock of *The New York Times*

[40] *Ibid.*, p. 13.
[41] *Ibid.*, p. 15.
[42] Nixon, *Six Crises,* p. 109.
[43] Nixon, *Vital Speeches,* October 15, 1952, p. 14.
[44] Nixon, *Six Crises,* pp. 133–34.
[45] "Doggone Gifted," *New Republic,* October 13, 1952, p. 2.
[46] *New York Times,* September 29, 1952.

was convinced, moreover, that had the fund been known to the delegates at the Republican National Convention it "would certainly have caused them to look elsewhere" for a Vice Presidential candidate.[47]

Nixon also argued that by accepting this money he had somehow saved the taxpayers $18,235. Actually, however, the Senator had already spent all of the approximately $60,000 allowed to his office for expenses and could not have charged the government with any additional ones unless, perhaps, he misused his franking privilege by sending out material of a political nature under the guise of official business.[48] But even this possibility was eliminated when Nixon told his radio and television audience specifically that he refused to abuse his franking privilege because "the taxpayers shouldn't be required to finance items which are not official business." Yet, it was a matter of record that before the Republican National Convention Nixon had used his franking privilege to poll 23,000 of his California constituents on their choice for the Republican nominee for President. Since Nixon distributed the questionnaires in his capacity as an official delegate, and since he admitted that the poll was for his "own personal information," it could hardly be claimed that it constituted legitimate government business.[49]

As the final, irrefutable proof that he had done no wrong Nixon offered an independent audit by the famous firm of Price, Waterhouse and Company and a legal opinion by Gibson, Dunn and Crutcher, the largest, and unquestionably one of the most reputable, law firms in Los Angeles. Nixon quoted a passage from the legal opinion which concluded, "Senator Nixon did not obtain any financial gain from the collection and disbursement of the fund by Dana Smith; that Senator Nixon did not violate any Federal or state law by reason of the operation of the fund." "That's an independent audit which was requested because I want the American people to know all the facts," Nixon told his audience, "and I'm not afraid of having independent people go in and check the facts, and that is exactly what they did."[50]

Throughout the telecast Nixon made extensive use of the debating technique which is generally described by the Latin phrase *tu quoque*.[51] Literally translated, *tu quoque* means "you're another" and refers to the classic retort of accusing one's accuser of the same crime or impropriety. Nixon told the audience, for ex-

---

[47] Arthur Krock, "Fund Raised For Nixon Has Boomerang Effect," *New York Times*, September 21, 1952.

[48] "The Defense of Checkers," *Commonweal*, October 10, 1952, p. 3.

[49] "Answering Back," *Newsweek*, October 13, 1952, p. 33. See also "The Shape of Things," *Nation*, October 11, 1952, p. 313.

[50] Nixon, *Vital Speeches*, October 15, 1952, p. 13.

[51] Costello, *The Facts About Nixon*, p. 111.

ample, that Stevenson had "a couple" of campaign funds which he used to supplement the salaries of several of his top state officials in Illinois, and that his running mate, Senator Sparkman, had had his wife on the payroll for the past ten years. And although Nixon was careful to explain that he did not necessarily "condemn" such practices, he did suggest that "under the circumstances both Mr. Sparkman and Mr. Stevenson should come before the American people as I have and make a complete financial statement as to their financial history." Moreover, he said, "if they don't it will be an admission that they have something to hide."[52]

Actually Nixon never came to grips with the crucial question raised by his acceptance of the fund, i.e., whether it was "wise" or "proper" for a United States Senator to accept more money from private sources than he received from the public in salary.[53] To borrow from the Kantian categorical imperative, was the propriety of his act such that it could be accepted as a universal rule of conduct for all those who strive for the just society? The answer to such a question surely must be a resounding "no." "What kind of a Congress would the country have if some of its members were taking expense funds from the C.I.O., others from wealthy manufacturers, bankers, and real estate interests?" asked the *Washington Post* in a lead editorial. "It would be only a matter of time before the representative principle would be destroyed, for no man can faithfully serve two masters," it answered.[54]

But Nixon never so much as admitted that he was guilty of even an error in judgment in accepting the $18,235. Yet, only a year before, the California Senator had himself demanded that William Boyle and Guy Gabrielson, the Democratic and Republican National Chairmen, resign because of allegations that they used their positions to influence Reconstruction Finance Corporation loans. Nixon argued at the time that party officials must "set an example of propriety and ethics which goes beyond the strict legal minimum required by law." His behavior after the fund disclosure seemed to indicate that the standards of morality which govern members of the party hierarchy are more rigorous than those which govern a Vice Presidential nominee.[55]

At the conclusion of the telecast Nixon was convinced that it had been a failure. Indeed, shortly after the program left the air he told the members of his immediate staff, "I loused it up and I'm sorry." And even as he spoke those on the scene noticed that tears had welled up in the candidate's eyes.[56] Later, as the Nixon car

[52] Nixon, *Vital Speeches*, October 15, 1952, p. 14.
[53] "Sir Mordred," *New Republic*, September 29, 1952, p. 5.
[54] Quoted in "The Mess Is In Us," *Christian Century*, October 8, 1952, pp. 1149–50.
[55] "An Issue of Principle," *Nation*, October 4, 1952, p. 287.
[56] Mazo, *Richard Nixon*, p. 131.

pulled away from the studio, carrying an apprehensive and even disconsolate candidate, a huge Irish setter bounded playfully after the automobile and wagged its tail. "Well at least we got the dog vote tonight," Nixon told his wife.[57] But by the time he arrived at his hotel it was obvious that this appeal had captured a good deal more than canine support. "The telephones are going crazy," one of his supporters yelled as Nixon entered the hotel, "everybody's in your corner." Minutes later Darryl Zanuck called to say that the telecast "was the most tremendous performance I've ever seen."[58] It had become clear that the speech, far from being a failure, was nothing short of a tremendous histrionic and political triumph.

General Eisenhower, who had delayed his scheduled address in Cleveland so that he might catch the Nixon telecast, was reported to be "jumping with fight" as a result of his running mate's remarks. Both Mrs. Eisenhower and her mother were reported to have wept openly, so moved had they been by the Nixon appeal. Thirty minutes after Nixon left the air Eisenhower strode into the Public Auditorium where 17,000 wildly enthusiastic Republicans were chanting "We want Nixon," "We want Nixon."[59] "I happen to be one of those people who when I get into a fight, would rather have a courageous and honest man by my side than a whole boxcar of pussyfooters," the General told the Republican throngs. "I have seen brave men in tough situations. I have never seen anyone come through in better fashion than Senator Nixon did tonight."[60]

Still Eisenhower reserved judgment on the fate of his running mate until he had had a chance to talk with him "face to face." He told the assembled Republicans that he needed "something more than a single presentation of thirty minutes" and had sent a telegram to Nixon requesting just such a confrontation for the following evening in Wheeling, West Virginia.[61] Eisenhower's telegram, which termed Nixon's performance "magnificent," explained to him that in order "to complete the formulation of [my] personal decision, I feel in need of talking to you, and would be most appreciative if you could fly to see me at once."[62] Unfortunately for Nixon, however, the Eisenhower message got lost in the flood of telegrams coming into the hotel, and Nixon, who had fully expected an immediate and decisive decision, was thus left completely in the dark as to the reason for the delay. "What more does [Eisenhower] want?" Nixon asked an aide. "I'm not going to crawl on my hands and knees to him."[63]

---

[57] Nixon, *Six Crises*, p. 125.
[58] Mazo, *Richard Nixon*, p. 131.
[59] "Behind Nixon's Speech," *Newsweek*, October 6, 1952, p. 25.
[60] Nixon, *Six Crises*, p. 127.
[61] *Newsweek*, October 6, 1952, p. 25.
[62] "The Acquittal," *Time*, October 6, 1952, p. 21.
[63] *Newsweek*, October 6, 1952, p. 25.

All that night and the next day the Western Union offices around the country were "taxed to full capacity" handling the incoming messages, and the newspapers were flooded with similar calls. Both reported that the sentiment expressed was overwhelmingly in favor of the Vice Presidential candidate. A telephone operator for *The New York Times* reported that shortly after the conclusion of Nixon's speech "the board lit up like a Christmas tree." Most of the callers wanted to know the address of the Republican National Committee, although she conceded that some wanted only to know the outcome of the Rocky Marciano–"Jersey" Joe Walcott championship fight which had taken place the same evening.[64] It was possible to argue, of course, that the results were similar in the two cases, i.e., Marciano knocked out Walcott in thirteen, and Nixon the Democrats in thirty.

Of members of the Republican National Committee who could be reached after the telecast, 107 of the total of 138, every one favored keeping Nixon on the ticket. And one committeeman, J. Russell Sprague of New York, seemed almost in a state of euphoria as he told newsmen that the speech had transformed the Vice Presidential candidate into nothing less than a "national hero."[65] The Republican national headquarters in Washington reported that it too was "completely swamped" with letters, telegrams, and phone calls concerning the Nixon candidacy.[66] And what was particularly striking was the fact that the messages were running approximately 200 to one in favor of Nixon's retention.[67]

Editorial comment throughout the country was also overwhelmingly favorable. "Extraordinary" said the *New York World Telegram;* "magnificent" said the *Los Angeles Herald-Express;* "eloquent" said the *Pittsburgh Sun Telegraph.* "The man who faced his critics down," the *Dallas Morning News* editorialized, "was the sort of man who made this country what it is." And the *New York Journal American* was of the opinion that Nixon had fought like a "man," a "gentleman," a "patriot," and just "plain Joe."[68] But perhaps even more significant than these favorable comments by the Republican-oriented newspapers was the fact that the critical ones also conceded, even if somewhat grudgingly, that the telecast had been singularly effective. "Poor boy struggling against adversity, devoted wife and kiddies, the family pet, hero traduced by sinister Red plots—these are always good," commented the *St. Louis Post-Dispatch.* "They always bring in the box tops."[69]

[64] *New York Times,* September 24, 1952.
[65] *Ibid.,* September 25, 1952.
[66] *Ibid.,* September 24, 1952.
[67] Clayton Knowles, "Messages Pour in Backing Nominee," *New York Times,* September 25, 1952.
[68] Excerpts of editorial comments taken from *St. Louis Post-Dispatch,* September 24, 1952.
[69] *Ibid.*

When Nixon's plane finally touched down in Wheeling, West Virginia, late Wednesday night, Eisenhower completely ignored protocol and rushed up the ramp and extended his hand to his running mate. A startled Nixon gasped, "Why General, you shouldn't have come out here." "Why not," beamed Eisenhower, "you're my boy."[70] Thus was a new page added to American folklore. Later, at the Wheeling stadium, the General told an enthusiastic crowd of supporters that "as far as I am concerned, [Nixon] has not only vindicated himself, but I feel that he has acted as a man of courage and honor and so far as I am concerned stands higher than ever before."[71] Yet, it was Nixon, not the famous General, who held center stage at Wheeling that night. "Eisenhower was very glad to play the slow violin accompaniment," a somewhat embittered Murray Kempton wrote, "to 'Richard Faces Life.' "[72]

At Wheeling, moreover, Nixon even managed to gain some hard political capital out of his week's ordeal and Eisenhower's indecisiveness. After passing references to such things as V-E Day, ticker-tape parades for the General, the General's natural warmth and personal magnetism, the General's "hound's tooth" comment, and his own tour of duty in the South Pacific, Nixon told the crowd that "a lesser man [than Eisenhower] . . . would, at the outset, have said 'this is just a smear; I am not going to listen to any of these charges; and . . . I am not even going to wait until the evidence is in before I make up my mind.' " The Vice Presidential candidate said he was "glad General Eisenhower didn't do that because there has been too much of that in the present Administration." And Nixon's final *tour de force* was nothing short of a masterpiece of political ingenuity. "Folks," he said, "if [Eisenhower] will do that with me just think what he is going to do when he becomes President. It is going to be the cleanest, the most honest government America has ever had."[73]

It will be recalled that only twenty-four hours earlier Eisenhower told the Republicans gathered in the Cleveland Public Auditorium that he needed "more than one single presentation of thirty minutes" to reach a decision on his running mate. Yet, there is no evidence that the General received any additional "presentation" from any source, and certainly not from Nixon, between the telecast and their meeting at Wheeling. Thus, without any additional dialogue between the Presidential and Vice Presidential

[70] *Time*, October 6, 1952, p. 21.

[71] "Remarks of General Eisenhower at Wheeling, W. Va.," *U.S. News and World Report*, October 3, 1952, p. 72.

[72] "Time Bomb," *Time*, October 6, 1952, p. 73.

[73] "Remarks of Senator Nixon at Wheeling, W. Va.," *U.S. News and World Report*, October 3, 1952, p. 74.

candidates Nixon had, by some unknown alchemy, become Eisenhower's "boy."[74]

However, inasmuch as the intervening twenty-four hours had produced conclusive evidence of the success of the Nixon performance, it seemed fairly clear that the "propriety" of the fund had been determined solely by audience response. *Commonweal*, one of Nixon's most outspoken critics throughout the controversy, commented sadly that "somewhere along the line the Great Crusade had lost a leader who had once showed such high promise. In his place was a man who decided great issues by counting telegrams."[75] And as *The New Republic* so succinctly stated the case, "a campaign can be waged in many ways, a crusade in only one way. Either a crusade is a search without compromise for its ideals, or it is a mockery."[76] Thus did Eisenhower, as the leader of the Great Crusade for morality in government, meet his first real test. He failed. It would be, moreover, neither his last test nor his last failure.

[74] Costello, *The Facts About Nixon,* p. 113.
[75] *Commonweal,* October 10, 1952, p. 4. See also "The Affair Nixon," *Commonweal,* October 3, 1952, p. 620.
[76] *New Republic,* September 29, 1952, p. 5.

Chapter 4

THE TEN PERCENTER

I'll tell you this. I'm going to roar clear across the country for a clean decent operation. The American people deserve it.

DWIGHT EISENHOWER

ALVIN S. McCOY, a highly regarded reporter for the *Kansas City Star,* pointed out in his column of February 10, 1953, that even though the Kansas legislature had, in 1951, appropriated $110,000 for the purchase of a privately owned hospital building standing on the grounds of the State Tuberculosis Sanatorium near Norton, Kansas, records filed with the State Insurance Commission by the building's owner, a fraternal insurance company called the Ancient Order of United Workmen, indicated that it had received only $99,250 in the transaction. State Insurance Commissioner Frank Sullivan told McCoy that he could not explain the $10,750 discrepancy between the amount received and the amount appropriated. AOUW President Edgar Bennett's recollection was similarly muddy; he said he could not remember "offhand" where the money had gone but did recall that there had been "some expenses, commissions and attorney's fees," although he did not know "how much." Thus, McCoy's question remained unanswered. What had happened to $10,750 of the taxpayer's money?[1]

McCoy's question had a rhetorical ring to it, for there was every reason to believe that he already knew what had happened to the taxpayer's money and, further, was fully prepared to divulge names and details should he be unable to obtain public disclosures from Sullivan, Bennett *et al.* Subsequent stories by McCoy and John McCormally of the *Hutchinson News-Herald* were sufficient to force a none-too-eager Sullivan to undertake a departmental investigation of the discrepancy.[2] The information did not prove to be especially difficult to obtain, for at a press conference three days later the com-

---

[1] Alvin S. McCoy, *Kansas City Star,* February 10, 1953.
[2] Kenneth S. Davis, "The Press and Wesley Roberts," *New Republic,* March 23, 1953, p. 10.

missioner disclosed that the entire $10,750, plus an additional $250 for "expenses," had been paid to C. Wesley Roberts as a fee for negotiating the sale of the hospital building to the state. Moreover, Roberts had been retained, and his $11,000 fee agreed to, by president Bennett himself, the man who only a few days earlier had been unable to tell McCoy "offhand" where the money in question had gone.

Less than a month before McCoy's first story on the hospital transaction broke, C. Wesley Roberts had been appointed National Chairman of the Republican Party with the "hearty approval" of President Eisenhower.[3] Since Roberts had been long identified with the Eisenhower cause, his selection had not been a surprising one. It was Roberts, for example, who had opened and directed Eisenhower's Washington headquarters, once Republicans began to campaign openly for Ike's nomination. Following the Republican Convention, Roberts had been rewarded with the office of Director of Organization of the Republican National Committee.[4] The discovery of a Republican "ten percenter" so soon after President Eisenhower's inauguration promised no small embarrassment for a party which had so substantially pitched its campaign against the "five percenters" of the Truman Administration. Indeed, Kansas' Lieutenant Governor, Fred Hall, was quick to chide Roberts for having demonstrated that he could "double a Democrat."[5]

Once Roberts' name became involved in the matter, politicians and reporters alike checked the records of the Kansas Secretary of State in an effort to determine whether Roberts had been registered as a lobbyist at the time of the sale. Kansas law provided that an individual who was retained by a person, firm, association, organization, or corporation having an interest in any measure or measures pending before the state legislature, and who attempted to influence the vote of any legislator on such measure or measures, was deemed to be a "legislative counsel or agent." All such persons were required to register, under penalty of fines up to $5,000, a jail sentence up to one year, or both.[6] The records of the Secretary of State revealed no registration by Roberts.

Roberts explained this simply by saying that he had not been a lobbyist. He insisted that he had been retained by the Ancient Order of United Workmen, not as a "legislative agent or counsel," but as a "public-relations counsel" in order "to prepare the facts concerning the hospital building for presentation by my client to the proper state agencies."[7] Roberts also pointed out that at the

[3] *New York Times*, January 17, 1953.
[4] Anthony Leviero, "Roberts Reported Set for the G.O.P. Post," *New York Times*, December 20, 1952.
[5] "Storm in Kansas," *Time*, March 30, 1953, p. 18.
[6] Kansas, *General Statutes*, (1949) c. 46, secs. 201–5.
[7] "Cyclone Over Kansas," *Newsweek*, February 23, 1953, p. 29. See also *New York Times*, February 13, 1953.

time of his retention by AOUW he had been a "private citizen," holding no governmental or political position whatsoever. Roberts never once wavered from this position despite the fact that his public relations firm didn't seem to have an office, a secretary, or any business stationery.[8] Still, something more than a semantical argument could be advanced on Roberts' behalf. For he contended that he had never attempted to influence the vote of any legislator on the hospital purchase. "I was scrupulous in making no lobby approach to the legislators," he said.[9] Certainly, contact with legislators appeared to be, by statutory definition, the *essential* function of the "legislative agent or counsel."

The reaction to Roberts' explanation of his role in the transaction was surprisingly mixed even within his own party. Republican state senator William D. Weigand, an old intra-party foe, charged that the transaction had been a "false sale, and the whole $110,000 misspent, since it appears that the state already owned the property." At the time, rumors were rampant, in fact, that the title to the building had already reverted to the state and that the legislature had allowed itself to be bamboozled out of $110,000 without debate or dissent. At the very least, senator Weigand contended, the affair "definitely needed furthur investigation."[10] Governor Edward Arn, a long-standing political ally of Roberts, disagreed sharply with the senator. The Governor told reporters that he "doubted" that Roberts had been engaged in lobbying and personally thought that the state senate had "acted wisely" in rejecting a motion to conduct an immediate inquiry into the affair.[11] President Eisenhower, remaining above the controversy, regarded it as nothing more than a factional fight among Kansas Republicans and announced through Press Secretary James Hagerty that he was "satisfied" with Roberts' explanation.[12]

Indeed, Kansas Republicans that year were busily devouring each other in one of the most bitter internecine struggles in the state's history. The fight was generally regarded as a battle between the more progressive "young Turks," of whom, paradoxically, one of the most vigorous happened to be the aging Alf Landon, against the more conservative "palace guard." The titular leader of the progressive revolt was Lieutenant Governor Fred Hall. Hall had handily defeated Old Guard opposition in the Republican primary of the previous summer and, moreover, in the fall had proved a considerably more popular candidate than his Old Guard

[8] W. H. Lawrence, "C. W. Roberts Deal Brings Kansas Suit to Regain $110,000," *New York Times*, March 19, 1953.
[9] *Time*, March 30, 1953, p. 18. See also *The New York Times*, February 14, 1953.
[10] *Ibid.*, February 13, 1953.
[11] *Ibid.*, February 14, 1953.
[12] *Ibid.*

running mate, Governor Arn. Among the recognized leaders of the anti-Hall wing of the party were Roberts, Arn, and United States Senator Frank Carlson. Most people even suspected that columnist McCoy's informant had been motivated not by considerations of ethics, but rather by a desire to embarrass and weaken the Arn-Carlson-Roberts faction. Under ordinary circumstances, Roberts would probably have had little to fear. Republican politics in Kansas had long been, as one writer cast it, "a cozy affair, a perpetual Era of Good Feeling." The Republican hierarchy simply ran the state as it saw fit; neither the poorly organized Democratic minority nor the Kansas one-party press posed a fearsome threat.[13] But the circumstances of 1953 were anything but ordinary.

It was Alf Landon, the former Governor of Kansas and unsuccessful Republican Presidential candidate in 1936, who refused to be quieted even by President Eisenhower's "satisfaction" with Roberts' statement. Within twenty-four hours of the White House news release, Landon charged publicly, "President Eisenhower's satisfaction with the ridiculous explanation of National Republican Chairman C. Wesley Roberts for his prostituting of his political influence in a raid on the public treasury of Kansas, which stinks to high heaven, does not satisfy the people of Kansas by a long shot." Landon continued that he understood the American people to have voted for a change in the "loose standards of public honesty and morality" of the pre-1952 years.[14] "The more [the Roberts affair] is ignored and smoothed over," he contended, "the more devastating will be the explosion in the end to President Eisenhower and the Republican party."[15] Lieutenant Governor Hall "agreed with Landon" and told reporters that "the whole matter deserved further consideration than the President has given it."[16]

The Judiciary Committee of the Kansas Senate, somewhat belatedly and apparently quite reluctantly, succumbed to the pressure and recommended that a joint legislative committee be established to inquire into the hospital sale. The investigatory committee which was ultimately established was composed of five House members and four senators, with but a single Democrat from each chamber.[17] Moreover, the Arn wing of the Republican party was reported to have a clear majority on the committee. Landon was so dismayed over the committee's composition that he stated publicly he feared a "whitewash."[18] Thus, there was reason to suspect that the promised exposé would be stillborn. Indeed, Roberts himself was so confident of a favorable—or at the very least a neutral—committee

[13] Davis, *New Republic*, March 23, 1953, p. 9.
[14] *New York Times*, February 15, 1953.
[15] *Ibid.*, March 2, 1953.
[16] *Ibid.*, February 16, 1953.
[17] Davis, *New Republic*, March 23, 1953, p. 11.
[18] *New York Times*, March 2, 1953.

report, that he offered to resign as National Chairman should it
prove to be in any way critical of his activities.[19] Appearing on
NBC's "Meet the Press" a few days before the committee opened its
investigation, Roberts told the newsmen that he personally wel-
comed the inquiry and hoped that it would clarify his role in the
transaction. "I will certainly welcome that," he said.[20]

Before the investigatory committee, Roberts' tactics hardly
seemed calculated to "clarify" his role in the hospital sale. From
the very outset of the hearings, Roberts seemed bent on diverting
the committee's attention away from the specific facts of the affair
by impugning the motives of newsmen McCoy and, to a lesser degree, McCormally. He charged, for example, that McCoy had de-
vised a "calculated plot" to destroy him as Republican National
Chairman and had stooped to "slanted" reporting to accomplish
that end.[21] Apparently Roberts believed, as did others, that McCoy
wanted to play the same important role in Republican affairs as
had his predecessor on the *Star*, Lacey Haynes.[22] Claiming to be a
victim of a "ruthless and persistent attack conceived with obvious
malice," Roberts asked that the charges against him "be weighed in
the balance of the personal vindictiveness and political ambition"
which had motivated them.[23]

Governor Arn espoused a conspiratorial view of the controversy
similar to that of Roberts. He told members of the committee that
McCoy had "stirred up, distorted and slanted" the true facts of the
hospital transaction for political reasons. Arn argued that the reporter had known of Roberts' connection with the hospital sale for
a full eight months but had waited to publicize the fact until Roberts had been appointed National Chairman. Throughout the controversy, the Governor said, McCoy had altered Associated Press
stories, without dropping the byline, in order to make a more damaging case against the Chairman. McCoy was also reported to have
stated in the presence of the Executive Secretary of the Kansas Republican Central Committee, McDill Boyd, that he would "get
Roberts" because he "would not stand for him running Kansas
politics from Washington."[24] McCoy's response to the Governor's
charges was simple and direct. He said that Arn had simply testified "untruthfully" in an attempt to divert the committee's attention away from the "sorry Roberts affair." "Please remember,"
McCoy told the committee members, "I did not create these facts.
Mr. Roberts did that."[25]

[19] "A Wise Decision," *Newsweek,* April 6, 1953, p. 28.
[20] *New York Times,* March 2, 1953.
[21] *Ibid.,* March 14, 1953.
[22] W. H. Lawrence, "Reporter Defends Story on Roberts," *New York Times,*
March 20, 1953.
[23] *New York Times,* March 14, 1953.
[24] *Ibid.,* March 17, 1953.
[25] Lawrence, *New York Times,* March 20, 1953.

The favorable report confidently awaited by Roberts never came. On March 27, 1953, a unanimous committee charged both Roberts and Edgar Bennett with "deliberately and intentionally" violating the "spirit" of the Kansas lobbying law if not its actual "letter." To prohibit similar future activities, it recommended that the statutes be revised to define lobbying as "an attempt to influence, in any manner, the act or vote of any member of the legislature, *directly or indirectly.*" The report also censured every state official who had been involved in the transaction for what it termed their "lack of diligence and thoroughness." Officials specifically named in the report included members of the Social Welfare Board, the superintendent of the State Sanatorium at Norton, the Attorney General and his staff, the state architect, and members of the House Ways and Means Committee.[26] There were rumors that the committee had sharpened the report considerably after it received a letter from the AOUW requesting reimbursement for the expenses it had incurred in preparing its case for the committee. One member of the committee termed the company's suggestion "a most arrogant proposal."[27]

Established conclusively by the hearings was the fact that Roberts had once contacted Representative Chris Green, Chairman of the Kansas House Ways and Means Committee, about the hospital sale. Unabashedly, Roberts admitted as much, but insisted that he had not attempted to influence Green in any way. He insisted that he had simply inquired about the procedure for obtaining committee consideration of the proposed hospital purchase and asked Green if his committee "would consider a proposal to purchase the AOUW hospital building at Norton if it were made by the proper state agencies and with their recommendation?"[28] Since a good many people had long considered AOUW's position at Norton to be both irregular and undesirable, it was not surprising that the Chairman told Roberts that he was confident his committee would be most happy to consider the matter.[29]

Interestingly, until August, 1950, or only shortly before this conversation with Green, Roberts had been State Chairman of the Republican party in Kansas. It seems unlikely that Roberts' great influence in party affairs ended with his resignation as State Chairman. The Kansas Attorney General, for example, was of the opinion that "Wes Roberts, while holding no political office, was [still] one of the most powerful political figures in and around the Governor's office and the legislative halls."[30] Green conceded as much when he

[26] The committee report is reprinted in Kansas, *Senate Journal*, 38th Sess., 1953, pp. 267–77.
[27] W. H. Lawrence, "Roberts is Scored by Kansas Inquiry," *New York Times*, March 28, 1953.
[28] Kansas, *Senate Journal*, 1953, p. 273.
[29] *Ibid.*
[30] *New York Times*, August 7, 1953.

said that, at the time of his conversation with Roberts, he thought of him as State Chairman. The magnitude of Roberts' influence is dramatized even more by the fact that Roberts had failed to tell Green that he had been retained by AOUW as its "public-relations counsel."[31] In fact, the chairman actually thought that Roberts was representing the state of Kansas in the transaction. During the hearings, Green said that, had he known that Roberts was to receive an $11,000 fee from the sale, he would have been "absolutely against it."[32]

Roberts had also approached the members of the State Board of Social Welfare. He told them that if the state chose not to purchase the company's unit, at a price to be determined by the state architect, AOUW planned to initiate a new campaign to publicize its insurance program. Moreover, it was made quite clear that such a campaign might result in occupancy of all of the unit's thirty-six beds by company-insured patients. The welfare officials did not look upon such a prospect "with any degree of happiness" for at least two reasons.[33] First, virtually all of the beds in the unit were then occupied by state patients, who could not easily be moved to the state hospital because of the crowded conditions there. Second, it was estimated that the state actually lost six dollars per day for every AOUW patient it admitted to the sanatorium.[34] Everything considered, Roberts' technique for forcing the transaction upon the state was anything but subtle.

The committee also discovered that Roberts' fee had been significantly affected by the state's decision concerning the hospital sale. Bennett, it seems, had agreed to pay Roberts a retainer fee of $1,000 at the time of his employment and an additional $10,000 should the hospital sale go through. If the state decided not to buy the unit at Norton, the $10,000 was to apply on Roberts' salary as head of the company's proposed publicity campaign to expand its insurance sales.[35] It was argued that, stripped to the barest essentials, the $10,000 was simply a "contingency fee." Certainly, only if the legislation passed, did Roberts receive the whole $10,000 with no strings attached; if it did not pass, he had to perform some additional work to earn the money. The argument, moreover, was not mere semantics, for Kansas law strictly prohibited the acceptance by lobbyists of any contingency fee.[36]

Were this not sufficient, Roberts also disclosed to the committee that he had accepted at least one other fee for "public-relations" work during the 1951 session. The Cities Service Gas Company,

[31] Kansas, *Senate Journal*, 1953, p. 273.
[32] *New York Times*, March 19, 1953.
[33] Kansas, *Senate Journal*, 1953, p. 273.
[34] Lawrence, *New York Times*, March 19, 1953.
[35] Kansas, *Senate Journal*, 1953, p. 272.
[36] Kansas, *General Statutes*, (1949) c. 46 sec. 204.

at the suggestion of Governor Arn, retained Roberts to provide an "informational service" on bills pending before the legislature. Roberts was paid $3,750 for his work.[37] Since a legislative reporting service could be obtained for as little as forty dollars, this too looked suspiciously like a lobbying fee.[38] Some thought it more than mere coincidence that the legislature that session had passed a law, long sought by the gas companies, authorizing their use of abandoned underground wells for storage purposes. Several months later, these doubts were intensified when an investigation by State Attorney General Harold R. Fatzer revealed that Roberts had personally contacted several legislators concerning the oil storage bill and that at least three lawmakers had been asked to confer with Roberts on the subject in the Governor's outer office. Some legislators reported that Roberts openly solicited their support on the bill, while others "inferred" that theirs was expected. Despite the requirements of the Kansas lobby law, none were told that Roberts was an employee of the Cities Service Gas Company.[39]

Only a "loophole" in the Kansas lobbying law prevented the Attorney General from taking legal action against Roberts for his failure to register as a lobbyist. In a statement to the press, the Attorney General admitted that "to the average layman, what occurred was lobbying pure and simple." But with "a feeling of real frustration," he said, he had to inform them "that Roberts' conduct did not violate our statute as it now is written." Lacking, he continued, was the "one essential element, namely that Roberts was actually employed by Cities Service Gas Company for the purpose of influencing legislation." Fatzer felt that he could not prove "beyond a reasonable doubt" that a contract of employment actually existed between Roberts and Cities Service. Roberts' imperceptibility can fairly well be judged by his reaction to Fatzer's news release. "It is gratifying," he said, "that after an exhaustive investigation of over four months' duration, my original word has been made good and that grounds for complaint do not exist."[40] Although Roberts had, by a technicality, escaped indictment for violation of the Kansas lobbying act, the general nature of his devious dealings was emphatically clear.

Sufficient evidence was uncovered during the hearings to raise "a legal question as to the title and ownership of said building," according to the report. At the least, the arrangement between the state and the insurance company proved unusual. By the terms of the original contract, the company was to have assumed the cost of construction, furnishing, and routine maintenance of the build-

[37] *New York Times*, March 17, 1953.
[38] Kenneth S. Davis, "Chairman Roberts Leaves the Crusade," *New Republic,* April 6, 1953, pp. 7–8.
[39] *New York Times*, August 7, 1953.
[40] *Ibid.*

ing. In addition to providing the land on which the building was
to be constructed, the state had agreed to administer the unit in
the same manner as others within the hospital complex, and to
furnish utilities. Tubercular patients insured by AOUW would be
admitted to the beds in the unit on a preferential basis but, in the
event that some beds were unoccupied, they were to become available for use by other patients admitted to the state sanatorium. The
company paid a flat rate of one dollar per day for each of its patients.[41]

Though the contract between the state and the insurance company did not note explicitly that title to the structure would revert
to the state should AOUW ever choose to withdraw from Norton,
many people had apparently deduced as much. In a letter to the
Kansas Attorney General dated July 13, 1927, for example, the
Chairman of the State Board of Administration stated categorically
that "should the AOUW in the future wish to withdraw its interest, the pavilion will become the property of the state for the use
of the sanatorium."[42] Furthermore, an examination of the records
of the Norton county clerk's office revealed that the company had
never paid taxes on the building. Norton County Clerk G. V.
Sarvis testified that inasmuch as the building was not on the tax
rolls when he took office in 1937, he and the county assessors had
always assumed that it was owned by the state. If the structure, in
fact, was privately owned "it should have been taxed, as a building
on leased ground, as personal property," he concluded.[43] Finally,
State Supreme Court Justice William A. Smith, who had been
Attorney General of the state when the hospital unit at Norton was
constructed, testified that the contract provided for state ownership
"because when you build a building on property, the building goes
with the real estate."[44]

Before the committee concluded its hearings Attorney General
Fatzer initiated proceedings against AOUW to recover the $110,000
plus six percent interest. Judge Beryl Johnson of the Shawnee
County district court dismissed the suit, however, and his decision
was later upheld by the Kansas supreme court. The supreme court
held that in the absence of facts clearly indicating intention to the
contrary, when one person allows another to place a building on his
property, title to the building does not follow title to the land on
which it was constructed. And "solely for the sake of argument,"
the court said, even if the state had lacked the authority to permit
private construction on public grounds, it, nevertheless, had recognized AOUW ownership for over twenty years. Thus, "in good

[41] Kansas, *Senate Journal*, 1953, p. 269.
[42] *Ibid.*, p. 267.
[43] Davis, *New Republic*, March 23, 1953, p. 11.
[44] *Ibid.*, p. 12.

conscience and equity and in recognition of its moral obligation" the state had little alternative but to purchase the building.[45] The shocking thing about the purchase, however, was that there existed no hint of any question of ownership prior to its execution. The legislature, with neither debate nor dissent, simply had appropriated the necessary $110,000.

A few hours after the committee released its report, Roberts presented a letter of resignation to President Eisenhower. His career as National Chairman had lasted but slightly more than two months. The decision to resign, Roberts said, had been strictly a "personal one" and he had "been influenced by no one in reaching it." And although he still maintained his innocence on all charges, he said he was practical enough to know that his "usefulness as National Chairman had been destroyed" by the adverse report of the state investigating committee. In his letter of resignation Roberts told the President, whom he termed the "greatest leader the Republican party and the nation has had since the day of Abraham Lincoln," that he earnestly believed that he had never in his life "committed a dishonorable act." Yet, despite this "clear conscience," he felt that his resignation was in the "best interest of the President, the Administration, and the Republican party." President Eisenhower's statement to the press also stressed the point that the Chairman's decision to resign had been "his own." Under the circumstances, the President conceded that Roberts' decision to resign had been a "wise one."[46]

In retrospect, one is somewhat surprised that Roberts did not emerge from the battle completely unscathed. For even though the National Chairman of a major party had been accused of "influence peddling," the controversy did not rocket into the front pages of the nation's newspapers. In fact, the scant attention the Roberts story received by the press, with such notable exceptions as the *St. Louis Post-Dispatch* and the *Christian Science Monitor,* stood in ironic juxtaposition to exhaustive newspaper coverage of earlier charges that Democratic National Chairman William Boyle had used his position to influence loans by the Reconstruction Finance Corporation.[47] Noting the paucity of coverage, one journalist charged that much of the early Associated Press material failed to get beyond its Kansas City headquarters. *Time* magazine, which ordinarily revels in scandals, failed to find anything sufficiently important in the Roberts case to report any of the first 4,500 words filed by its correspondent in Kansas.[48] It was not until March 30,

[45] 283 P. 2d 461
[46] Anthony Leviero, "Roberts Resigns," *New York Times,* March 28, 1953.
[47] See U.S., Congress, Senate, Senate Permanent Subcommittee on Investigations, *American Lithofold Corp., William M. Boyle, Jr., Guy George Gabrielson,* Report No. 1142, 82d Cong., 2d Sess., 1952.
[48] Davis, *New Republic,* March 23, 1953, p. 9.

1953, over a month and a half after reporter McCoy's first column, that this national "news magazine" printed a word about Roberts' difficulties.[49] Following the release of the committee's report and Roberts' resignation, *Time* could report only that "the outcome of this borderline case was tough on Roberts."[50]

The truth of the matter would appear to be that a large segment of the nation's press underplayed the significance of Roberts' role in the hospital transaction, much as it had discounted the significance of Vice Presidential candidate Nixon's political slush fund in 1952.[51] The Americans for Democratic Action documented the news differential by publishing the results of its survey comparing newspaper coverage in the Boyle and Roberts cases. Specifically, it examined the coverage given the two cases by six metropolitan dailies, *The New York Times*, the *New York Herald Tribune*, the *Washington Post*, the *Washington Star*, the *Pittsburgh Press*, and the *Baltimore Sun*, for comparable ten-day periods. The survey disclosed that these newspapers had devoted only one-third as much space to the Roberts story as they had to Boyle. Moreover, Boyle had received front page treatment a full seventy percent of the time, whereas the Roberts stories had received such attention only slightly over sixteen percent of the time and, frequently, were buried on the back pages.[52] In fact, the two cases were quite comparable, albeit that Roberts himself saw "no parallel."[53]

The journalistic indifference to the ethical questions arising from the Roberts affair was equaled only by the indifference of most Republican officials. The Republican National Committee, which accepted Roberts' resignation with "the utmost reluctance and deep regret," insisted on passing a resolution terming Roberts a "friend of integrity whom we hold in high esteem." Indeed, perhaps the crowning irony of this sorry tale was that, even after his resignation, Mrs. C. Y. Semple, Kansas National Committeewoman, insisted that "at least ninety percent of Kansas Republicans have the utmost faith in Wes Roberts."[54] It was also rather ironical that while the legislative committee hearings were being held in Kansas, Senator Frank Carlson, the man responsible for Roberts' appointment as National Chairman, was making news in the nation's capital by demanding a congressional investigation of leave payments to officers in the Truman Administration.[55] Apparently, the Senator believed the old adage, "the best defense is a good offense."

[49] *Time*, March 30, 1953, p. 18.
[50] "Curtain for Mr. Roberts," *Time*, April 6, 1953, p. 30.
[51] "Extra! Extra!" *New Republic*, March 30, 1953, p. 6.
[52] *New York Times*, April 22, 1953.
[53] *Ibid.*, March 2, 1953.
[54] W. H. Lawrence, "G.O.P. Elects Hall," *New York Times*, April 11, 1953.
[55] *New York Times*, March 14, 1953.

The President himself, for the most part, responded to the
affair with profound silence. The extent of the press' efforts to
present the President in only the most favorable light can be well
judged by an editorial in the *New York Herald Tribune,* which
dealt in part with this Presidential silence. Eisenhower, it said, had
"meticulously avoided prejudicing the case or attempting to influence its outcome by [making] public statements." But once all
the facts in the case were clear, the editorial concluded, the problem
had been "met with vigor, speed and effectiveness by the party
leadership."[56] Democratic Senator Neely of West Virginia viewed
the President's response somewhat differently. To the Senate, he
commented that it was indeed remarkable that the "Crusader" who
had promised to "roar across the country" for political purity had
offered no word of censure throughout the controversy. The President "roared out" against Roberts, the Senator observed, like the
bumpkin Bottom in "Twelfth Night"—"as gently as a sucking
dove."[57]

[56] *New York Herald Tribune,* March 29, 1953.
[57] U.S., *Congressional Record,* 83d Cong., 1st Sess., 1953, 99, Part 3, p. 3095.

Chapter 5

THE POWER AND THE GLORY

From its very inception, Dixon-Yates was destined to end in public disgrace and disrepute. Its purpose was unwholesome; the methods used devious, and in carrying out the scheme every concept of decent government and fair and impartial administration of applicable law was ignored.

Report of the Senate Subcommittee on
Antitrust and Monopoly

SUCCESFUL POLITICIANS seldom speak disparagingly of our national heroes. They have discovered, no doubt, that such criticism simply is not compatible with continued success. Yet, Democratic National Chairman Stephen Mitchell began the 1956 congressional campaign by attacking not one but two of the most venerated of American folk heroes, President Dwight Eisenhower, who represented something of a "father image" to a sizeable percentage of the American public, and golfer Bobby Jones, four-time winner of the American Open. As James Reston of *The New York Times* remarked, the chairman could hardly have chosen a more reckless approach unless, perhaps, he had accused the President of befriending Willie Mays.[1]

The Mitchell attack on Eisenhower and Jones stemmed from his debate with Republican National Chairman Leonard Hall before the Seventy-Seventh Annual Convention of the American Bar Association in Chicago. During one heated exchange, Hall challenged Mitchell to cite a "single instance" of corruption in Washington since the Eisenhower Administration took office. Wisely or

[1] James Reston, "Mitchell Spurns a Rule," *New York Times*, August 18, 1954. Two weeks after the above paragraph was written, *Esquire* magazine listed some four dozen personalities who seem to be immune from malicious gossip. "By common consent," it claimed, "these are the O.K. people: no magazine knocks them, no newspaper exposes. Their names may be uttered without producing a sneer. They are the sum of human virtue . . . and shine like good deeds in a naughty world." The first person listed was golfer Bobby Jones. "The Unknockables," *Esquire*, June, 1966, pp. 84–85.

not, Mitchell picked up the gauntlet. "All right. Let's look at the Dixon-Yates scandal. A competing syndicate offered to provide the power for $90,000,000 less than Dixon-Yates and the Tennessee Valley Authority would provide the power for $140,000,000 less," Mitchell charged. "It so happens that a director of one of the two companies favored in the syndicate [Bobby Jones], is one of the President's closest friends—with a cottage next to President Eisenhower's at the Augusta golf course."[2]

This so-called scandal to which Mitchell referred in mid-August had already been given intermittent coverage in the newspapers for some two months, although for reasons unexplained, periodicals had made no mention of it and did not do so until early September.[3] Indeed, as late as November, 1954, *Life* magazine reported that "the Senate-House Committee on Atomic Energy is preparing to judge something called the Dixon-Yates contract,"[4] while *U.S. News and World Report* reported that "people almost everywhere wonder what [Dixon-Yates] are all about."[5] The central figures in this emerging controversy were Edgar H. Dixon, president of Middle South Utilities, Inc., and Eugene A. Yates, chairman of the Board of Directors of the Southern Company. Early in 1954, their respective companies had formed the Mississippi Valley Generating Company to construct and operate a coal-fueled steam generating plant at West Memphis, Arkansas. The plant was to supply the Atomic Energy Commission with 600,000 kilowatts of power annually.

Technically, the term Dixon-Yates was something of a misnomer. Certainly it would have been much more appropriate to have referred to the Dodge-Hughes-Strauss contract after its three principal architects, Joseph M. Dodge and Rowland R. Hughes, Eisenhower's first two directors of the Bureau of the Budget, and Admiral Lewis Strauss, chairman of the Atomic Energy Commission.

---

[2] Actually, Mitchell had his figures reversed. On June 17, 1954, Representative Chet Holifield of California charged before the Joint Congressional Committee on Atomic Energy that power generated by TVA would cost at least $90,000,-000 less than power generated by the Dixon-Yates combine. U.S., Congress, Senate-House, Joint Committee on Atomic Energy, *Hearings, S. 3323 and H.R. 8862, To Amend the Atomic Energy Act of 1946*, Part 2, 83d Cong., 2d Sess., 1954, p. 985. On the following day Lucius E. Burch, Jr., counsel for a New York power syndicate headed by Walter von Tresckow, testified before the Committee that the von Tresckow proposal would save the government a minimium of $150,000,000. *Ibid.*, p. 1084.

[3] The first article indexed under "Dixon-Yates" in the *Readers Guide to Periodical Literature* was "Mitchell's Charges," *America*, September 4, 1954, p. 530. It is interesting to note that six of the next ten articles which dealt with the controversy appeared in the *New Republic*. Had the President read this liberal journal, he may well have been spared a good deal of embarrassment.

[4] "Meet Dixon and Yates," *Life*, November 8, 1954, p. 34.

[5] "The ABC's of Dixon-Yates," *U.S. News and World Report*, November 19, 1954, p. 27.

The contract stemmed from the President's rejection, in 1954, of the Tennessee Valley Authority's request for funds to build a steam generating plant near Fulton, Tennessee, in order to meet the growing demands for power in the Memphis area. President Truman had rejected an identical request in 1953, and not a few of Truman's critics charged that he included the project in the 1954 budget only to embarrass the incoming Republican Administration. Regardless, Dodge promptly removed the Fulton proposal and the President promised, in his budget message of January, 1954, to solve the problem by "reducing, by the fall of 1957, existing commitments of the Tennessee Valley Authority to the Atomic Energy Commission by 500,000 to 600,000 kilowatts."[6]

The Atomic Energy Commission had previously contracted with private utility companies for needed power, once with Electric Energy, Inc., at Joppa, Illinois, and once with Ohio Valley Electrical Corporation at Portsmouth, Ohio. Thus, that aspect of the contract was not unique. However, it may be pointed out that the performance of both EEI and OVEC had been anything but spectacular. Construction costs and annual power charges at Joppa, for example, exceeded the original estimates by $58,000,000 and $2,800,000 respectively. Indeed, the ill-fated Joppa venture ultimately became known as the "Ebasco fiasco," after the company which was retained by EEI to construct the plant, Ebasco Services. The performance of OVEC at Portsmouth was little better. There construction costs and annual power charges exceeded the original estimates by $32,000,000 and $1,600,000.[7]

The fundamental difference, other than perhaps the clandestine manner in which the Dixon-Yates contract was negotiated, lay in the fact that the power generated by MVGC was not to be delivered to the Atomic Energy Commission installations as had been the case at both Joppa and Portsmouth. Under the terms of the Dixon-Yates contract, all of the power purchased from MVGC by the AEC was to be resold to the Tennessee Valley Authority so that it could be used in the Memphis area. In the lexicon of the Bureau of the Budget and the Atomic Energy Commission, this was "replacement power" for the like amount used by the AEC at its Paducah-Joppa installation some two hundred miles upstream. Thus, for the first time in its history, the AEC was to function as something of a power broker. This was, pure and simple, a "lunatic arrangement" editorialized *The New Republic.*[8] Even the staunchly Republican Scripps-Howard papers opposed the AEC's "broker role" and ad-

[6] For the text of the President's budget message see *The New York Times,* January 8, 1954.
[7] Senate-House Joint Committee on Atomic Energy, *Hearings To Amend the Atomic Energy Act of 1946,* 1954, p. 1003.
[8] "Hear No Evil, See No Evil, Speak No Evil," *New Republic,* September 13, 1954, p. 3.

vised the President to "toss [the Dixon-Yates contract] into the ash can."[9]

The competing syndicate to which Mitchell had referred was headed by Walter von Tresckow, a New York financial and economic consultant and formerly President of the Central Hanover Bank. It should be stressed, however, that this von Tresckow bid was not solicited by either the Bureau of the Budget or the Atomic Energy Commission. Aparently, by the sheerest of coincidences, von Tresckow read of the AEC's impending contract with the Dixon-Yates combine in a New York newspaper. He then dispatched a telegram to the Atomic Energy Commission requesting permission to submit an alternative proposal. His scheme was, in essence, quite simple. With the Federal Government underwriting the project, any risk to the contracting syndicate was virtually nonexistent. With this factor in mind, von Tresckow proposed to finance the entire project with low interest, three and one-half percent bonds, and limit the syndicate's profit to a flat fee of four million dollars. Finally, the plant was to be amortized over a thirty-year period, then sold to the Tennessee Valley Authority for one dollar.[10]

To say that the von Tresckow proposal was received unenthusiastically at the Bureau of the Budget and the Atomic Energy Commission would be an understatement. Indeed, it was only after more than a month of waiting and much correspondence that the syndicate officials were granted a hearing. Even then, its representatives were unable to meet with any of the top officers in the two government agencies. Less than two weeks after receiving the von Tresckow proposal, the AEC recommended against its adoption. The recommendation came in the face of the New York syndicate's insistence that its proposal would save the government a minimum of $150,000,000 over a thirty-year period. It was rejected, according to the director of the Bureau of the Budget, Roland R. Hughes, because of "elements of uncertainty and indefiniteness in the proposal" and because the Federal Government was forced to take the "entire financial risk with no real ceiling on the Government's liability."[11]

There is little doubt that Mitchell gleaned this political morsel from the pages of the *Congressional Record*. Senator Wayne Morse had, exactly one month earlier in the course of a debate on amendments to the Atomic Energy Act of 1946, made the identical charge. On July 17 the Oregon maverick remarked to his Senate colleagues

[9] The Scripps-Howard editorial was reproduced in "Ike Should Cancel Dixon-Yates Contract," *Time*, November 22, 1954, p. 39.
[10] Senate-House Joint Committee on Atomic Energy, *Hearings To Amend the Atomic Energy Act of 1946*, 1954, pp. 988, 1083.
[11] *Ibid.* See also William M. Blair, "President Revives T.V.A. Power Issue By Order to A.E.C.," *New York Times*, June 18, 1954.

that he had recently read an article in *Look* magazine which listed Bobby Jones as one of the President's "cronies."[12] "I am not blind to the fact, however, that [Jones] is also director of . . . the Southern Company, and I also know that it is a major member of the Dixon-Yates combine, with which the President has directed the Atomic Energy Commission to enter into a contract," he exlaimed. "It raises a question in my mind if what we are doing is substituting the golf stick for the public power yardstick."[13] Unlike Mitchell's charges, however, the Senator's remarks received little attention from the nation's press.

Chairman Hall refused to comment directly upon Mitchell's charges because, he said, he had "no knowledge" of the Dixon-Yates contract or the congressional discussion of it. Inasmuch as *The New York Times* had already devoted just under fifty news items to the Dixon-Yates controversy, this was certainly an amazing admission. "But I am sure of one thing," Hall exclaimed, "when Steve Mitchell or anyone else tries to show by implication that the President is doing a favor for one of his neighbors, the American people will condemn that statement."[14] Later, Bobby Jones termed the charges "utterly ridiculous and without foundation." "I would be very much surprised if [President Eisenhower] was even aware of the fact that I was on the Board of Directors of the Southern Company," he told the press, "because I have never had any conversation [with him] about that fact."[15]

Predictably, the initial question at the Presidential press conference the following day concerned the Mitchel allegations. "Mr. President, do you care to comment on that matter?" asked Marvin Arrowsmith of the Associated Press. A "wry smile" flashed across Eisenhower's usually benign face. It was immediately clear that the President had anticipated the question and had prepared his answer. He had expected, he said, to be exposed "to many kinds of innuendo and allegations" when he entered politics. However, he was a "little astonished" that the attack included a private citizen of the stature and character of Bobby Jones. "Of course I approved the recommendations for this [Dixon-Yates] action," the President told the assembled newsmen, and in a much firmer voice suggested, "Anyone of you present might singly or in an investigation group, go to the Bureau of the Budget, to the Chief of the Atomic Energy Commission, and get a complete record from the inception of the idea to this very minute, and it is all yours."[16]

As directed by the President, the Bureau of the Budget re-

[12] Fletcher Knebel, "Ike's Cronies," *Look,* June 1, 1954, p. 59.
[13] U.S., *Congressional Record*, 83d Cong., 2d Sess., 1954, 100, Part 8, p. 10794.
[14] Luther A. Huston, "Mitchell Implies G.O.P. Corruption," *New York Times*, August 17, 1954.
[15] *Ibid.*
[16] Joseph A. Loftus, "President Scorns Mitchell Attack on A.E.C. Contract," *New York Times*, August 18, 1954. For the text of the President's news conference see *The New York Times*, August 18, 1954.

leased, on August 21, what it termed the "full and complete" account of the negotiations which led to the signing of the Dixon-Yates contract.[17] Journalist Douglass Cater pointed out, however, that "someone around the White House was . . . blessed with genius in timing the release of this material,"[18] for the release, which ran to a total of 134 mimeographed pages, came at 4:30 on Saturday afternoon. Thus, reporters found themselves with the almost impossible task of assimilating the huge mass of detailed and complex material and writing their respective stories in the few short hours before the deadline for filing their weekend copy. As a result, much of the material relevant to Dixon-Yates never made the nation's press. Moreover, a disapportionate amount of what did get published dealt with that material which exonerated the President of any improper relations with the famous Georgia golfer.

Unquestionably, the documents proved that there was not a scintilla of truth to Mitchell's suggestion that the Dixon-Yates contract may have been conceived on the Augusta fairways. In fact, the documents indicated quite clearly that the President was not even informed of the particulars of it until long after the negotiations had begun. Thus, the purity of the President's own relations to the contract seemed assured; he remaind "as clean as a hound's tooth." However, a careful reading of the documents did reinforce a growing suspicion that there had been a serious lack of Presidential knowledge of and control over the Dixon-Yates negotiations from the very outset.

The idea that Eisenhower was less than well informed about the details of the whole affair had first been suggested by his comments in a July 22 press conference.[19] Syndicated columnist Doris Fleeson had asked Eisenhower whether he thought that the President had the power to order a supposedly independent regulatory commission like the Atomic Energy Commission to execute a contract which a majority of its members opposed. Specifically, she said, she was referring to the revelations of the Joint Committee on Atomic Energy that three of the five AEC commissioners had initially opposed the Dixon-Yates contract. Considering the fact that Commissioners Henry D. Smith and Eugene M. Zuckert had, in an April 16, 1954, letter to the director of the Bureau of the Budget, termed the contract "awkward and unbusinesslike" and "irrelevant to the mission of the commission,"[20] the President's response was

[17] *Ibid.*, August 19, 1954.

[18] Douglass Cater, "The ABC of Dixon-Yates, Or, How To Get Less for More," *Reporter*, October 21, 1954, p. 16.

[19] For the text of the President's press conference see *The New York Times*, July 22, 1954.

[20] A full disclosure of the contents of the letter from Zuckert to Hughes had been made before the Joint Committee on Atomic Energy on June 17, 1954. Senate-House Joint Committee on Atomic Energy, *Hearings to Amend the Atomic Energy Act of 1946*, 1954, p. 958. The existence of the letters had, moreover, been reported in a page-one story in *The New York Times* the following day. See Blair, *New York Times*, June 18, 1954.

shocking. "Now, in this one [question] you are telling me things and you are giving me a premise that I didn't know existed."[21]

That the officials in the Bureau of the Budget and the Atomic Energy Commission had never solicited any alternative private proposals was clearly established long before the release of this "full and complete" account of the Dixon-Yates negotiations. But these new documents also brought to light the even more startling revelation that the Tennessee Valley Authority, whose operations would be so fundamentally affected by the terms of the agreement, had not been informed of the negotiations until the contract was virtually a *fait accompli*. In a letter of July 2 to Director Hughes, the vice-chairman of the TVA's board of directors complained that TVA had not been afforded the courtesy of examining and commenting upon the President's instructions to the AEC before they were released. In concluding his remarks, he attacked the terms of the contract as "seriously prejudicial both to TVA and to the interests of the Government."[22]

Administrative officials, it will be recalled, had justified their rejection of the von Tresckow proposal, at least in part, on the grounds that the Federal Government would have been forced under its terms to assume the "entire financial risk." Yet, these same officials rejected a proposal of the Tennessee Valley Authority despite the fact that their own estimates indicated that the cost of TVA generated power would result in an annual savings to the Federal Government of some $3,685,000.[23] TVA's estimates, incidentally, indicated an annual savings of $5,567,000.[24] According to the lexicon of a 5,000 word analysis issued by the Bureau of the Budget on July 7, 1954, to allow the TVA to perform all such functions simply because it could do it more cheaply would be contrary to what it termed "our basic conception of the private enterprise economy." The facts "demonstrate clearly," the report continued, "that [the Dixon-Yates contract] is the best possible solution of the immediate problem."[25]

At this stage of the controversy, one fact had become crystal clear: Eisenhower Republicans, no less than the Roosevelt and Truman Democrats, were extremely rigid ideologists on the question of public versus private power. Indeed, officials of the Eisen-

[21] For the text of the President's press conference see *The New York Times*, July 22, 1954. At this time, White House rules required that the President's remarks be reported in "indirect discourse." Obviously, however, *The New York Times* simply changed the transcript from first person to third person. The Eisenhower diction and syntax are quite unmistakable. The author of this study took the liberty in this chapter of changing the quoted statements to first person.
[22] Elie Abel, "Two Agencies Open Files in Dispute on A.E.C. Contract," *New York Times*, August 22, 1954.
[23] Senate-House Joint Committee on Atomic Energy, *Hearings To Amend the Atomic Energy Act of 1946*, 1954, p. 957.
[24] *Ibid.*, p. 1063.
[25] *New York Times*, July 11, 1954.

hower Administration, and of course the President himself, reacted to the need for additional power in the Tennessee Valley like so many Pavlovian dogs; i. e., they simply assumed that private power, regardless of the cost of production, was inherently preferable to public power. Therefore, a way had to be found to deliver the contract to a private utility and, thereby, strike a blow for free enterprise. Dixon-Yates represented, as one author so succinctly put it, "a tenacious administrative devotion to ideology in defiance of economic fact and correct procedure which matches or surpasses any ideological fixation imputed to the most doctrinaire of the New Dealers."[26]

Of course, the extent of the President's commitment to public power in general and the Tennessee Valley Authority in particular had long been a subject of debate. An examination of Eisenhower's statements on the subject seemed to suggest that he stood firmly on both sides of the issue; he was both for and against public power. As a Presidential candidate in 1952, Eisenhower told a Memphis, Tennessee, audience, "There is no disposition on my part to impair the effective working out of the T.V.A."[27] At a press conference of June 17, 1953, he told reporters, "I have stated a thousand times that I am not out to destroy T.V.A."[28] Further, in defending the Dixon-Yates contract during his press conference of July 21, 1954, the President insisted, "I am prepared to support the T.V.A. as it now stands, with all the strength I have, and anyone who says this is any attempt to destroy the T.V.A. is, to say it in the mildest way I know, in error."[29]

On the other hand, at the McNary Dam dedication ceremony of September 23, 1954, Eisenhower exhibited a pronounced hostility toward "the believers in centralization," i.e., the advocates of public power. "As Federal power expands in a region . . . local enterprise becomes increasingly intimidated and discouraged even though the needs for energy continue to grow," the President told his audience. "Thus, still more Federal intervention becomes necessary. Such a conversion of local regions [into] Federal satel-

[26] Cater, *Reporter*, October 21, 1954, p. 13. It seems not unfair to point out that at least from Adam Smith to Herbert Hoover *competition* has been regarded as a fundamental principle of the free enterprise system. And while admitting that unrestricted competition in the utility field is seldom feasible, it was somewhat incongruous that an administration so publicly committed to the advancement of free enterprise would repress so completely every alternative proposal to Dixon-Yates, whether it originated in the public or private sector. So it appeared that all, or at least a major part, of the enterprise was eliminated and, without any real competition, Messieurs Dixon and Yates were simply granted a contract which virtually assured them a nine to eleven percent return on their equity investment for a period of twenty-five years. See Gordon R. Clapp, "Dixon-Yates Deal," *Nation*, October 2, 1954, pp. 286–87.
[27] E. W. Kenworthy, "Dixon-Yates: The Riddle of a Self-Inflicted Wound," *Reporter*, January 26, 1956, p. 19.
[28] *New York Times*, June 18, 1953.
[29] *Ibid.*, July 22, 1954.

lites poses a threat deadly to our liberties. The Administration in Washington . . . is unalterably opposed to such malignant growth of bureaucracy."[30] Emmet John Hughes, chronicler of the Eisenhower Administration, later quoted the President as having said in his cabinet meeting of July 31, 1953, "By God, if ever we could do it, before we leave here I'd like to see us sell the whole [TVA] thing, but I suppose we can't go that far."[31]

The single bright spot for Dixon-Yates critics toward the latter part of 1954 stemmed from revelations before the Senate Subcommittee on Antitrust and Monopoly that Middle South, the utility company headed by Edgar H. Dixon, and its subsidiary, the Mississippi Power and Light Company, had for years engaged in a variety of questionable activities such as excessive charges and dual bookkeeping.[32] Indeed, testimony before the subcomittee raised a very real question as to whether the companies had not continually violated provisions of the Holding Company Act of 1935. James D. Stietenroth, secretary-treasurer of MPLC, opined, for example, "I think the way we have operated down there is certainly in violation of the spirit of the Holding Company Act."[33]

At the time, the subcommittee was headed by maverick North Dakota Republican William Langer. On the Dixon-Yates issue, as well as a good many others, Langer was anything but an organization man. Organizational Republicans did not want an investigation. Indeed, the lack of enthusiasm within the party hierarchy for an investigation of the monopolistic practices among Dixon-Yates subsidiaries can well be judged by the fact that the Republican Policy Committee, according to Langer, had blocked his request for funds to conduct his proposed investigation.[34]

Langer, however, was not to be denied. He simply told his fellow Republicans that he would finance the investigation out of his own pocket. "As long as I pay the bills, who's going to stop me?" he said. Nonetheless, Everett Dirksen, Republican Senator from Illinois and chairman of the Republican Campaign Committee, questioned the legality of using private funds for an official inquiry. Should Langer carry out his threat to finance such an investigation, Dirksen solemnly told reporters, "it would become a

[30] *Ibid.*, September 24, 1954.

[31] Emmet John Hughes, *The Ordeal of Power* (New York: Atheneum, 1963), p. 152.

[32] U.S., Congress, Senate, Subcommittee on Antitrust and Monopoly Legislation of the Committee on the Judiciary, *Hearings, Power Policy: Dixon-Yates Contract*, Part 2, 83d Cong., 2d Sess., 1954, p. 185. See also Michael Straight, "New Light on Dixon-Yates," *New Republic*, October 11, 1954, pp. 8–10. See also Straight, "More Light on Dixon-Yates," *New Republic*, October 18, 1954, pp. 6–11.

[33] Senate Subcommittee on Antitrust and Monopoly, *Dixon-Yates Hearings*, 1954, p. 280.

[34] *New York Times*, August 22, 1954.

matter of public interest."[35] After the Langer hearings began, John
M. Butler, the Republican Senator from Maryland and the man
who professed to be "representing the distinguished Senator from
Illinois, [Everett Dirksen],"[36] interrupted the testimony repeatedly
to suggest that the investigation was being conducted without the
approval of the Senate, e.g., "is this the subcommittee that the
Congress refused funds for?"; "I think in all fairness, the chairman
must put on this record that the Senate of the United States refused
the funds for this hearing"; "the Senate itself has refused this committee and its chairman funds to hold this investigation."[37]

Even after the revelations before the Langer subcommittee,
however, it seemed likely that the Democrats' attack on the Dixon-
Yates contract would fall short of success. Certainly, the Stietenroth
testimony had virtually no impact on the President. At the Presidential press conference of October 27, for example, Clark R. Mollenhoff of the *Des Moines Register and Tribune* asked Eisenhower
if the unethical behavior of the Dixon-Yates subsidiaries had had
any "effect on his thinking." He also asked if the fact that competitive bids had not been solicited "bothered him." "Well, I can't think
of any man in Government whom I trust more as to his integrity,
his common sense, and his business acumen than Lewis Strauss,"
answered the President.[38] Apparently, if it did not bother Chairman
Strauss, it did not bother Eisenhower. Still, Senator Kefauver, the
ranking Democrat on the Langer subcommittee was quite bothered
and termed the Dixon-Yates contract "bad business, bad government, and bad morals."[39] In the end, of course, it was to be the
Senator's judgment, not the President's, which would prevail. But
that was still several months away.

Indeed, throughout the fall and winter of 1954, the chances of
voiding the Dixon-Yates contract appeared to be rather bleak. Of
course, the critics of the contract had received a near fatal blow
at the very outset of the controversy when Chairman Mitchell
made his ill-conceived attack on the beloved President. *The New
York Times* was moved to comment editorially, "Chairman Stephen
A. Mitchell of the Democratic National Committee has done his

[35] *Ibid.* See also *ibid.*, August 31, 1954. A White House aide would later
remark, "[Dirksen] was one of the few men up there who stood by us all through
the Dixon-Yates affair—and those were pretty rough days around here," William
Barry Furlong, "The Senates Wizard of Ooze: Dirksen of Illinois," *Harpers*, December, 1959, p. 45.
[36] Senate Subcommittee on Antitrust and Monopoly, *Dixon-Yates Hearings*,
1954, p. 186. During the latter part of September, Senator Dirksen was in Massachusetts and was, thus, unable to attend the subcommittee hearings. Before his
departure, however, he designated Senator Butler to be his personal representative.
[37] *Ibid.*, pp. 187, 188, 227.
[38] For the text of the President's press conference of October 27, 1954, see *The
New York Times*, October 28, 1954.
[39] *Ibid.*, July 5, 1954.

best to reduce this year's political campaign to the lowest possible
level. . . . It outrages one's sense of fairness."[40] Then, too, early
in the controversy the President had released what was purportedly
the "full and complete" record of the contractual negotiations. The
President's stratagem, at least for the short run, was immensely
successful. For such a maneuver made it appear, to many viewers,
that the Dixon-Yates negotiations had been completely correct and
aboveboard.

The Democratic dilemma of the time was succinctly stated by
Douglass Cater in an article which appeared in the October 21, 1954,
issue of *The Reporter* magazine. "[The Democrats] have as yet
been unable to prove any collusion or direct malfeasance in the
Dixon-Yates affair," he wrote. "Their problem is to explain through
a maze of technical detail just how awkwardly, arbitrarily, and at
what cost to the taxpayer the Administration has gone about ex-
pressing its doctrines in practice."[41] Apparently, only Governor-
Elect James Folsom of Alabama had had any degree of success
in explaining the intricacies of the Dixon-Yates contract to the
American voters. In explaining his technique to fellow Democrats
in Indianapolis, Indiana, "Kissin Jim" asserted, "I just tell them
that Mistuh Eisenhower is trying to take TVA away from the
people and give it to Mistuh Dixon and Mistuh Yates!"[42] Still,
some members of the audience expressed some doubts as to the
universality of such an appeal.

Admittedly, the released documents indicated that the Tennessee Valley Authority would have produced the power more cheaply
than the Dixon-Yates syndicate, but the President had justified the
award, it will be recalled, in the name of private enterprise. It
appeared more than barely possible that in any case the typical
American and, more importantly, the typical newspaper and periodical editor were not necessarily committed to an unlimited ex-
tension of public power.[43] As late as December, 1954, for example,
The Saturday Evening Post could still editorialize, "no evidence
was presented to suggest that the Dixon-Yates contract was unusual
or that it was disadvantageous to the Government." It concluded,
moreover, that "the question is not 'What is immoral about the

[40] *Ibid.*, August 19, 1954.

[41] Cater, *Reporter,* October 21, 1954, p. 16.

[42] *Ibid.*

[43] The editorial silence on the Dixon-Yates contract caused Democratic
standard-bearer Adlai Stevenson to remark that "some historian is going to have
trouble figuring out why one President's letter to a music critic got the American
press so much more excited than the next President's writing a check for scores
of millions on the American taxpayers to a group of private utility companies."
Lawrence C. Davies, "Stevenson Says Democrats Save Policy for G.O.P.," *New
York Times,* July 11, 1954.

Dixon-Yates contract?' but 'Do we or don't we want nationalization of our electric-power industry?' "[44]

In late 1954 and early in 1955 the controversial contract cleared three major hurdles. On October 20, 1954, Attorney General Herbert Brownell, Jr., ruled the proposed contract, the text of which even at this late date had not been released by the Administration, to be valid under the Atomic Energy Act of 1954.[45] To that point a number of the Dixon-Yates critics had insisted that the contract was invalid on at least two counts. First, they argued that Section 164 of the Act prohibited the Atomic Energy Commission from assuming the role of "power broker," and, second, they argued that Section 165b prohibited the Commission from reimbursing contractors for federal income taxes.[46] The Dixon-Yates contract, incidentally, provided that federal income taxes be included in computing and adjusting the base rate and cost structure at West Memphis.

On November 13, 1954, the Joint Committee on Atomic Energy voted to waive a provision of the Atomic Energy Act which requires that all atomic energy contracts lie before the committee for thirty days unless a majority of its members specifically rules otherwise.[47] The vote, which was along straight party lines, had come after a week of hectic testimony punctuated with acrimonious exchanges between Administration spokesmen, especially Strauss and Hughes, and Democratic members of the committee. It hardly seems an exaggeration to say that the Administration failed utterly to justify the necessity for such haste.[48] *The New Republic* reported, for ex-

[44] "The Dixon-Yates Row Was a TVA Diversion," *Saturday Evening Post*, December 11, 1954, p. 10. As late as April, 1955, an article in *Reader's Digest*, which was subtitled "A Study in Political Frenzy," could argue, "Dr. Eisenhower, who has a degree in 'middle-of-the-road' philosophy, is not prescribing the death of public power. He is simply suggesting that it should walk more on its own feet. And that is all that there is to the furor over the Dixon-Yates contract." William Hard, "Washington's Big Brawl: Dixon-Yates," *Reader's Digest*, April, 1955, p. 22.

[45] *Ops. Att'y Gen.* 187 (1954). For the sake of accuracy, it should be mentioned that the *St. Louis Post-Dispatch*, on October 12, 1954, published the essentials of the contract. Richard Dudman, "Dixon-Yates Contract Gives Risk-Free 9 Percent Return," *St. Louis Post-Dispatch*, October 12, 1954. The accuracy of its release was confirmed a few days later by *The New York Times*. See Anthony Leviero, "Dixon-Yates Pact Put to Brownell for Legal Ruling," *New York Times*, October 16, 1954. It was never revealed just who leaked the story to the newspapers, but in his press conference of October 27 the President told Raymond P. Brandt, "If I had anything to do with it, I would discipline the person who gave [the paper] the copy. . . . I don't know [the person]." For the text of the President's press conference remarks see *The New York Times*, October 28, 1954.

[46] 68 *Stat.* 919 (1954).

[47] William M. Blair, "Committee Clears Dixon-Yates Pact By G.O.P. Majority," *New York Times*, November 19, 1954.

[48] U.S., Congress, Senate-House, Joint Committee on Atomic Energy, *Hearings, Utility Contract Between Atomic Energy Commission and Mississippi Valley Generating Company*, 83d Cong., 2d Sess., 1954, pp. 3, 11, 214, 254, 292, 572, 619.

ample, that the ten Republican members were "understandably glum" following the testimony by Strauss and Hughes and had admitted, privately, that the Administration was behaving "outrageously."[49]

Indeed, the favorable vote had come only after Chairman W. Sterling Cole received a letter from the President in which he specifically requested the waiver of the thirty day rule. To that point, there was reason to believe that at least two of the ten Republican members of the committee were prepared to join the eight Democrats in opposing it. Since the incoming Congress was to be controlled by the Democrats, the switch of these two Republicans would, in effect, have killed the Dixon-Yates contract. Once the President put his power and influence behind the proposal, however, all ten Republicans quickly fell into line. In the President's letter to Cole, which began "Dear Stub,"[50] Eisenhower pointed out that his Administration was opposed to "fastening on the Federal Government a continuing and never-ending responsibilty which I frankly do not believe is logical nor, in the long run, in the best interests of the country." And although he indicated his desire for the committee to give the proposal its "fullest consideration," he did emphasize the fact that "the Administration plan and all facts concerning its development, have been before the public for months."[51] The veracity of the latter remark would, in a few short weeks, be vigorously challenged.

On February 9, 1955, the Securities and Exchange Commission removed the final obstacle to the Dixon-Yates contract when, in a four to one decision, it approved the financing proposal of the Mississippi Valley Generating Company.[52] Democratic Commissioner Paul Rowen was the lone dissenter. Many of the opponents of the Dixon-Yates scheme had hoped that the SEC would void MVGC's admittedly unusual plans for financing the project. Indeed, the ratio of bonded indebtedness to equity capital, i.e., capital to be raised by the Dixon-Yates group, was an extraordinarily high ninety-five to five percent. It was, according to the lexicon of Wall Street, a "high leverage" operation. Typically, in such ventures, the percentage of equity capital to be put up by the promoter never runs under forty percent, unless an emergency situation exists, and it frequently runs as high as sixty percent. However, under the financing arrangement approved by the SEC, Dixon-

[49] Michael Straight, "Dear Stub . . . Signed Dwight," *New Republic,* December 27, 1954, p. 13.
[50] *Ibid.*
[51] For the text of the President's letter to Chairman Cole see *The New York Times,* November 11, 1954.
[52] William M. Blair, "Dixon-Yates Wins Approval of S.E.C.," *New York Times,* February 10, 1955.

Yates would be required to put up only $5,500,000 of the total $105,415,000.[53]

But on February 18, 1955, the Democrats uncovered what eventually proved to be the fundamental chink in the Administration's seemingly impregnable armor. On that day Senator Lister Hill of Alabama asserted from the floor of Congress that "facts [concerning the Dixon-Yates deal] have been deliberately concealed from the Congress and the American people." Specifically, he charged that one Adolphe H. Wenzell, a vice president and director of the First Boston Corporation, the banking firm which had arranged the Dixon-Yates financing, was acting as a consultant to the director of the Bureau of the Budget during the very period in which the Dixon-Yates negotiations were in progress. According to the Senator, "There exists persuasive evidence that this man participated in conferences and meetings on the Dixon-Yates matter, which were held in the Budget Bureau at the very time when the First Boston company was making arrangements for financing the Dixon-Yates plant."[54]

At this point, Senator Hill's "persuasive evidence" consisted largely of a single confidential memorandum which had been drafted by T. G. Seal, the Ebasco Services official in charge of plant construction at West Memphis, and which dealt with one of Adolphe Wenzell's visits to the Dixon-Yates office in Washington. The memorandum had initially been uncovered in the course of hearings before the Securities and Exchange Commission. Two of Seal's remarks in the next-to-last paragraph were particularly revealing: "Following my visit with Mr. Cook [Deputy Manager of the AEC], Mr. Wenzell rejoined me in our office about 5 P.M., when he had finished his day with the Budget Bureau people." This comment is even more startling when one considers the fact that the sole purpose of Wenzell's visit to the Bureau of the Budget was, admittedly, to make certain that the officials there were "thoroughly posted" for their "anticipated argument with TVA." Later, the Seal memorandum stated, "Mr. Clapp of the TVA and General Nichols of the AEC and the Budget Bureau people were to get together today, March 3, in Mr. Hughes' office at 9 A.M. for

---

[53] Kenworthy, *Reporter*, January 26, 1956, p. 23.
[54] U.S., *Congressional Record*, 84th Cong., 1st Sess., 1955, 101, Part 2, p. 1714. It is interesting to note that on the very day that *The New York Times* printed the Senator's charges, it also carried a news item which indicated that Eugene A. Yates had issued a thirty-four page statement defending the terms of the power contract. According to the Yates release, "the facts show that the contract is sound, reasonable and in the best interests of the Government, the public and the sponsoring companies. The contract and related transactions have been meticulously studied and checked by all Government agencies concerned." *New York Times*, February 19, 1955.

further intra-Government discussion. We hope to hear how these discussions eventuate later today."[55]

Hill told his colleagues that as soon as he became aware of the possibility that Wenzell had served in such a dual capacity he telephoned Hughes's office for an explanation. Although Hughes could not be reached at that time, the Senator described the nature of his inquiry to the assistant director and subsequently received a letter from Hughes. "Bureau of the Budget records show that on May 20, 1953, Mr. Wenzell was invited to serve as a consultant, without compensation, to Mr. Joseph M. Dodge, then Director of the Bureau of the Budget," Hughes said in a letter dated February 11, 1955. "Mr. Wenzell's consultative services were used intermittently for a total of 34 days between May 20, 1953, and March 2, 1954, when he completed his work." Finally, the director stated, "Mr. Dodge advises me that Mr. Wenzell was engaged as a technical expert . . . regarding the accounting system of the Tennessee Valley Authority."[56] On March 16, 1955, Hughes wrote a second letter to Hill. "Although the condition and nature of Mr. Wenzell's services are as set forth in that letter [of February 11], supplementary information as to the period when [Wenzell's] services were used has come to my attention," the director said. "Our records show that Mr. Wenzell attended a few meetings between March 2 and April 3, 1954. Our records show further that these meetings were concerned with the technical aspects of the [Dixon-Yates] proposal.[57]

In a statement released by the First Boston Corporation some three days after Hill's initial charges, the president of the company, James Coggeshall, asserted that Wenzell's role as an "unpaid consultant" to the Bureau of the Budget between May, 1953, and March, 1954, had "long been known in Government, financial, and utility circles." Insofar as Coggeshall was concerned, First Boston's role in the Dixon-Yates controversy could be explained quite simply: "We were asked to advise and assist in the financing. We agreed and the needed financing was subsequently arranged." Moreover, the corporation executive stressed repeatedly that neither First Boston nor Wenzell had, or would, receive a fee for the services performed.[58]

Still, if Wenzell's role in the Dixon-Yates negotiations had been so well known in government circles, critics asked, why had Wenzell's name not appeared in the Budget Bureau's release of August 21, 1955? It will be recalled that on that date the Bureau had released, with great fanfare, the "full and complete" chronology

[55] U.S., *Congressional Record*, 84th Cong., 1st Sess., 1955, 101, Part 2, p. 1716.
[56] For the text of the Hughes letter of February 11, 1955, see *ibid*. See also William M. Blair, "Facts Concealed on Dixon-Yates Senator Asserts," *New York Times*, February 19, 1955.
[57] Quoted from Kenworthy, *Reporter*, January 26, 1956, p. 24.
[58] *New York Times*, February 22, 1955.

of the facts concerning the Dixon-Yates contract.[59] Why, also, had Hughes's two letters to Hill evinced such a fragmentary knowledge of Wenzell's participation in the negotiations? A cursory examination of the letters made the Hughes tack readily apparent. The director was making a heroic effort to convey the impression that Wenzell's role in the negotiations had been relatively insignificant— so insignificant, in fact, that Hughes had not even been particularly aware of it until after the Senator's inquiry. Ultimately, answers to both of these questions were to come, but not for some four months.

On June 23, 1955, Memphis voted to build its own $100,000,000 municipally owned electric generating plant. Mayor Frank Tobey told reporters that the action had been taken so that the plant would be completed before the city's contract with the Tennessee Valley Authority expired in 1958.[60] This action should have come as no surprise to anyone even slightly familiar with the city's history, for it had been a base of strength for the advocates of public power since the days of Edward H. "Boss" Crump. Memphis, for example, was the first major city to enter the TVA system.[61] Crump, who according to W. C. Handy's immortal "Memphis Blues" did not " 'low no gee-tar playing in Memphis," also did not " 'low no" private power companies in Memphis either, at least not after 1939. The motive behind the city's action was made abundantly clear by Major Thomas H. Allen, president of the Memphis Light, Gas, and Water Division, who stated categorically, "we do not intend to use Dixon-Yates power, and that's that."[62]

In a letter dated June 30, 1955, TVA Board Chairman Herbert D. Vogel informed Director Hughes that, following the decision by the Memphis city commission, the power to be developed by the Dixon-Yates combine was no longer needed. Apparently, electricity generated at the West Memphis plant could be distributed, economically, only in the Memphis area. Unlikely as it may seem, the Administration gave every indication that it was surprised by this turn of events. The President, for example, when informed by telephone of the Vogel letter, even interrupted his golf game at the Burning Tree Golf Club and quickly returned to the White House.[63]

[59] *Ibid.*, August 19, 1954. See also *ibid.*, August 22, 1954. On November 4, 1954, Hughes testified before the Joint Committee on Atomic Energy that "all basic information that I have on the subject is already public knowlege. . . . The complete facts on the background of this problem have been publicly available for more than two months." Joint Committee on Atomic Energy, *Hearings on the Utility Contract Between AEC and MVGC,* 1954, pp. 11, 14. Strauss later testified before the same committee, "I have no knowledge of any consultants that Mr. Dodge may have had, or whether he had any." *Ibid.*, p. 249.

[60] *New York Times,* June 24, 1955.

[61] "The End of Dixon-Yates?," *Time,* July 11, 1955, p. 15.

[62] "Dimout?" *Newsweek,* July 11, 1955, p. 27.

[63] W. H. Lawrence, "Dixon-Yates Doom Seen As President Orders a Review," *New York Times,* July 1, 1955.

Reporters were told to stand by for "an important story." Finally, at what *The New York Times* called the "unusually late hour" of 7:00 P.M., the White House issued a news release to the effect that the President had requested Hughes "to confer promptly with the Atomic Energy Commission and the Tennessee Valley Authority to determine whether it is in the interests of the people of that area now to continue or to cancel the Dixon-Yates contract." From their talks with Hughes, reporters "suspected cancellation"— suspicions which were to be confirmed ten days later when the President officially cancelled the contract. The White House news release came, interestingly, just one hour before Hughes was to appear before an "extraordinary and well-heralded" night session of Senator Kefauver's Subcommittee on Antitrust and Monopoly to explain Wenzell's role in the Dixon-Yates negotiations.[64]

Following Hughes's appearance before the Joint Committee on Atomic Energy in November, 1954, the editors of *The New Republic* had remarked that the director "proved to be as inept a witness as reporters could remember. He appeared to know so little about the major provisions of the Dixon-Yates contract, which he had approved, that with some justification Senator [Clinton] Anderson asked him if he had ever read it."[65] Hughes's appearance before Senator Kefauver's subcommittee in July, 1955, did little to soften this judgment. Indeed, a report later issued by the subcommittee stated categorically, at one point, "the testimony that Hughes gave before the subcommittee defies understanding."[66]

When questioned as to why Wenzell had never been mentioned as being a participant in the Dixon-Yates negotiations in the Bureau's "full and complete" chronology, Hughes testified that he thought the executive's role had been too insignificant. None of those in "technical-advisory" capacities had been listed, he said. Wenzell "never had anything to do with the policy of Dixon-Yates or anything of that nature."[67] When asked why Wenzell's name had also failed to appear anywhere on the chronology released by the Atomic Energy Commission, the director replied, "I imagine

[64] "The Day It Got Hot At Burning Tree," *New Republic,* July 11, 1955, p. 3.
   [65] *New Republic,* November 15, 1954, p. 3.
   [66] U.S., Congress, Senate, Subcommittee on Antitrust and Monopoly, *Power Policy: Dixon-Yates Contract,* Staff Report Pursuant to S. Res. 61 as extended by S. Res. 170, 84th Cong., 2d Sess., 1956, p. xviii. The director's testimony was replete with ambiguity and contradictions. At one point, for example, he insisted that President Eisenhower "knows . . . we had an expert working on this thing, and he knows his name and his connection and all about him. In fact, he approved him before we got him down here." U.S., Congress, Senate, Subcommittee on Antitrust and Monopoly of the Committee on the Judiciary, *Hearings, Power Policy: Dixon-Yates Contract,* 84th Cong., 1st Sess., 1955, p. 53. At the same time, however, he argued that he had "no recollection" that he had called Wenzell and asked him to come to Washington as a consultant. *Ibid.,* p. 22.
   [67] *Ibid.,* p. 18.

[Strauss] decided it for the Atomic Energy; I decided it for the Budget Bureau."[68] These comments were especially revealing inasmuch as the assistant manager of the AEC, R. W. Cook, would later testify that Wenzell's name had been deleted from the commission's chronology at the specific request of the Bureau of the Budget.[69]

Chairman Kefauver also asked the director, quite pointedly, what he thought of Wenzell's having arranged for the First Boston Corporation to act as the financial agent for the Dixon-Yates combine. The exchange which followed was nothing short of amazing. "Did he do that?" the beleaguered Hughes answered. "You have been acquainted with this thing all through, and you did not know First Boston was the financial agent?" the Senator asked. "I don't believe they are, but maybe they are, I don't know. I would have to check it up. That is not our part of the job," Hughes said. The Senator, slightly aghast by this time, pressed on. "Well, you read Senator Lister Hill's speech in February, [1955]?" (It should be stressed that Senator Kafauver's question was being posed on June 27, 1955, slightly over four months after Hill had made his celebrated speech on the floor of the Senate.) "I was told it was not true," the director answered lamely.[70]

On July 8, 12, and 19, the key figure in the controversy, Adolphe Wenzell, testified before the subcommittee.[71] Considering the nature of the testimony by previous witnesses, especially Hughes, Wenzell proved to be a refreshing change. The former First Boston executive, who had resigned from the firm on June 1, some four years before he reached the compulsory retirement age,[72] proved to be a blunt, outspoken advocate of what he styled rugged individualism, a man who believed with all his heart that the Tennessee Valley Authority was a horrendous example of creeping socialism. His testimony gave the distinct impression that he would have regarded it as a great public service to have turned the entire TVA system over to private enterprise. Although his political and economic views may have been more appropriate in the Coolidge-Harding-Hoover era, his testimony was invariably precise and to the point.

Wenzell testified that he had been called to Washington by Hughes on January 18, 1954, to serve as an expert on questions of financing for the Bureau of the Budget. Two days later Wenzell brought First Boston Vice President Paul L. Miller to Washington

[68] *Ibid.*, p. 43.
[69] *Ibid.*, p. 703.
[70] *Ibid.*, pp. 40–41.
[71] For an excellent account of Wenzell's testimony before the Senate subcommittee see Walter Goodman, "About Face on Dixon-Yates," *New Republic*, July 18, 1955, pp. 6–8.
[72] Subcommittee on Antitrust and Monopoly, *Dxion-Yates Hearings*, 1955, p. 116.

to aid him in this capacity.[73] From his testimony before the Securities and Exchange Commission and the Senate subcommittee, it was apparent that, throughout the negotiations, Miller regarded himself as a representative of First Boston. At the SEC debt finance hearings, for example, Miller stated that he "certainly personally hoped" that his company would be named the financial agent for Dixon-Yates.[74] "[The Dixon-Yates package] showed the potentiality of being a large piece of financing, an interesting piece of financing, which would attract notice among private utility executives," Miller told the members of the subcommittee, "and we were glad to be associated with it whether we got a fee or not."[75] Finally, George D. Woods, chairman of the board at First Boston, testified that Miller went to Washington as a "First Boston man."[76]

Wenzell himself attended some twenty meetings which were connected, in one way or another with the Dixon-Yates contract. Indeed, the consultant must have moved like a whirling dervish between his Bureau of the Budget office in Washington and his First Boston office in New York from January 14 to April 10, 1954. During most of the month of February, for example, he was spending Monday and Friday at First Boston and Tuesday, Wednesday, and Thursday at the Bureau of the Budget. On February 23, Wenzell, along with other officials of the First Boston Corporation, completed the financing proposal for the Dixon-Yates combine in the firm's New York offices. A few days later Mr. Dixon sent the plan to the Bureau of the Budget, where financial consultant Wenzell was on hand to aid in its evaluation for the government.[77] This duplicity is even more amazing when one considers the fact that Wenzell insisted, under oath, that he had made it "abundantly clear" to Hughes that First Boston was to be the financial agent for Dixon-Yates. Moreover, he had previously testified before the Securities and Exchange Commission that he was the "mouthpiece" for First Boston during this period.[78]

Eventually, the duplicity of his position became so obvious to Wenzell that, on February 23, 1954, he approached Hughes about

[73] *Ibid.*, pp. 211–12.
[74] *Ibid.*, p. 90.
[75] *Ibid.*, p. 86.
[76] *Ibid.*, p. 548. Both Wenzell and Miller testified that Miller had conferred with Hughes in his office on at least one occasion. This was of particular importance inasmuch as Hughes insisted throughout the hearings that he had never met, or even heard of, Miller, e.g., "as far as I am concerned, Miller is an unknown party to me." *Ibid.*, p. 40.
[77] Subcommittee on Antitrust and Monopoly, *Dixon-Yates Contract*, Report Pursuant to S. Res. 61 & 170, 1956, p. xxix. See also Goodman, *New Republic*, July 18, 1955, p. 6.
[78] Subcommittee on Antitrust and Monopoly, *Dixon–Yates Hearings*, 1955, p. 287. Throughout Wenzell's term of employment for the Bureau of the Budget, he received his full salary from First Boston. However, he received only travel and per diem expenses from the government.

its propriety. He said he told the director that it could conceivably cause "some embarrassment later on." It was his view, Wenzell told the members of the subcommittee, that the director "didn't think . . . it was as serious or had the implications, possibly, that I had."[79] A few days after his talk with Hughes, however, Wenzell again brought up the subject, this time with a lawyer for Sullivan and Cromwell, the law firm which represented First Boston Corporation. The counsel with whom he spoke, John Raben, advised Wenzell to resign, "preferably in a formal letter" and "as promptly as possible." He also suggested that, under the circumstances, First Boston should decide, "as a matter of policy . . . whether or not they wanted to act as an agent or if they decided to act as an agent, whether they wanted to take a fee."[80]

The circumstances surrounding First Boston's decision not to charge Dixon-Yates a fee for marketing some $120,000,000 in securities were especially interesting, and quite possibly unique in the history of American capitalism. For if we are to believe the testimony of Paul Miller, assistant vice president of First Boston, the firm decided against a fee solely because such a decision "was in the public interest."[81] Upon questioning, however, the thirty-five-year old Miller was unable to cite another instance in which his firm had displayed such beneficence, despite the fact that it had handled similar financial transactions for the World Bank, the Federal Government, state governments, and a number of municipalities.[82] In fact, when First Boston had handled the bond issue for the Ohio Valley Electric Company at Portsmouth, Ohio, certainly an analogous situation, the firm had earned the extremely lucrative fee of $150,000.[83]

The Democratic members of the subcommittee, as well as the maverick Republican member, Senator Langer, suggested that the corporation's sudden burst of public spirit may have been motivated by the fact that the Senate was preparing to investigate Wenzell's role in the controversy. Miller denied this, insisting that First Boston's executive committee had decided against charging a fee at its July 1, 1954, meeting. Although no such resolution appeared in the minutes of the July 1 meeting, the minutes for October 21 did refer to "our earlier decision not to accept compensation."[84] Senator Joseph O'Mahoney, Democrat from Wyoming, suggested that the peculiar phrasing had undoubtedly been motivated by the fact that by October Dixon-Yates had become a national controversy. He could not believe, he said, that such a major decision, if actually

[79] *Ibid.*, p. 571.
[80] *Ibid.*, pp. 573–74.
[81] *Ibid.*, p. 86.
[82] *Ibid.*, p. 100.
[83] *Ibid.*, p. 78.
[84] *Ibid.*, p. 91.

made in the July 1 meeting, would have gone unrecorded. Interestingly, Dixon-Yates received its first written indication that First Boston would not charge a fee in May, 1955, only a few weeks after Senator Hill had made his speech from the Senate floor.[85] Some suggested, moreover, that the two events were not entirely unrelated.

One of the most damaging points raised before the Kefauver subcommittee concerned not Wenzell, but Presidential Assistant Sherman Adams. Just prior to the House of Representatives vote on a $6,500,000 transmission line which was to carry the power generated by the West Memphis plant to the middle of the Mississippi River where it was to be fed into the TVA system,[86] Adams phoned the chairman of the Security and Exchange Commission, J. Sinclair Armstrong, and requested a delay in the Commission's scheduled hearings. It is interesting to note that one Adolphe Wenzell was scheduled to appear before the Commission on June 13, or two days after Adams made his call. The SEC postponed the hearings, as requested, and Wenzell did not testify until after the House approved the appropriation.[87] Thomas L. Stokes was moved to write, "Adams knew that [the SEC investigation] would show, as it did, that an agent of a Wall Street investment firm that was involved in Dixon-Yates financing was also a consultant for the Budget Bureau in negotiating the Dixon-Yates deal."[88]

Following the disclosures before the Kefauver subcommittee, the Atomic Energy Commission ruled that Wenzell's role in the Dixon-Yates negotiations voided all of the Federal Government's contractual obligations and refused to pay the Mississippi Valley Generating Company for its expenditures at West Memphis prior to the official cancellation of the contract. Predictably, of course, MVGC brought suit in the United States Court of Claims to recover a reported outlay of $3,534,778.45.[89] Ultimately, the Justice De-

---

[85] *Ibid.,* pp. 161–63.

[86] "Dixon-Yates Push," *Newsweek,* June 27, 1955, p. 24. See also "Sluice and Bobble," *Time,* June 27, 1955, pp. 15–16. Although the Democrats controlled the House of Representatives at the time of the vote, many New England Democrats, long angered by the fact that southern states were luring away their textile industries with the offer of cheap public power, joined the Republicans to give the Administration a surprising 198 to 169 victory.

[87] Subcommittee on Antitrust and Monopoly, *Dixon-Yates Hearings,* 1955, p. 379.

[88] Stokes's remarks were quoted from Richard L. Strout, "Tom Stokes and Sherman Adams," *New Republic,* July 7, 1958, p. 11. Stokes was also quoted as saying, "We [reporters] have become familiar too, with the way the White House, chiefly through Sherman Adams, Assistant to the President, meddles constantly in the business of these [regulatory] commissions, which is really none of his business." *Ibid.* Adams unquestionably played a particularly significant role in the Dixon-Yates affair. However, the Presidential Assistant refused to testify before the Senate Subcommittee despite the insistent pleas of Senators Kefauver, O'Mahoney, and Langer. Langer became so incensed at Adams' refusal to appear that he demanded that he be subpoenaed. Subcommittee on Antitrust and Monopoly, *Dixon-Yates Contract,* Report Pursuant to S. Res. 61 & 170, 1956, p. xxix.

[89] William Blair, "U.S. Sued By Dixon-Yates for $3,534,778 Expenses," *New York Times,* December 14, 1955.

partment asked that the Court dismiss the suit, contending that, when Wenzell served simultaneously as consultant to the Bureau of the Budget and vice president of the First Boston Corporation, he was involved in a "conflict of interest so contrary to public policy as to render the alleged agreement null and void." This was, ironically, exactly what critics of the Dixon-Yates contract had been contending for some eighteen months. Thus, the Justice Department had come full circle and was, in effect, repudiating most of the contentions which had been made by the Administration in its previous vigorous defense of the contract.[90]

Initially, both Brownell and Strauss favored paying MVGC the requested cancellation costs. Later, however, the AEC chairman discovered that a lowly counsel in his own office, Herzel H. Plaine, had recommended that the AEC reject the claim on the grounds that Wenzell's dual role had negated all of the Federal Government's obligations under the contract.[91] According to the testimony before the Kefauver subcommittee, Strauss then called for the counsel's security file to make certain that he was not a subversive![92] He was not. In fact, it may have surprised the chairman just how many singularly patriotic Americans there were throughout the United States who were opposed to that particular outlay of public funds. Ultimately, however, the Acting Comptroller General, Frank H. Weitzel, and the top lawyer in the AEC, William Mitchell, agreed, substantially, with Plaine's position.[93] Following these developments, both the AEC and the Justice Department had very little choice but to reject payment of the claim.

On July 15, 1959, a badly divided United States Court of Claims rejected the Federal Government's contention that the contract had been, from the very outset, "unlawful, null and void, and contrary to public policy" and awarded the MVGC $1,867,545.56.[94]

[90] Anthony Lewis, "U.S. Now Denies Dixon-Yates Basis," New York Times, July 13, 1956.
[91] T.R.B., "Washington Wire," New Republic, December 19, 1955, p. 2.
[92] Senate Subcommittee on Antitrust and Monopoly, Dixon-Yates Hearings, Part 2, 1955, p. 1165. Strauss told the members of the Senate Subcommittee that Plaine's attack on the Dixon-Yates contract had had absolutely nothing to do with his calling for the security file. Moreover, he suggested that the newspaper accounts which had suggested such a thing were "distorted and very nasty." He had called for the file, he said, after a member of the United States Senate, whose name was not revealed, had told him that the counsel's file contained "derogatory information of a subversive nature." Ibid.
[93] In a letter to Strauss dated October 3, 1955, Weitzel stated, "It is our view . . . that no settlement of the liability of the United States in connection with the Dixon-Yates contract should be made which does not save to the Government the right to have the public policy issue judicially determined should it later be decided to follow that course of action." Subcommittee on Antitrust and Monopoly, Dixon-Yates Contract, Report Pursuant to S. Res. 61 & 170, 1956, p. 38. In a memorandum to the AEC dated November 15, 1955, Mitchell stated, "My conclusion is that there is a substantial question as to validity of the contract which can only be settled in the courts." Senate Subcommittee on Antitrust and Monopoly, Dixon-Yates Hearings, Part 2, 1955, p. 1131.
[94] Mississippi Valley Generating Company v. United States, 147 Ct. Cl. 1 (1959).

The Justice Department appealed, according to the President, because "it believed that until the Supreme Court had acted on the matter it would never be finally settled."[95] It was not until January 9, 1961, that the Supreme Court handed down its ruling which set aside the decision of the Court of Claims.[96] It was, at the very least, a "strange" victory for the Administration and, quite possibly, a victory it really had not wanted to win. In his first volume of *The White House Years,* for example, Eisenhower wrote, "I felt that the Court of Claims decision was right. . . . Dixon-Yates became the losers in the whole affair—on a technicality."[97]

Even a cursory examination of the record indicates quite clearly that the President was never fully aware of the extent to which Wenzell was involved in the Dixon-Yates affair. For example, in his press conference of June 29, 1955, he insisted, quite incorrectly, that officials in his Administration had "got together every single document that was pertinent to this thing and put it out." He also insisted, again quite incorrectly, that "Wenzell was never called in or asked a single thing about the Dixon-Yates contract."[98] A week later, when Charles Bartlett of the *Chattanooga Times* asked the President if he thought Wenzell's role proper in light of the subcommittee revelations, Eisenhower answered, "Indeed yes."[99] Finally, in his memoirs, published in 1963, Eisenhower still insisted, despite all evidence to the contrary, that "Wenzell was not involved in or consulted on any major policy decision. . . . Neither Mr. Hughes nor Mr. Dodge, moreover, knew that Wenzell at times was simultaneously consulting with the Budget Bureau and advising Dixon and Yates on its financing as a representative of First Boston."[100]

To many observers, the President emerged from the Dixon-Yates episode as something of a contemporary Ulysses S. Grant, i.e., a man who was disposed to do the right thing but who was so totally uninformed about the affairs in his own Administration that he was unable to carry out his altruistic goals. In a very real sense,

[95] Dwight D. Eisenhower, *The White House Years: Mandate For Change* (Garden City, New York: Doubleday and Company, Inc., 1963), p. 384.

[96] United States v. Mississippi Valley Generating Company, 364 U.S. 520 (1961). The statute on which the case revolved states, "Whoever, being an officer, agent or member of, or directly or indirectly interested in the pecuniary profits or contracts of any corporation, joint-stock company, or association, or of any firm or partnership, or other business entity, is employed or acts as an officer or agent of the United States for the transaction of business with such business entity, shall be fined not more than $2,000 or imprisoned not more than two years, or both." 18 *U.S.C.* 434.

[97] Eisenhower, *The White House Years: Mandate For Change,* p. 384.

[98] For the text of the President's press conference remarks of June 29 see *The New York Times,* June 30, 1955.

[99] For the text of the President's press conference remarks of July 6 see *ibid.,* July 7, 1955.

[100] Eisenhower, *The White House Years: Mandate For Change,* p. 383.

the blame must be placed squarely on the President. It was Eisenhower, for example, who instituted the military "chain of command" to handle the tedious administrative details he found so distasteful.[101] It was Eisenhower, too, who displayed such an aversion to perusing the nation's newspapers and periodicals. And, finally, it was Eisenhower who surrounded himself with assistants who had so little compunction about withholding vital information from the President. As a result of the Dixon-Yates controversy, more and more people were wondering aloud, "Who's running things?" It would not be the last time such a sentiment would be expressed!

[101] The President's aversion to details caused T.R.B. to remark, "Eisenhower's past indifference to lesser details of his office has frightened some people. Sometimes he seems to glory in not knowing what was happening." T.R.B., *New Republic*, December 19, 1955, p. 2.

Chapter 6

THE MAN WHO KNEW EVERYBODY

The law locks up both man and woman
Who steals the goose from off the common,
But lets the greater felon loose
Who steals the common from the goose.

Medieval English stanza

AT THE VERY HEIGHT of the Wenzell scandal Charles Bartlett of the *Chattanooga Times* and W. H. Lawrence of *The New York Times* reported that Secretary of the Air Force Harold Talbott might have used his official position to solicit business for the Paul Mulligan Company. The firm, which specialized in clerical efficiency studies, was owned equally by Talbott and Mulligan. The Lawrence column of July 15, 1955, revealed that, as a result of a ninety-day preliminary investigation conducted by its counsel, Robert Kennedy, the Senate Permanent Investigation Subcommittee planned to hold full-scale hearings upon the affairs of Secretary Talbott. The hearings were intended to determine whether Talbott had violated either the "letter or spirit" of the conflict of interest laws.[1]

In a telephone conversation with *The New York Times*, Talbott admitted that he had maintained his ownership of the Mulligan Company, but stated that he had not received any profits from the Company earned in defense contracts. When asked whether he had ever solicited any business for the Company, he answered that "solicitation is a strange word. I did not solicit any business. I have talked to some of my intimate friends about the work of Mulligan. My business associations have been proper and ethical in my opinion."[2]

Curiously, few newspapers gave the *Times* report much coverage; some ignored it altogether. Most Washington correspondents

[1] W. H. Lawrence, "Senate To Query Secretary of Air on Business Ties," *New York Times,* July 15, 1955.
[2] *Ibid.* See also *The New York Times,* July 16, 1955.

seemed to have been convinced that there was nothing illegal or improper in Talbott's activities on behalf of the Mulligan Company. The *Chicago Tribune,* for example, a subscriber to the *Times* wire service and certainly one of the most outspoken newspapers during the "Truman scandals," failed to print any part of the Lawrence report. To most newspapers, it was simply another "back-page story with a front-page name."[3]

On July 18 the subcommittee hearings began with the questioning of Talbott for two hours in closed session. Since the testimony given was secret, newspapers could speculate only vaguely as to what had transpired. Subcommittee Chairman John McClellan indicated that the investigation was "not closed" but would say further only that Talbott had admitted that the Mulligan Company's profits were "substantial."[4] Within forty-eight hours, however, *The New York Times* managed to obtain virtually the entire confidential transcript of the closed session. Its exposé showed that Talbott had actively promoted the business of the Mulligan Company from his Pentagon office, frequently writing letters to prospective clients on Air Force stationery. Included in the story were photographs of letters from Talbott to various businessmen, some written under Air Force letterheads, and all marked "CONFIDENTIAL."[5]

This leak of confidential testimony brought immediate repercussions. Talbott told one reporter, "I don't want to talk to you. I don't care what you print. I have nothing to say." His wife was even more increased, telling the same reporter, "it's a pretty snide, low, sneaking group that has done this. My husband is tired. Don't you call him anymore."[6] Because of the leak, the subcommittee voted to conduct the remaining hearings in public. Several of its members inserted into the record their personal regrets for the damage to Talbott's reputation. Ironically, the strongest statement of regret came from a curious source, Senator Joseph McCarthy of Wisconsin. He asserted, "I think it is extremely important that we have this public hearing to make sure that by innuendo, or otherwise, that the Secretary does not get an unfair deal and a smear."[7]

The subsequent public hearings did cast some additional light on the establishment of the Talbott-Mulligan partnership. It was revealed, for example, that the Mulligan Company had been estab-

[3] "Front-Page Name," *Newsweek,* August 1, 1955, p. 74.

[4] W. H. Lawrence, "Senators Question Talbott Two Hours," *New York Times,* July 19, 1955.

[5] Lawrence, "Talbott Pushed Firm's Business, Letters Indicate," *New York Times,* July 21, 1955.

[6] *Ibid.*

[7] U.S., Congress, Senate, Permanent Subcommittee on Investigations of the Committee on Government Operations, *Hearings, Harld E. Talbott–Secretary of the Air Force,* 84th Cong., 1st Sess., 1955, p. 2.

lished in 1947, specializing originally only in "clerical cost control" studies. Later, it expanded its services to include "general management engineering." At the time of the congressional inquiry the company had a seventeen-man staff, all employed in its single office in New York City. Records indicated that it had, at one time or another, performed studies for over fifty large American corporations, its active accounts including such companies as Oscar Mayer, Electric Auto-Lite, and Libby-Owens-Ford.[8]

Mr. Mulligan recalled that his interest in efficiency began one morning years before when he realized that his left hand always remained idle as he brushed his teeth. "Pretty soon," he said, "I was screwing the cap back on the toothpaste with the left hand while brushing with the right. I still do it." Following this rather modest beginning in the field of efficiency studies, Mulligan developed an approach to the study of office procedures which entailed the use of motion pictures. He did not attempt to establish his own consulting firm because he lacked the necessary business contacts. But when Mulligan met industrialist Harold Talbott in 1946, he sensed immediately that a man with Talbott's extensive acquaintances in the business world would make an ideal partner, for as Mulligan said, "Harold knew everybody."[9] Thus, from the birth of the partnership, corralling prospective customers seemed to be Talbott's sole *raison d'être* in the company.

The hearings clearly indicated that Talbott had continued to function as a recruiter of prospective clients for the Mulligan Company, even after his appointment as Secretary of the Air Force. The Secretary, for example, had been instrumental in securing new contracts with such firms as Avco Manufacturing Corporation, Baldwin-Lima-Hamilton Corportation, Olin Industries, Greyhound Corporation, and Owens-Illinois Glass Company.[10] Furthermore, the profits of the Mulligan Company had risen from $84,327 in 1963 to $133,317 in 1955. Talbott's personal income from the company had averaged over $50,000 per year after his appointment as Secretary of the Air Force.[11]

Talbott readily admitted that he had approached many of the company's new clients, but argued that without exception the people involved had been personal friends for ten to twenty-five years. Furthermore, he contended, he had never used his official position to bring pressure on them. He contended that, with the possible exception of the contract with Avco Company, none of his activities had been "improper." In that particular case, he admitted that the

    [8] "Talbott Business Connection Questioned," *Aviation Week*, July 25, 1955, p. 13.
    [9] "Talbott's Mulligan Stew," *Life*, August 1, 1955, p. 75.
    [10] Senate Permanent Subcommittee on Investigations of the Committee on Government Operations, *Talbott Hearings*, 1955, p. 199.
    [11] *Ibid.*, p. 198.

contract was "questionable" and probably should not have been made inasmuch as over fifty percent of Avco's business was with the Defense Department. In order to correct any irregularities which the subcommittee may have felt had occurred, Secretary Talbott announced that he was "giving, not selling," his interest in the Mulligan Company to his partner.[12]

The Republican Senators on the subcommittee differed appreciably in their reactions to this proposal by Talbott. Senator McCarthy argued against it on the grounds that such action could be construed as an admission that something was wrong. Senator Bender of Ohio saw no impropriety in Secretary Talbott's past conduct, but felt that he should divest himself of his interest in the Mulligan Company.[13] The Senator hastened to tell reporters that he did not want it to appear that he was taking part in a whitewash. "Look here boys," he said, "I'm not trying to cover up anything. . . . I don't hold any brief for Talbott. I've only spoken to him once, and that time he insulted me."[14]

But it was not the Avco Manufacturing Company's contract, or even the letters soliciting business for the Mulligan Company, which proved to be the most damaging charge leveled against Talbott. During the hearings, it was discovered that the Radio Corporation of America had refused to renew a contract with the Mulligan Company six months previously because it could not secure an advisory opinion from the Attorney General clearing it of any impropriety under the conflict of interest laws. Talbott testified that as soon as he had learned of the RCA request he had told his personal lawyer, Murray Smith, "my goodness, if there is any suspicion forget it. We won't do the contract or have anything to do with it."[15]

Counsel Robert Kennedy then asked Talbott if he had not, in fact, asked the Air Force General Counsel, John Johnson, to investigate the question of possible conflict of interest. Talbott answered, "I told Johnson about this, but I didn't tell him to do anything, I don't think." Finally, Kennedy asked Talbott whether he had ever told RCA attorney, Sam Ewing, over the telephone that their position at RCA was "foolish" and that they should "come off their high horse and stop acting so high and mighty." Although Talbott admitted that his memory was "hazy," it was his opinion that no such discussion had ever taken place; he was certain that he had never made the statement attributed to him.[16]

[12] Ibid., pp. 19–21. See also W. H. Lawrence, "Talbott Offers To Give Up Share in New York Firm," New York Times, July 22, 1955.

[13] Senate Permanent Subcommittee on Investigations of the Committee on Government Operations, Talbott Hearings, 1955, p. 24.

[14] "Return Engagement," Reporter, August 11, 1955, p. 4.

[15] Senate Permanent Subcommittee on Investigations of the Committee on Government Operations, Talbott Hearings, 1955, pp. 28–29.

[16] Ibid., pp. 29–30.

Later testimony by Air Force General Counsel Johnson and by Mr. Ewing revealed that Talbott had indeed been "hazy" as to the circumstances surrounding the RCA contract negotiations. First Johnson testified that at the request of Secretary Talbott he had investigated the possibility of any conflict of interest in the prospective contract between RCA and Mulligan, even to the extent of meeting with Attorney General Brownell in an effort to obtain his official approval of the contract. Although it was Johnson's opinion that such a contract would be neither illegal nor improper under existing conflict of interest laws, he was never able to secure an official approval from the Attorney General.[17] *The New York Times* reported that Brownell told Talbott at a social function a few days after his meeting with Johnson that granting such an opinion to an outside private firm would be contrary to the policy of the Justice Department.[18]

RCA attorney Sam Ewing later testified that Talbott had spoken to him in a three-way conversation involving Talbott, Johnson, and Ewing. This was subsequently corroborated by Johnson. During this telephone conversation, Ewing testified, Talbott had mentioned twelve or fifteen companies which were doing work for the Air Force and which were also under contract to the Mulligan Company. Then Talbott asked him, "If all of these other companies could take contracts with Mulligan and Company, why was RCA acting so high and mighty"[19]

In the face of of the evidence gathered in four days of testimony, Talbott was virtually compelled to admit to the subcommittee, "In retrospect . . . I now see that I was mistaken in permitting myself to make phone calls or write letters about the Mulligan Company."[20] However, by this time, Talbott, like the Dixon-Yates affair, had become a center of political controversy. From a cursory examination of newspaper coverage, it was apparent that the Secretary's belated admission of his past mistakes would be inadequate to calm the furor ignited by the hearings. Partisan charges were numerous, typical of such attacks being those from Minnesota's Democratic Senator Eugene McCarthy and Democratic National Chairman Paul Butler. McCarthy taunted the Republicans that "the crusaders have one or two rough spots in their shining armor."[21] Butler, with obvious reference to Eisenhower's campaign promises, remarked that "it is easy to set high standards, but the proof of integrity comes not in setting up the rules but in living up to them."[22]

[17] *Ibid.*, pp. 93–100.
[18] W. H. Lawrence, "Talbott May Quit," *New York Times*, July 27, 1955.
[19] Senate Permanent Subcommittee on Investigations of the Committee on Governmental Operations, *Talbott Hearings*, 1955, pp. 85–109.
[20] *Ibid.*, p. 179.
[21] *New York Times*, July 25, 1955.
[22] W. H. Lawrence, "Democrats Prod the White House To Oust Talbott," *New York Times*, July 29, 1955.

At President Eisenhower's press conference of July 27 Robert Clark of International News Service asked the President if he saw anything improper in Secretary Talbott's activities. Although he refused to comment specifically on Talbott until he had seen the "whole record," Eisenhower did give the standard of ethical behavior which he expected from the public officials serving in his Administration. "I do not believe that any man can hold public office merely because he is not guilty of any illegal act," he said. "His action has to be impeccable, both from the standpoint of law, [and] from the standpoint of ethics."[23]

Nevertheless, *The New York Times* reported that in fact several of the President's advisers, including Vice President Nixon, Attorney General Brownell, and Presidential Assistant Sherman Adams, had met to settle the fate of Secretary Talbott.[24] "High Republican officials" reported confidentially to the *Times* that there was strong party pressure being exerted upon Talbott to submit his resignation in order to avoid embarrassment to the President.[25] The Republican Senate Policy Committee also met and, though no official pronouncements were uttered, reputable sources reported that a majority of the members had advised Nixon that they felt Talbott should either resign or be fired.[26] Talbott responded to his critics, saying that he had "no more idea than a jackrabbit of resigning."[27]

Ultimately, Talbott did succumb to the pressures being exerted upon him and, in a letter to President Eisenhower dated August 1, 1955, asked to be relieved of his duties as Secretary. He emphasized, once again, that he thought his conduct always to have been "within the bounds of ethics," and, blaming his predicament largely upon what he termed "distorted publicity," categorically asserted that he had "never used that office to further [the Mulligan Company's] business." In accepting the resignation, President Eisenhower thanked the Secretary for his "tireless energy and effort" and stated that he was of the opinion that Talbott's administration of the Department had been "unexcelled." However, the President admitted that, under the circumstances, Secretary Talbott's decision to resign had been "the right one."[28]

In less than two weeks Secretary of Defense Charles Wilson had located a replacement for Secretary Talbott and given Talbott him-

[23] "The President: 'I Will Decide,'" *U.S. News and World Report,* August 5, 1955, p. 99.
[24] W. H. Lawrence, "Talbott's Future Weighed by Aides of the President," *New York Times,* July 23, 1955.
[25] Lawrence, "President Stresses Ethics over Law in Talbott Case," *New York Times,* July 28, 1955.
[26] "Behind the Scenes: Ike and the Talbott Affair," *Newsweek,* August 8, 1955, p. 20.
[27] Allen Drury, "Talbott Quitting, Perhaps at Once, G.O.P. Sources Say," *New York Times,* July 30, 1955.
[28] The texts of both letters are reproduced in "The End of the Talbott Story," *U.S. News and World Report,* August 12, 1955, p. 72.

self a rousing send-off from Bolling Air Force Base, just outside Washington. The new Secretary of the Air Force was a mild-mannered Assistant Secretary of Defense for Research and Development, Donald Quarles, who seemed to fit perfectly the requisites established by Secretary Wilson: "A man who sits next to God, has financial and engineering experience, and who can be confirmed by the Senate."[29] One Pentagon aide warned Wilson that the introverted Quarles "might not put up a good front." Wilson remarked that, at the moment, he was more interested in someone who could "look after his rear."[30]

Meanwhile, across the Potomac at Bolling Air Force Base, official Washington planned one of its most spectacular farewells for retiring Secretary Talbott. One hundred and fifty planes were to fly over the ceremony at which Secretary Wilson would present Talbott with the Defense Department's highest civilian award, the Medal of Freedom, for "meritorious service." Although Hurricane Connie reduced the overflight to ten planes, the ceremony, nevertheless, was impressive, with 1,800 troops parading and the Air Force band playing "So Long, It's Been Good To Know Yuh." Talbott's clever advice for the day was "do right and don't write." Two days later, Talbott received a second medal, the Navy's Distinguished Public Service Award.[31] With his two medals and apparently not the slightest idea that he had done anything wrong, Talbott returned to the business world "to make a little dough."[32]

Technically, Talbott's activities on behalf of the Mulligan Company had not been prohibited by the express provisions of the conflict of interest laws, inasmuch as Section 434 of the Criminal Code prohibits an officer only from using his official position in such a way as to transmit *government* contracts to a firm in which he has a pecuniary interest. All of Talbott's activities were directed toward the procurement of *private* contracts for the Mulligan Company.[33] But certainly his activities violated the spirit of the law. Moreover, public officials generally have long recognized that, at the very least, to engage in activities such as Talbott's risks publicity which would undermine their authority and, thereby, impair their effectiveness. Certainly, no responsible administrator would encourage such behavior among officials in his department.

As it turned out, however, this was not a unique experience in Talbott's career. During World War I, for example, he had served as president of an airplane company which had engaged in dubious

[29] "Air Secretary Quarles: He Can Do Anything," *Newsweek*, August 22, 1955, p. 20.
[30] "Hail and Fancy Farewell," *Time*, August 22, 1955, p. 19.
[31] *Ibid.*
[32] Walter Goodman, "The Innocence of the Executive-on-Loan," *New Republic*, September 19, 1955, p. 9.
[33] 18 *U.S.C.* 434.

practices on government aircraft contracts. At that time, Charles Evans Hughes conducted an official investigation into the United States' aircraft program. Later, similar investigations were held by committees of the House and Senate.[34] All three reports strongly censured the Dayton Wright Airplane Company, which had been incorporated by E. A. Deeds, C. F. Kettering, Harold E. Talbott, Sr., and Harold E. Talbott, Jr., "manifestly with the expectation of obtaining government contracts."[35]

A month after the incorporation, Colonel Deeds had ostensibly resigned as vice president of the company in order to accept a position as head of the Aircraft Production Board in Washington. It was remarkable that the Hughes hearings, which filled over twenty volumes with testimony, produced no hint as to the reasons for Deeds's appointment. Deeds knew little, if anything, of the aircraft industry and had never been connected with the government previously. Yet, this official had, in the words of the Hughes Report, "important, if not commanding, influence" in directing the placement of aircraft contracts.[36]

Shortly after Deeds assumed his duties in Washington, the Dayton Wright Company received a government cost-plus contract which, after subsequent modification, involved an estimated profit of approximately $3,500,000. This was most remarkable inasmuch as the company had been incorporated only a few months before with a capital stock of but $500,000. Interestingly, the three remaining stockholders of the company increased their profits by voting themselves $100,000 in salaries. These salaries were charged to the government as part of the cost of production. Although this was not illegal under existing laws, the Hughes Report strongly criticized the propriety of the action.[37]

It also was discovered that from the time Deeds assumed his duties in Washington there had been a continuing stream of telegrams exchanged between him and his former associates. It was clearly evident from telegrams inserted into the Hughes Report that such information would give the Dayton Wright Company a decided advantage over competitors in bidding on government contracts. Especially damaging was the telegram from Deeds to Kettering which stated that all confidential telegrams would thereafter be

---

[34] The Hughes Report is reproduced as Appendix A in U.S., Congress, House, Select Committee on Expenditures in the War Department, *Expenditures in the War Department—Aviation*, Report No. 637, 66th Cong., 2d Sess., 1920, pp. 73–122. See also U.S., Congress, Senate, Subcommittee of the Committee on Military Affairs, *Aircraft Production in the United States*, Report No. 555, 65th Cong., 2d Sess., 1918.

[35] House Select Committee on Expenditures in the War Department, *Expenditures in the War Department—Aviation*, Report No. 637, 1920, p. 83.

[36] *Ibid.*, p. 84.

[37] *Ibid.*, pp. 83–84.

sent to Harold E. Talbott, Sr., rather than to the Dayton Wright Company.[38]

The Hughes Report to the Attorney General concluded that the conduct of these men was of a "reprehensible" nature but admitted that their activities did not make them criminally liable under existing statutes. It did, however, recommend that Deeds be court-martialed under the Articles of War.[39] However, Newton Baker, the Secretary of War, refused to prosecute Deeds, saying that since he had come to Washington at such a great personal and pecuniary sacrifice he should be honored rather than chastised.[40]

The final chapter of the Dayton Wright controversy was written in 1922 when the government brought suit for over three million dollars against the Dayton Wright Company for overcharges and improper charges in government contracts. In the District Court Judge Hickenlooper rendered a decision which upheld most of the government's claims. However, counter claims were filed and, on appeal to the Circuit Court of Appeals, it was held that the contracts were of such a broad and general nature as to cover the items charged against the government. The case was remanded to the lower court with instructions to dismiss the bill.[41] Since Talbott's involvement with the Dayton Wright Company was a matter of public record, it seems curious that a man of Eisenhower's announced concern with honest government and honorable officials would select such a man for a subcabinet level position. That the Senate should consent to such a selection is, perhaps, a matter of less curiosity.

During the Senate hearings on Talbott's confirmation, only Senator Estes Kefauver subjected Talbott to intensive interrogation about his role in the Dayton Wright affair. Time and again Kefauver asked Talbott whether he thought that the exchange of telegrams was proper. Talbott's view of the exchange, and one is struck by his fragmental knowledge of the whole affair, was that the telegrams were "perfectly proper" but "unfortunate in their implication."[42] Because of the implication of such exchanges, Talbott assured the Senators that he would never allow such a practice to occur in any department which he headed.

Senator Kefauver also questioned Talbott as to his views on the propriety of the Dayton Wright Company's practice of charging certain items to the government as a portion of the cost of aircraft

[38] *Ibid.*, pp. 85–92.
[39] *Ibid.*, p. 122.
[40] *New York Times*, January 17, 1919.
[41] Dayton Airplane Company v. United States 21, Fed. 2n 675.
[42] U.S., Congress, Senate, Committee on Armed Services, *Hearings, Nomination of Harold E. Talbott, To Be Secretary of the Air Force*, Part 4, 83d Cong., 1st Sess., 1953, p. 10.

production. Specifically, he asked Talbott about the $100,000 per year in salaries which the three stockholders had voted themselves as executive officers in the company. Talbott answered that his position was unquestionably worth its $30,000 salary, adding that it was for others to determine whether he was the proper man for the job.[43]

Kefauver then presented a portion of the Hughes Report which described a rather complicated procedure whereby the two Talbotts and Kettering had formed a syndicate in order to buy a plant in Miamisburg, Ohio, for $60,000. According to the Hughes investigation, this plant was immediately sold to the Dayton Wright Company, owned by the same three people, for $127,000. The profit was then split among the stockholders, and the cost of the plant charged to the government. Talbott, surprisingly, could not recall such a transaction, but again assured the Senators that such practices would be unacceptable as future public policy.[44]

Kefauver's final questions related to certain dubious bidding practices by the Chrysler and Electric Auto-Lite Companies which occurred during a period in which Talbott was a director of both corporations. It seems that, after the government had called for bids on 1,000 automobile generators of a certain design, Chrysler had submitted a bid of $77.20 and Electric Auto-Lite one of $87.00 per unit. Thus, Chrysler was awarded the contract. Later, it was discovered that the Electric Auto-Lite Corporation actually had manufactured all of the generators used by Chrysler, and had sold the particular type in question to the automobile company at a set price of $54.00 per unit. In this instance Chrysler simply notified Electric Auto-Lite to ship 1,000 of these generators to the Radford Arsenal and pocketed the difference of over $100,000. Again Talbott professed ignorance of such a transaction but came down firmly against such a practice as a matter of principle.[45]

Despite these rather striking disclosures concerning Talbott's past activities, Kefauver was the only member of the Senate Armed Services Committee to oppose confirmation. Repeatedly Kefauver expressed his willingness to forgive Talbott for any improprieties committed over thirty-five years earlier, but the Senator was unable to conscience Talbott's continuing equivocation about the Dayton Wright affair, e.g., the telegrams were "perfectly proper" but "unfortunate in their implication."[46] On the floor of the Senate,

[43] *Ibid.*, p. 11.

[44] *Ibid.*, pp. 17–18.

[45] *Ibid.*, p. 30. Senator Kefauver's material concerning the practices of these two companies was taken from U.S., Congress, House, Subcommittee of the Committee on Expenditures in the Executive Departments, *Hearings, Inquiry into the Procurement of Automotive Spare Parts by the United States Government,* 82d Cong., 1st Sess., 1951.

[46] U.S., *Congressional Record,* 83d Cong., 1st Sess., 1953, 99, Part 1, pp. 825–26.

Wayne Morse vigorously attacked Talbott's appointment, asserting, "it stinks."[47] Yet, this opposition was to no avail, and the appointment was approved with only six dissenting votes.[48]

Had Talbott been even passingly sensitive to the maintenance of respectable ethical standards in public service, one would think the Kefauver-Morse attack would have made him hypersensitive to any question of ethics or morality which might arise in his new post as Secretary of the Air Force. Yet, Talbott's proselytizing for the Mulligan Company indicated that the lesson passed unlearned. It seems manifestly certain that companies dependent upon government contracts could not afford to antagonize the Secretary for fear of jeopardizing future government business. Consequently, they were susceptible to Talbott's "persuasion" in the employment of the services of the Mulligan Company. The periodical *America* editorialized that it would take a "colossal naiveté" to think that the companies would have acted otherwise.[49] Actually, there was substantial evidence that Talbott did possess just such a lack of political and moral sophistication.

It would be difficult to argue that Talbott accepted the government position only for its income of $30,000 a year. Certainly, the loss he incurred from his stock sales, as well as the loss of his salary as a top executive, overshadowed any financial gain deriving from the Mulligan Company's increased volume of business. Moreover, any clever crook or scoundrel would certainly not have operated so openly as did Talbott. It may be that Talbott's past dealings with government and his forty-five year pursuit of profits in the business world had dulled his sensitivity to and his appreciation for the ethical considerations which must govern the conduct of an honorable public official.[50]

In retrospect, it is evident that Talbott did not possess the stringent ethical code promised the American public by candidate Eisenhower in the 1952 campaign. Furthermore, in light of the confirmation hearings, his deficiency could have come as no surprise. The hearings alone, it would seem, should have raised serious misgivings in the President's mind about Talbott. Seldom, to be sure, had any newly appointed official indicated such an insensitivity to questions of ethics in the public service. No evidence exists that Attorney General Brownell reported to the President Secretary Talbott's efforts to obtain an advisory opinion on the RCA contract. The *St. Louis Post-Dispatch* asked editorially, "Why did Mr. Brownell stand mute?"[51]

[47] *Ibid.*, p. 828.
[48] *Ibid.*, p. 868.
[49] "Washington Front," *America*, August 6, 1955, p. 445.
[50] Walter Lippmann, "Talbott, Two Men in One Job?" *St. Louis Post-Dispatch*, August 3, 1955.
[51] *St. Louis Post-Dispatch*, August 2, 1955.

If Eisenhower's moral sense was not stirred as greatly by Talbott as by the mink coats and deep freezers of his presidential predecessor, much the same can be said for the press. Most newspapers treated the Talbott controversy much differently than they had handled the conflict of interest cases arising under President Truman. Generally, the newspapers ignored the earliest Talbott disclosures and, thereafter, limited their coverage to a rather pedestrian accounting of the factual material, stressing the fact that the Secretary had broken no laws but failing to mention that those involved in the infamous Truman scandals had broken no laws either. In retrospect, it appears that the typical editor's ethical sensibility was nowhere nearly as shaken by a businessman's imprudence as it had been by that of stenographers and office boys under President Truman. Ralph McGill, writing for the *Atlanta Constitution*, charged that the American newspapers never became excited or critical about the Talbott controversy. Editorially, he asserted that many papers gave the whole affair "the soothing syrup cure, the once-over-lightly hair singe, or the well-reasoned boys-will-be-boys touch."[52]

Typical of the editorial response to the Talbott affair was one in the *Chicago Daily Tribune*, which exhibited an almost Alice-in-Wonderland character. Noting that President Eisenhower's handling of the Talbott case was in sharp contrast to President Truman's handling of similar cases, the *Tribune* continued, "in those not so distant days very little attention would have paid to a Talbott case because there were so many more flagrant ones at hand, involving downright bribe-taking and stealing."[53] The *Tribune*'s observation is an astonishing inversion of history. Talbott, as Secretary of the Air Force, had realized $50,000 per year from the Mulligan Company, indubitably a more substantial sum than the value of a twelve-pound ham, a deep freezer, or a fur coat. Moreover, Secretary Talbott was a member of the subcabinet, not merely one of the "hired hands."[54] Undaunted by reality, however, the *Tribune* pursued the point. "Mr. Eisenhower does not withhold judgment month after month in hope that with the passing of time the public will forget," it said. "He does not stall, he does not act on the assumption that members of his party are entitled to special privileges, and he does not quibble."[55]

There is evidence that, in the end, Eisenhower did ask for Talbott's resignation. *Newsweek* reported confidently that the Presi-

[52] This column is reprinted in Ralph McGill, "There was a One-Party Press in the Talbott Scandal," *Democratic Digest*, October, 1955, p. 17.
[53] "Wholesome Change in Washington," *Chicago Daily Tribune*, August 3, 1955.
[54] Gerald W. Johnson, "Morals For Gentlemen," *New Republic*, August 15, 1955, p. 16.
[55] *Chicago Daily Tribune*, August 3, 1955.

dent had done so after reading the testimony of RCA attorney Samuel Ewing.[56] It is also a matter of record that no Republican of any stature defended Talbott throughout his ordeal. The absence of support was nowhere more striking than in the silence of Talbott's immediate superior, Defense Secretary Charles Wilson. At a news conference shortly before Talbott's resignation, Secretary Wilson said he "was very distressed about the whole business. I don't like any part of it. . . . I feel I have gotten one year older."[57]

If the President asked for Talbott's resignation, he did so quietly. Even in accepting the resignation he did not indicate any moral indignation comparable to that displayed in the 1952 campaign when he promised repeatedly to "clean up the mess in Washington." Curiously, Eisenhower praised Talbott at the time of his resignation, saying, "your diligence in the administraton of your Department has been unexcelled. . . . I commend you for your fine accomplishments as Secretary."[58] It would seem that the Administration at least tacitly condoned Talbott's conduct in office by awarding him the Medal of Freedom and the Navy's Distinguished Public Service Award, hardly appropriate rewards for activities which, by most standards of measurement, were more disreputable than the "mink coat" and "deep freezer" scandals of the Truman years.

[56] "Behind the Scenes: Ike and the Talbott Affair," *Newsweek,* August 8, 1955, p. 20.
[57] *Time,* August 22, 1955, p. 19.
[58] *U.S. News,* August 12, 1955, p. 72.

Chapter 7

THE GRATEFUL IMMIGRANT

With respect to corruption, it is my purpose, if you should assign me to that high post, to clean out every vestige of crookedness from every nook and cranny of the Federal Government. . . . I promise we'll use the scoop-shovel—not the whitewash brush.

DWIGHT EISENHOWER

THE ECHOES of the Talbott case had hardly quieted when the fifth conflict of interest case to haunt the Eisenhower Administration was uncovered, again by a solitary, enterprising political columnist. On September 1, 1955, Drew Pearson's column, "Washington Merry-Go-Round," charged that Peter Strobel, Commissioner of Public Buildings and number two man in the General Services Administration, had not dissolved his connection with the consulting engineering firm of Strobel and Salzman after accepting the government post. The column also asserted that Strobel had refused to provide his superiors with a list of the firm's clients, making it virtually impossible to determine whether the government was doing business with any of the clients of Strobel and Salzman.[1] As Commissioner of Public Buildings, Strobel had the responsibility of letting the contracts for all new buildings and for alterations and repair of the older ones. The importance of this position can be fairly measured by the fact that Strobel had submitted to the Bureau of the Budget projects totalling 346 million dollars during the fiscal year ending June 30, 1955.[2]

Pearson's role in the Strobel case was significant for a number of reasons. First, the content of his September 1 column was subsequently corroborated in hearings conducted by the House Antitrust Subcommittee. Second, he scooped the newspapers of the

[1] Drew Pearson, "The Washington Merry-Go-Round," *Harrisburg* (Ill.) *Daily Register,* September 1, 1955.
[2] U.S., Congress, House, Antitrust Subcommittee of the Committee on the Judiciary, *Hearings, Activities of Peter Strobel,* 84th Cong., 1st Sess., 1955, p. 11.

country by just slightly less than two months. *The New York Times,* for instance, contained no reference to Strobel's conflict of interest difficulties until October 27.[3] Moreover, before the House subcommittee held its initial hearings, a second Pearson column appeared which presented additional charges against the Commissioner of Public Buildings. This column stated that Strobel had pressed his consulting firm's $3,000 claim against the Corps of Engineers, had refused to sign the Departmental conflict of interest form until "practically ordered" to do so by his superior, Edmund Mansure, and had given government contracts to clients of Strobel and Salzman.[4]

Following the first Pearson column, Commissioner Strobel "bitterly complained" that he was not given an opportunity to give his side of the controversy. Upon hearing of Strobel's anger, Pearson invited him, by both letter and telephone, to present a rebuttal to his column of September 1. Although Pearson was promised an interview, it was never granted. Just prior to the release of his second column, Pearson again invited Strobel to present his case. However, Strobel's secretary reported that he was much too busy and, furthermore, was about to catch a train. It was later learned that Strobel caught the train to New York City for a weekend with his family.[5]

If Strobel was not particularly cooperative with Pearson, he was extremely so with staff members of the House Antitrust Subcommittee, who also were carrying on an investigation into Strobel's affairs.[6] Strobel's cooperation with the subcommittee was apparently predicated upon the sincere feeling that he had nothing to hide. He appeared before the subcommittee as the successful business executive who had come to Washington, at a great financial loss, solely to serve his country. And in many respects this was an accurate picture, for he had given up a yearly income in excess of $100,000 in order to accept the $14,800 government post. "My wife thinks I'm crazy," Strobel said at the time of his appointment, but "perhaps I can partly pay back this country for what it has done for me."[7] It is worthy of note that Strobel, his wife, and child had immigrated to the United States years before with little more than his engineering degree from Copenhagen's Technical University.

In his introductory statement to the subcommittee, Strobel readily admitted that he still retained his interest in the engineering consulting firm of Strobel and Salzman, but insisted that, upon

[3] *New York Times,* October 27, 1955.

[4] Drew Pearson, "The Washington Merry-Go-Round," *Harrisburg* (Ill.) *Daily Register,* October 26, 1955.

[5] *Ibid.*

[6] Antitrust Subcommittee of the Committee on the Judiciary, *Strobel Hearings,* 1955, p. 1.

[7] "Uncle Sam's Landlord," *Time,* June 28, 1954, p. 18.

coming to Washington, he had given up "the active management of the business."[8] He said that he had devoted "some time" to the firm since he came to Washington but had never attended to the affairs of the company on government time. With the Talbott case obviously in mind, he told the subcommittee that he never used government stationery to transact his private business.[9] The meanings of "active management" and "some time" would later become focal points of the inquiry.

Clearly, Strobel was never evasive about his desire to retain his partnership in Strobel and Salzman, candidly maintaining from the outset that, if forced to choose between the partnership and the government position, he would choose the former. The firm is "a personal thing, a matter of pride," he said; "I built the firm and in all modesty I must say it is vitally important to its continuance that I remain connected with its operations."[10] The head of GSA, Edmund Mansure, indicated that Strobel discussed the situation with him before accepting the government position. He reportedly told Strobel that, since the commissioner's post was a "very demanding job and full-time work," Strobel must give up any "active management" of the firm.[11]

There was some question, however, as to whether Strobel discussed the problem with other officials in the Administration. At the hearings, both Herbert Maletz, chief counsel for the subcommittee and Joseph Moody, assistant general counsel of the General Services Administration, testified that Strobel stated in their presence that both Attorney General Brownell and Thomas Stevens, Assistant to the President, had approved of the arrangement whereby he would keep his interest in the firm. Yet, Strobel testified that he could not recall having told anyone, much less Maletz and Moody, that Brownell and Stevens had concluded that his continuing connection with Strobel and Salzman was "perfectly proper."[12]

Strobel had formulated three rules which were to govern the activities of Strobel and Salzman as long as he held public office. First, the firm would not accept any contract from the General Services Administration; however, it might properly seek contracts with other governmental agencies. Second, the firm would take no new clients if they were interested in seeking contracts with the Public Buildings Service. Prospective clients with which the firm was negotiating prior to Strobel's taking office were not to be con-

[8] Antitrust Subcommittee of the Committee on the Judiciary, *Strobel Hearings,* 1955, p. 2.
[9] *Ibid.,* p. 5.
[10] *New York Times,* October 27, 1955.
[11] Antitrust Subcommittee of the Committee on the Judiciary, *Strobel Hearings,* 1955, pp. 182–83.
[12] *Ibid.,* pp. 16, 17, 244.

sidered new clients. Finally, the firm would have no financial interest in any architectural or construction firm.[13]

Despite these safeguards, Strobel clearly found it ethically difficult to sign the Standards of Conduct statement required of all employees of the General Services Administration. Although he became commissioner on July 1, 1954, he did not sign this code until December 27, 1955, and then only after a special inquiry by his superior, Edmund Mansure. He told the subcommittee initially that he did not sign the Standards of Conduct form because he could not "just as it is." Later he recalled that the Code was not signed earlier because it "got covered up under a pile of work."[14]

Strobel's phrase "just as it is" referred to sections four and six of the Code. Section four states that the Director of Personnel must grant prior, written approval before an employee could engage in outside employment or business activity. Section six states that each employee must submit a written statement of all outside business connections to his immediate superior.[15] Certainly, Strobel failed to comply with either of these regulations. Thus, when he finally signed the Code he checked sections four and six and attached a memorandum to the Director of Personnel listing certain reservations. The gist of the memo was that he wanted it clearly understood that he was a partner in the consulting firm of Strobel and Salzman, but that this firm would not "directly or indirectly" perform any work for the General Services Administration.[16]

Strobel also was dilatory in providing his superiors with a list of his firm's clients. The Office of Compliance of the General Services Administration requested, on two separate occasions, that Strobel submit such a list. Joseph Moody, Assistant General Counsel of the GSA, stated that after the second attempt to get this information, the Office of Compliance filed a memorandum which "did not expressly state that Strobel refused either request but clearly so implied."[17] Eventually, Strobel submitted the requested information, but not until August of 1955, which was over one year after he had taken office and, again, only after some prodding from his superior, Mansure.[18] "I didn't want anybody snooping around my private business," he said. "I had other things to do."[19]

Perhaps the most damaging evidence uncovered by the subcommittee concerned Strobel's role in pressing his firm's claim with the Corps of Engineers. In April, 1953, Strobel and Salzman secured a $100,879 contract with the Corps of Engineers for draw-

[13] *Ibid.*, pp. 2–3.
[14] *Ibid.*, pp. 28, 67.
[15] *Ibid.*, p. 30.
[16] *Ibid.*, p. 29.
[17] *Ibid.*, p. 202.
[18] *Ibid.*, p. 32.
[19] "Conflict of Interest?"*Time*, November 14, 1955, p. 106.

ings and specifications for warehouses and heating plants. Subsequently, the Corps enlarged the scope of the project, and this change necessitated additional work on the part of Strobel and Salzman. For its extra work the company later submitted a bill to the Corps for $7,500.

Although all work on this job was completed before Strobel became Commissioner of Public Buildings, the Corps had not acted on the firm's claim for additional payment. Strobel candidly admitted that, after becoming commissioner, he contacted Mr. Lyn Hench of the Corps of Engineers "two or three times" in order to press his firm's claim against that agency. Ultimately it was settled for $3,097. Strobel viewed his activity as being perfectly proper because he always contacted the Corps of Engineers on his "lunch hour, not on government time."[20]

This remark, which surely rivals in awkwardness Secretary Wilson's "bird dog" comment, suggested that the commissioner devoted precious little of his time to examining the conflict of interest laws. Sections 281 and 283 of the United States Criminal Code prohibit a government employee from accepting compensation for services performed before a government agency,[21] as well as from serving as an agent in a claim against a governmental agency.[22] Conviction carries a maximum fine of $10,000, imprisonment for one year, or both. From a cursory examination of these statutes, which have been on the books since 1862, it is clear that they are applicable to government officials twenty-four hours per day.

The only question open to debate was whether Strobel was acting as an "agent" for the firm of Strobel and Salzman or as the "principal" in the case. The conflict of interest statutes do not prohibit a public employee from seeking relief from an agency of the Federal Government. Thus, any public official, for example, might legally protest an adverse tax ruling before the Internal Revenue Bureau. Therefore, one could argue the point that Strobel was not violating the conflict of interest laws since he owned ninety percent of the consulting firm and was, consequently, acting as the "principal" in the case. Evidently the Department of Justice agreed since it did not initiate criminal procedures against Strobel when the case was turned over to it.[23]

Strobel also became involved in a second controversy with the Corps of Engineers. On March 31, 1954, he had personally negotiated a $71,050 contract with the Corps to design helicopter hang-

[20] Antitrust Subcommittee of the Committee on the Judiciary, *Strobel Hearings*, 1955, pp. 24–26.
[21] 18 *U.S.C.* 281.
[22] 18 *U.S.C.* 283.
[23] Charles Egan, "Strobel Inquiry Started by F.B.I.," *New York Times*, October 29, 1955.

ars.[24] Although Strobel did not become Commissioner of Public Buildings until July 1, 1954, it was revealed that he was retained as a "fulltime, 8-hour per day, 5-day a week consultant" by the General Services Administration on April 1, 1954, so that he might familiarize himself with the duties of the Commissioner of Public Buildings prior to the retirement of the incumbent commissioner, W. E. Reynolds. There was a clear understanding between Strobel and Mansure that Strobel would become commissioner on July 1.[25]

Thus, only one day before Strobel began his on-the-job training for the commissioner's post, he negotiated a contract for Strobel and Salzman with the Corps of Engineers. Moreover, Strobel did not inform the Corps that he had accepted government employment, despite the fact that the Corps placed certain restrictions on the granting of contracts to government employees. It was the opinion of Harold Rhind, an attorney for the Corps of Engineers, that had the Corps known Strobel was about to become a government employee, the contract with Strobel and Salzman would not have been granted.[26]

Harry B. Zackrison, chief of the Engineering Division of the Corps, would not say categorically that the contract would not have been granted, largely because of the importance of the hangar project and the four- or five-week delay which would have necessarily resulted in any subsequent renegotiation of the contract. However, he did admit that, had the Corps been in possession of the complete facts, they would have served as a "red light," thereby causing it to check more carefully into the whole matter so as to be certain of its legality.[27] Indeed, after Zackrison learned of Strobel's appointment as commissioner, he sent a letter of inquiry to Strobel and Salzman to ascertain whether Strobel was receiving any profits from the hangar contract. Failing to receive this clarification, the Corps informed the firm by telephone, some two weeks later, that it had directed all work on the hangar project to cease.

On being informed of Strobel's difficulty with the Corps of Engineers, Public Buildings Counsel Joseph Moody told Strobel that questions of public policy and ethics were involved and advised him to submit a detailed statement of his relationship with the consulting firm to the Corps of Engineers. Moody eventually prepared a rough draft of just such a statement for Strobel's use.[28] However, Strobel never submitted such a document. He told Moody that he had "decided to handle the matter in some other

[24] Antitrust Subcommittee of the Committee on the Judiciary, *Strobel Hearings,* 1955, p. 87.
[25] *Ibid.,* p. 6.
[26] *Ibid.,* p. 249.
[27] *Ibid.,* pp. 250–51.
[28] *Ibid.,* pp. 92–94.

way." Then after its Legal Division announced that it could find no legal objections to the contract in question, the Corps decided that it would be "in the best interests of the government" to rescind the stop order. However, the Corps decided not to grant any future contracts to the firm of Strobel and Salzman.[29]

Testimony at the hearings also confirmed Pearson's allegation that clients of Strobel and Salzman were granted government contracts after Strobel had become commissioner. One such company was the Serge Petroff architectural firm of New York City. In August, 1954, shortly after Strobel assumed his new duties, the Immigration and Naturalization Service requested approximately $360,000 in alterations on a building at 70 Columbus Avenue, New York City. It hoped to move its Ellis Island operation into that building by December 1 of the same year. Because of the urgency of the request, Strobel immediately contacted Edwin Lawton, deputy regional director of the Public Buildings Service and the man responsible for letting contracts in the New York area.[30] Exactly what transpired between the two is subject to interpretation.

Strobel, noting the urgency of the situation, reported that he "suggested" the Serge Petroff firm to Lawton because he knew it to be a reputable firm capable of completing the job by the December 1 deadline.[31] Lawton testified that, although he did not interpret the "suggestion" as "absolute instruction," he did feel that "Strobel inferred that I was to do business with Petroff and not any other firm." Lawton also admitted that, as a result of his talk with Strobel, he never considered any other architectural firm, though he agreed with Chairman Celler that there were undoubtedly many New York firms which would have been willing to undertake the project.[32]

Whether Strobel intended to use his superior rank as a subtle form of coercion is, of course, difficult to determine. Certainly, there is substantial evidence indicating that Strobel was motivated solely by his desire to get the building ready by the deadline. Still, the want of proof that he intended to use the prestige of his office improperly does not relieve Strobel from the charge of impropriety. Clearly, Strobel never informed Lawton that his consulting firm had been retained by the Petroff firm four separate times between 1953 and 1955. Lawton admitted that if he had known of this relationship, he would have consulted with his superiors before granting the contract.[33]

Yet, Lawton's handling of his job was not above criticism.

[29] *Ibid.,* pp. 254–55.
[30] *Ibid.,* p. 35.
[31] *Ibid.,* p. 36.
[32] *Ibid.,* pp. 99–101.
[33] *Ibid.,* p. 99.

During his five years with the Public Buildings Service he had
granted only one other contract to a New York architectural firm,
that one going to Chapman, Evans, and Delehanty for alterations
of another building in New York City. Subsequently, it was discovered that this firm was also a client of Strobel and Salzman and
that this contract had been let while Strobel was commissioner.
It is doubtful, however, that Strobel had any knowledge of the
contract negotiations until weeks after the firm's selection. Likewise, it is doubtful that Lawton, at the time of the negotiations,
was aware that the firm was a client of Strobel and Salzman. Yet,
there remained the very real question as to why this firm, which
did not submit the lowest bid, ultimately was granted the contract.
Lawton's testimony did not resolve this question. "It was just an
eeny, meeny, miney, mo basis," he said.[34]

During Strobel's term as commissioner, the Public Buildings
Service also granted a contract to Roberts and Company Associates
of Atlanta, Georgia. Again, the company was a client of Strobel
and Salzman. The $24,200 contract was for modifications and
additions to their original plans for the Communicable Diseases
Center in Atlanta. The original contract, which amounted to
$382,000, had been granted to the firm some time before Strobel
had become commissioner, and, it deserves mention, the Code of
Ethics among architects would dictate that the firm doing the
original work would also do all revisions and additions.[35] Again,
Strobel had not informed anyone of his relationship with the
Roberts firm. On the basis of "hindsight," he said, he at least
should have reported this relationship to Mansure.[36] Interestingly,
Mansure was criticized by prominent Republicans for granting a
contract to "Chip" Roberts, former treasurer of the Democratic
National Committee.[37]

Strobel, in at least one instance, did solicit business for Strobel
and Salzman while Commissioner of Public Buildings. Sol
Schwarz, business manager of his firm, testified that in November
or December, 1954, Strobel accompanied him to a meeting with
Mr. Ferrenz, of the architectural firm of Ferrenz and Taylor, for
the purpose of inquiring about business on a housing contract
which they understood the firm held. Strobel "was trying to get
business—he along with me," Schwarz said. But since the meeting
revealed that Ferrenz and Taylor held no housing contract, they
"could not solicit any work at that time."[38] They did, however,
leave a brochure on Strobel and Salzman, and, in August of 1955,

[34] *Ibid.*, pp. 53–55.
[35] *Ibid.*, pp. 76–82.
[36] *Ibid.*, p. 83.
[37] *Ibid.*, p. 194.
[38] *Ibid.*, p. 159.

received an $18,000 contract from Ferrenz and Taylor.[39] It is interesting to note that Ferrenz and Taylor submitted its own brochure to the Public Buildings Service only a month previously in hopes of obtaining government contracts.[40]

In late July, 1955, the Central Intelligence Agency requested that the Public Buildings Service prepare a list of "outstanding architects" who would be capable of designing its new $46,000,000 headquarters building.[41] With a project of this magnitude, it was estimated that the architectural fees alone might run as high as $2,000,000, a figure which prompted Mansure to refer to the project as an "architectural plum."[42] The Public Buildings Service submitted the names of fourteen architectural firms to the CIA, of which four were active clients of Strobel and Salzman, two were former clients of Strobel and Salzman, and two others had been approached by Strobel and Salzman.[43] Thus, of the fourteen names names submitted to the CIA, Strobel's firm had had some relationship with eight. Strobel remarked that "it goes to prove the high caliber of clientele Strobel and Salzman has been able to establish."[44]

The extent to which Strobel influenced the determination of these fourteen firms is difficult to ascertain. He first testified that he participated in the initial preparation of the list of architectural firms.[45] Later, he corrected his testimony because, he said, the record made it appear that he took an "active part" in the initial preparation of the list, whereas only his staff was responsible for the preliminary draft. He personally participated in the final draft, i.e., in the elimination of several firms which had appeared on the first listing.[46] After the hearings had concluded, however, he again altered his position, saying that his previous testimony was "in error" and that he did not, at any stage, participate in the preparation of the list. In substantiation of Strobel's final position, the Evaluation Committee of the Public Buildings Service submitted an affidavit to the subcommittee which said, in part, that "the Commissioner did not participate in the evaluation of these firms or in the preparation of this final list. He was not present when the final list was being prepared."[47] Again, however, Strobel unquestionably forgot to inform any of his associates of his relationship with these architectural firms.

[39] *Ibid.*, p. 162.
[40] *Ibid.*, p. 271.
[41] *Ibid.*, p. 116.
[42] *Ibid.*, p. 187.
[43] *Ibid.*, p. 188.
[44] *Ibid.*, p. 121.
[45] *Ibid.*, p. 116.
[46] *Ibid.*, pp. 153–54.
[47] *Ibid.*, p. 275.

The three days of testimony undeniably revealed that, knowingly or not, Strobel frequently used the power of his office in such a way as to put him in a compromising position. Possibly Strobel did not use this power as openly and as blantantly as did Secretary Talbott, e.g., he did not use government stationery to contact prospective clients. But the power of his office was there, despite the fact that he never seemed to be competely aware of the influence and authority which necessarily lie behind any important governmental post.[48] "If they want to get rid of me, they'll have to fire me," he said, "I'm not the kind of man who runs."[49]

There is no evidence to suggest that Mansure, initially, intended to fire the commissioner as a result of the subcommittee disclosures. However, a few days after the hearings concluded, Chairman Celler delivered what the *St. Louis Post-Dispatch* termed a "virtual ultimatum" to Mansure, demanding to know what, if any, action was to be taken by the General Services Administration. He called for an answer by November 22.[50] In addition, *The New York Times* reported that a "reliable informant" had said that direct pressure from the White House was being exerted to force Strobel's dismissal, although there was no hint as to the actual source of this pressure.[51] Certainly it did not come from the President, who at that time was in a Denver hospital recuperating from his heart attack.

But, pressured or not, Strobel finally did submit a letter of resignation to Mansure. He insisted that he never used his official position to advance his private interests. Still, he felt that, no matter how "honorable his conduct" or how "innocent his intentions," some people would use his private business connections to embarrass him and the Administration. Mansure accepted the resignation with "regret," saying that Strobel had brought to government "a high professional competence and experience that has been of great benefit" and commended the commissioner for his "fine attitude."[52] The very next day Strobel made a "hurried departure" for his home in New York City, taking with him only those things he could carry.[53] "In politics I was out of my element," he said.[54]

There were, obviously, many parallels between the Talbott and Strobel cases. First, there was the almost unbelievable naiveté on the part of each of these business men. In regard to the Petroff case, for instance, Strobel said, apparently with the utmost sin-

[48] "Questions That Remain," *St. Louis Post-Dispatch,* November 10, 1955.
[49] *Time,* November 14, 1955, p. 106.
[50] *New York Times,* November 7, 1955.
[51] *Ibid.,* November 10, 1955.
[52] Antitrust Subcommittee of the Committee on the Judiciary, *Strobel Hearings,* 1955, pp. 276–77.
[53] *New York Times,* November 10, 1955.
[54] "Smeared and Cleared," *Fortune,* June, 1956, p. 49.

cerity, "I don't think it entered my thought that there might be any conflict whatsoever. It was a matter of getting the job done."[55] Strobel, like Talbott, also never seemed to perceive any of his mistakes except in retrospect. In the Roberts contract, for example, it was only "on hindsight" that he was able to see that he should have disqualified himself during the contractual negotiations.[56]

In fact, throughout the hearings he exhibited a rather shocking inability to grasp the fact that a public official should not use his office in a manner which might bring pecuniary reward to either himself or his friends, or use it in such a way as to give the appearance that such was the case. Moreover, he failed to comprehend that his activities while commissioner were almost diametrically opposed to the uncompromising code of ethics promised by Eisenhower and other leading Republicans in the "Great Crusade."

Yet, Strobel was certainly not intentionally a dishonest man, motivated by a desire for financial gain. He had accepted the government post, at a considerable financial loss, from what seemed to be a real sense of public duty. Even Subcommittee Chairman Celler said that he believed that Strobel had always been convinced, in his own mind, that he was not guilty of any wrongdoing.[57] Besides, only a very foolish scoundrel would have cooperated with the subcommittee, "to the n'th degree" in the words of Celler, if he felt that he was guilty of either illegal or unethical acts.[58]

Inasmuch as the commissioner's position is not subject to Senate confirmation, Mansure must, it seems, accept much of the responsibility for the Strobel controversy. It is apparent, from Mansure's testimony at the hearings, that he never had a very clear understanding of Strobel's relationship with the consulting firm. He simply accepted Strobel's word that he would not take part in the activities of the firm. Mansure admitted that he did not check on this partnership arrangement with anyone in the Attorney General's office, saying that he was "under the impression that Mr. Strobel's counsel had taken the matter up and had advised him."[59] Moreover, there is little evidence which suggests that he made much of an effort to assure that Strobel's active management of the firm had ceased following the "danger signals," i.e., Strobel's failure to sign the Code of Ethics and provide the GSA with a list of his firm's clients.

Some months after Strobel's resignation, a unanimous subcommittee reported that his continuing relationship with his private engineering firm placed him in a "fundamentally inconsistent and

[55] Antitrust Subcommittee of the Committee on the Judiciary, *Strobel Hearings,* 1955, p. 51.
[56] *Ibid.,* p. 83.
[57] *Ibid.,* p. 198.
[58] *Ibid.,* p. 137.
[59] *Ibid.,* p. 184.

untenable position." In addition, all agreed that as a matter of public policy, the government should not hire people who retain private interests in firms with which they must deal as public officials. However, the subcommittee divided evenly along party lines as to whether Strobel's activities constituted either a conflict of interest or a violation of the General Services Administration's Code of Ethics. The three Democrats, Celler of New York, Rodino of New Jersey, and Rogers of Colorado answered "yes" on both counts, whereas the three Republicans, Keating of New York, McCulloch of Ohio, and Scott of Pennsylvania voted "no" on both counts.[60]

Nevertheless, more and more people were beginning to suspect that not all of the officials in the Eisenhower Administration were "as clean as a hound's tooth." Indeed, five highly publicized conflict of interest cases, four involving resignations, but none of them dismissals, would constitute a very high incidence of public corruption for any national administration in its first three years, but particularly one as aggressive in its protestations of morality as the Eisenhower Administration. Ironically, during the 1952 campaign the crusading general had told an Atlanta, Georgia, gathering, "If you are as tired as I am of picking up your newspapers about a fresh Government scandal, then let's get together and restore decency and honesty to the nation's capital."[61] The President seemed to be recovering his health in Denver, but at the same time his political halo was slipping badly.

[60] U.S., Congress, House, Antitrust Subcommittee of the Committee on the Judiciary, *Report Pursuant to H. Res. 22,* 84th Cong., 1st Sess., 1956, pp. 15, 26.
[61] For the text of the Atlanta speech see *The New York Times,* September 3, 1952.

Chapter 8

CROSSCURRENTS

The party that's in
Commits all the sin.
The party that's out
Is always devout.

ANONYMOUS

THE FRONT PAGE of *The New York Times* of November 15, 1955, was a study in contrasts. One article reported that President Eisenhower had just returned to his Gettysburg farm to convalesce from his heart attack. Reporters estimated that over 7,000 boisterous well-wishers, many of them carrying "Welcome Home Ike" placards, had crowded into downtown Lincoln Square to welcome the town's most celebrated citizen. Accompanied by the local high school band, the citizens sang "Happy Birthday Dear Mamie" for Mrs. Eisenhower, who happened to be celebrating her fifty-ninth birthday that day, and the mayor's daughter presented her with a beautiful bouquet of purple orchids and red roses. A beaming President thanked, in his words, "my future permanent neighbors, I hope."[1]

A second article, however, was more sober. It reported that Hugh Cross, chairman of the Interstate Commerce Commission, had been called before the Senate Permanent Subcommittee on Investigation for executive hearings. Executive hearings are, by definition, secret and closed to the public. A committee holding such a proceeding operates under the assumption that the official under suspicion may prove to be perfectly innocent and, thus, should not be needlessly exposed to public ridicule or censure. Chairman McClellan, therefore, refused to reveal the exact nature of the investigation, though he admitted that a conflict of interest problem might possibly arise in any case brought before his subcommittee.[2] The thought of another conflict of interest case was

---

[1] *New York Times*, November 15, 1955.
[2] *Ibid.*

hardly an enviable prospect for the Eisenhower Administration inasmuch as Strobel's resignation as Public Buildings Commissioner had occurred less than a week previously.

When sufficient evidence of misbehavior is elicited in committee executive session, a public hearings is in order. Also, the scheduling of a public hearings generally implies that at least a *prima facie* case has been made. After only one day in executive session, one from which Cross had emerged "white faced and in visible distress," the subcommittee voted unanimously to hold a public inquiry.[3] Senator George Bender, Republican of Ohio, wanted the public hearings to begin at once. "The President doesn't want anything concealed," he said. "His policy is to bring everything into the open—quickly."[4] Such a comment took on something of an Orwellian character in light of the President's rather ambivalent attitude in the Nixon, Roberts, Talbott, Wenzell, and Strobel cases.

From the outset most members of the subcommittee seemed not to agree with Senator Bender on the wisdom of holding public hearings immediately. In fact, the subcommittee deliberately delayed the inquiry, ostensibly to give Cross a chance to resign. "Responsible informants" reported to *The New York Times* that both Democratic and Republican members of the subcommittee had agreed not to pursue the investigation if only Cross would resign.[5] Eight days later, on November 23, Cross did submit his resignation and plans for the proposed public hearings were dropped.[6]

Fortunately, for those interested in this case, the subcommittee voted the following January to make the executive testimony available to the public. The vote was along straight party lines, with Democrats McClellan, Jackson, Symington, and Ervin voting for, and Republicans McCarthy, Mundt, and Bender against, public disclosure.[7] Surprising, perhaps, was the fact that Senator Bender had by this time, lost much of his zeal for public disclosure of the facts of the Cross controversy. When the subcommittee voted to release the executive testimony, the Senator told newsmen that he thought it was "grossly unfair to Mr. Cross."[8]

Testimony presented during the executive session indicated

[3] William S. White, "ICC Chairman to Face Open Senate Investigations," *New York Times,* November 16, 1955.

[4] *St. Louis Post-Dispatch,* November 17, 1955.

[5] William S. White, "Cross Expected To Resign, Quashing Senate Inquiry," *New York Times,* November 17, 1955.

[6] Allen Drury, "Cross Resigns as Head of ICC; Assails Charges," *New York Times,* November 26, 1955.

[7] U.S., Congress, Senate, Permanent Subcommittee on Investigations, *Hearings, Hugh W. Cross—Chairman of the Interstate Commerce Commission,* 84th Cong., 2d Sess., 1955, p. 1.

[8] *New York Times,* January 14, 1956.

that Chairman Cross had contacted at least three railway presidents on behalf of Railroad Transfer, Inc., a company owned by his longtime friend, John Keeshin. Keeshin's company was seeking the contract to haul passengers and baggage among Chicago's six widely scattered rail terminals. For over a century this contract had been held by the Parmalee Transportation Company and, though renegotiated from time to time, it had never been let on a competitive basis. In late 1954, however, the Western Passenger Association, a six-man committee which represented the twenty-one railroads serving Chicago in negotiations with Parmalee, decided to call for open bidding on a new five-year contract.[9]

Parmalee's continually rising costs and decreasing standards of service were largely responsible for the change to competitive bidding. The company's equipment, for instance, had deteriorated to such an extent that the transfer of both passengers and baggage was regarded by many as singularly inefficient. Yet, the costs of this service to the railroads had continued to rise throughout the many contractual renegotiations with Parmalee. One railway president testified that the change to competitive bids had been recommended because Parmalee's charges had simply gone "sky high."[10] Although at least nine different companies were asked to submit bids on the franchise, only three found the prospects sufficiently attractive to do so. These three companies included the Parmalee Transportation Company, Railroad Transfer, Inc., and the Willett Teaming Company.[11]

Cross seems to have developed an interest in this contract as soon as he heard that it might be negotiated. Howard Simpson, president of the Baltimore and Ohio Railroad Company, submitted an affidavit to the subcommittee which revealed that Cross had conversed with him a number of times about the Chicago transfer contract. In the spring of 1955, Cross made his first inquiry as to the details of the contract. At that time, Simpson said, he could advise the chairman only that the contract was to expire in 1955. Upon "further inquiry" from Cross, Simpson learned that the contract was to be let on a competitive basis. This information was relayed to Cross by telephone. The affidavit disclosed that Cross also made subsequent inquiries about the contract when conversing with Simpson "on other things."[12]

Subpoenaed telephone records corroborated at least part of Simpson's statement. For the records showed that between April 18 and June 8, 1955, Cross had placed four person-to-person calls

[9] "Star Crossed," *Time*, December 5, 1955, p. 23.
[10] Senate Permanent Subcommittee on Investigations of the Committee on Governmental Operations, *Cross Hearings*, 1955, p. 5.
[11] *Ibid.*, pp. 10, 28.
[12] *Ibid.*, p. 22.

to Simpson. While there is no record of the matters discussed in
these conversations, it seems reasonable to assume that Cross was
not calling in his capacity as chairman of the Interstate Commerce
Commission since he requested that all the calls be billed to his
private phone number.[13] Simpson insisted that Cross had never
attempted to influence him in any of these discussions. Moreover,
he had said that he had "no knowledge" that Cross had any connection with Railroad Transfer, Inc.

Paul E. Feucht, president of the Chicago and Northwestern
Railway, told the subcommittee that on May 13, 1955, he had
received a telephone call from Chairman Cross, who told him he
was "very much interested in seeing that J. L. Keeshin got the new
contract with the railroads." Speaking from a memorandum that
he had dictated some five or ten minutes after the telephone conversation, Feucht testified that Cross was intimately acquainted
with the details of both the Parmalee and the Keeshin bids. At
least, Feucht said, "he knew more about it than I did." His
memorandum was replete with comparisons of such contractual
details as rates, wages, equipment, financial backing, etc. Cross
had even pointed to a "joker" in the Parmalee contract which did
not appear in the Keeshin bid.[14] Subsequent inquiry proved that
the figures given by Cross were substantially correct.

Feucht admitted that he had been "quite puzzled" at the time
as to why the chairman of the ICC would call him about such a
contract. "I just thought it was kind of funny," Feucht said, "that
someone like that would call me about this contract."[15] For at
best Cross was only a "passing acquaintance," a person to whom
he had not even been introduced until after Cross had become a
member of the Interstate Commerce Commission. Moreover, Feucht
never conversed with Cross either before or after this one telephone
call.[16]

However, Feucht had not been concerned about the propriety
of the call from the chairman until later when, he said, "I thought
about it a little bit."[17] It seems neither inappropriate nor unfair
to inquire at this point as to why a railway president would think
only "a little bit" about such a call. Although the transfer of
passengers and baggage had been held to be involved solely in
intrastate commerce, thereby not subject to ICC regulation, all of
the twenty-one railroads interested in the transfer contract certainly
fell under ICC regulation. Feucht was well aware, for instance, that
his Chicago and Northwestern Railroad could make not even the
most rudimentary changes in rates or standards of service without

[13] *Ibid.*, pp. 25–26.
[14] *Ibid.*, p. 10.
[15] *Ibid.*, p. 9.
[16] *Ibid.*, p. 7.
[17] *Ibid.*, p. 9.

prior approval by the commission. A mere inquiry from such a powerful source might exert influence.

It is not meant to imply here that Feucht was guilty of any wrongdoing. As a matter of fact, there seems to be no evidence that he was. He simply turned the memorandum in question over to his company's representative on the Western Railroad Association, saying, "Here is what Hugh Cross gave me over the telephone, and I don't know what interest he has in this thing, but take it for what it is worth."[18] Feucht's failure to appreciate fully the question of propriety raised by the phone call fits neatly into the motif which was rapidly emerging from the Eisenhower conflict of interest cases, namely that the American businessman often displays an appalling insensitivity to questions of public morality.

The testimony of Wayne A. Johnston, president of the Illinois Central Railroad, was even more damaging to Cross. Whereas Simpson and Feucht indicated that they were unaware of Cross's intention to become associated with Railroad Transfer, Inc.,[19] Johnston stated that he had heard rumors around Chicago that Hugh Cross would resign his post on the commission and come to Chicago to head Railroad Transfer if it secured the new contract. He further testified that on one of his frequent trips to Washington, where, he always tried "to make the rounds to see the various commissioners," he had asked his friend Cross if this rumor were true. Cross reputedly replied that he would "if things worked out satisfactorily," i.e., if Keeshin got the contract. Johnston said that he had not pursued the question.[20]

Fred Gurley, president of the Atchison, Topeka, and Santa Fe Railroad Company, submitted an affidavit to the subcommittee which revealed that he too had heard rumors that Cross was unhappy in Washington and wanted to return to Illinois, where he had served as lieutenant governor from 1940 to 1948. Like Johnston, he had heard that Cross would resign his post on the Commission and become associated with Railroad Transfer if Keeshin were successful in securing the contract in Chicago. He stressed, however, that he had never spoken directly with either Cross or Keeshin concerning such an arrangement.[21]

Keeshin later testified that there never was an agreement, either expressed or implied, that Cross would become head of Railroad Transfer should it be awarded the contract. He readily admitted that he too had heard rumors that Cross might join his firm. He had assumed, he said, that the story had been circulated by his competitor, Parmalee Transportation Company. However, there is no evidence that Keeshin made any effort to quiet these

[18] *Ibid.*
[19] *Ibid.*, pp. 12, 22.
[20] *Ibid.*, pp. 18–20.
[21] *Ibid.*, p. 23.

rumors,[22] possibly because they might prove helpful in securing the contract.

In 1954, Keeshin had inquired as to Cross's interest in returning to Chicago to head a bus line which was then in receivership, and for which he had submitted a bid of $350,000. He had made the inquiry, he said, because it was "commonly known" that Cross wanted to leave government service and get back to Illinois, either in politics or business.[23] When Keeshin failed to gain control of the bus line, Cross was left with the impression that, if he ever wished to return to private business, a job with one of Keeshin's companies could always be provided.[24]

Keeshin testified that he had discussed the Chicago transfer contract with Cross but pointed out also that he frequently discussed business affairs with him. After all, he argued, Cross was an old friend, and a friend whose opinion he valued highly. But Keeshin denied categorically that he had attempted, in these discussions, to solicit the aid of the chairman in his struggle for the Chicago contract. However, he did concede that he had hoped that "if an occasion arises, he [Cross] could pass a good word for me."[25] Specifically, Keeshin hoped that if any of the railway people coming into the chairman's office inquired about "the way Keeshin operates," the chairman would give him a good recommendation.[26] He obviously thought this not unlikely, since he reported that Cross had told him that he hoped Railroad Transfer would get the contract.[27]

Actually, a substantial relationship between Keeshin and Cross had been reasonably well established before the subcommittee's executive session was called. The subcommittee had subpoened telephone records which indicated that between March 23 and September 18, 1955, Cross's telephone had called Keeshin's eighteen times, while Keeshin's had called Cross's fourteen times.[28] Some of these calls were probably placed by the men's wives and still others undoubtedly dealt with the commission's delay in granting Keeshin's trucking company temporary authority to operate along a new route.[29] Keeshin conceded, however, that he "might have made some calls pertaining to this particular [transfer] contract."[30]

However, he insisted that Cross had told him nothing about his having contacted rail officials on behalf of Railroad Transfer,

[22] *Ibid.*, p. 43.
[23] *Ibid.*, p. 33.
[24] *Ibid.*, p. 42.
[25] *Ibid.*, p. 40.
[26] *Ibid.*, p. 48.
[27] *Ibid.*, p. 41.
[28] *Ibid.*, p. 25.
[29] *Ibid.*, p. 37.
[30] *Ibid.*, p. 40.

Inc.[31] Keeshin's testimony on this point leaves one with a certain feeling of disquietude. Curiously, he admitted that, once he got the contract, he called Cross and "thanked him for what help he did give, if he did give any."[32] Even more curious, the telephone records indicate that on June 13, 1955, the day the contract was awarded, it was Cross who called Keeshin and not vice versa. Moreover, the records show that Keeshin did not call Cross until July 14, over one month after the letting of the contract.[33] There is the possibility, of course, that Keeshin called the chairman from some place other than his office or his home. But Senator McClellan did question Keeshin as to whether Cross might not have telephoned "to tell you that he had done the job."[34]

By this time Keeshin evidently had serious reservations about the contract. Subsequent to securing it his life had been threatened, the city of Chicago had attempted to negate the contract by city ordinance, Parmalee had refused to leave the rail stations, he had been subpoenaed by a Federal Grand Jury, and, finally, he had been called before a congressional subcommittee. Prior to landing the contract he had operated the largest truckline in the United States and, as he said, "didn't owe anyone any money" and was "enjoying life." Keeshin told the subcommittee, undoubtedly with the utmost sincerity, that he would gladly give the contract back to the railroads and Parmalee and "kiss them on both cheeks."[35]

When Cross appeared before the subcommittee he conceded that he had contacted the three railway presidents. He said that, at least "inferentially," Keeshin had requested that he "put in a good word for him" with the rail officials.[36] Cross could not recall, however, whether he had ever informed Keeshin that he had contacted Feucht, Simpson, and Johnston. "I would not say that I did, or that I didn't," he said.[37] He was certain, however, that Keeshin had never called to express his appreciation for whatever aid, if any, the chairman may have given him.[38] Cross maintained that he first learned of the contract from a trade publication around the latter part of June.[39]

Subsequent reflection on his communication with Paul Feucht caused Cross to term the phone call "indiscreet," and a mistake which should not have been made. However, he insisted that he had been motivated, not by a desire for personal gain, but rather

[31] Ibid., pp. 41, 46, 48.
[32] Ibid., p. 46.
[33] Ibid., p. 25.
[34] Ibid., p. 49.
[35] Ibid., p. 53.
[36] Ibid., p. 66.
[37] Ibid., p. 73.
[38] Ibid., p. 69.
[39] Ibid., p. 68.

by his interest in the Chicago and Northwestern Railroad, which had "unique" problems because of its extremely isolated rail terminal.[40] However, it must be said that the chairman's views as to what had transpired in the conversation differed significantly from those of Feucht.

Feucht, it will be recalled, had testified that in his telephone conversation with Cross, the chairman had displayed a thorough knowledge of the terms of both the Parmalee and Keeshin bids, one greater than that of Feucht himself.[41] Yet, early in the hearings, Cross maintained that he had little knowledge of the details of either the Parmalee or the Keeshin bids, saying, "I did not have any knowledge as to the specific terms." However, he later admitted that he had some general understanding of the provisions of the Keeshin bid, e.g., the "kind of service" proposed. But Cross seldom seemed able to give the subcommittee any of the "specifics" on the Keeshin bid.[42]

He denied having ever said that there were "jokers" in the Parmalee bid which did not exist in the one submitted by Keeshin, because, he said, he never possessed sufficient details of the two bids to make such a comparison. Also, he firmly rejected the contention that he had called one bid "superior" to another. For his assumption had always been that Feucht and other officials had "more knowledge" of the bids than he, largely because he had possessed information only "of one side." The telephone call, he maintained, was not made to recommend one company over the other, but simply to tell Feucht to be sure and "weigh the bids."[43] Although he admitted that he "could be wrong," he did not think that he had ever told Feucht that he was "very much interested in seeing that J. L. Keeshin got the contract with the railroads." But, regardless, he was positive that he had never intended to bring pressure on Feucht.[44]

Cross gave no particular significance to his conversation with Howard Simpson of the Baltimore and Ohio Railroad. He admitted that he had contacted Simpson about the transfer contract and had even met with him on one occasion in his Baltimore office. But, Cross said, he had been in Baltimore, not to meet with Simpson, but to see his tailor about a suit, the one, it seems, which he was wearing the very day he testified. Moreover, he had spent no more than twenty minutes with Simpson and some of that was spent in looking at the "old paneling and beautiful woodwork" in the rail offices. The Chicago transfer contract was only one of the "several" problems discussed at that time.[45]

[40] *Ibid.*, p. 59.
[41] *Ibid.*, p. 10.
[42] *Ibid.*, pp. 63–64.
[43] *Ibid.*, pp. 77–78.
[44] *Ibid.*, p. 65.
[45] *Ibid.*, p. 60.

Cross attached no more importance to his discussions with Wayne Johnston of the Illinois Central Railroad. He had, it seems, frequently talked with Johnston on business affairs, but perhaps even more often on private and social matters. Specifically, Cross said, he was interested in such things as Johnston's role as a trustee of the University of Illinois, a school he had once attended. He sometimes discussed a new building erected by the Illinois Central Railroad. He had referred to the transfer contract, "on probably more than one occasion," but only in "the most casual way." Moreover, Cross thought that it was "inconceivable" that the rail executives would have felt that these conversations were designed to exert undue pressure upon them.[46]

Testimony given by Chairman Cross conflicted in many respects with that given by Johnston. First, Cross maintained that there had never been an understanding between him and Keeshin that he would go to work with Keeshin's transfer company. He told reporter William S. White that he "denied categorically" that any such offer was ever made.[47] Certainly, he said, he had never told Johnston that he would go to work for Keeshin "if everything worked out satisfactorily." He admitted that Johnston had once inquired about the possibility, but he had assumed that the questioning was "in the spirit of levity." "I know Wayne Johnston," he said, "and we kid back and forth." Since the transfer company was a new operation, and an operation about which he felt he had limited knowledge, Cross maintained that it would have been the "last one in the world" he was interested in.[48]

Furthermore, Cross denied that Keeshin had left him with the clear understanding that a job with any of his firms could always be arranged if he desired to quit government service and return to private business. It was his understanding that the one job offer he had from Keeshin, to head the Chicago West Town Bus Line, had not been duplicated after that transaction fell through.[49] At any rate, Cross said, he could not have accepted a position with Keeshin at that time because he had already resolved to stay on the commission until his term as chairman expired. At that time he had "no other plans in mind; that was, of any kind, practicing law, or anything else."[50]

The calling of public hearings by the subcommittee set in motion a chain of events which was becoming increasingly familiar in these conflict of interest cases. First came the widespread rumors that Cross was being pressured by high officials to resign his post. It was reported that Warren Olney, chief of the Criminal Division of

[46] *Ibid.*, pp. 60–61.
[47] White, *New York Times*, November 16, 1955.
[48] Senate Permanent Subcommittee on Investigations of the Committee on Governmental Operations, *Cross Hearings*, 1955, pp. 78–80.
[49] *Ibid.*, pp. 67–68.
[50] *Ibid.*, p. 79.

the Department of Justice, had requested a transcript of the executive session proceedings, principally, according to *The New York Times,* to make the whole record available to the President. Eisenhower, it was solemnly reported, was "understood" to be ready to remove Cross even if guilty of only "inefficiency or neglect of duty." William S. White reminded his readers that officials under President Eisenhower "not only must be above any suggestion of lawbreaking but also must operate with unblemished ethical records."[51] The *Times* also "had reason to believe" that the case was being considered by Presidential Assistant Sherman Adams.[52]

Next came the predictable letter of resignation which Cross desired to be effective "immediately upon [the President's] acceptance." His stated reasons for the resignation at that particular time were threefold. First, he said that both he and his wife were in poor health. Second, he desired to protect the "unblemished reputation" of the Interstate Commerce Commission. And, finally, he had a sense of "regard and respect" for the President and his Administration. He emphasized, however, that had it not been for these considerations he would have remained at his post and defended "to the end" the "baseless charges" leveled against him.[53]

In a letter dated November 25, President Eisenhower accepted the resignation as of the close of business that day because, he said, "I understand that to be your wish." Even the President's letter of acceptance followed a stereotyped form. In fact, some of the more cynical of the Washington reporters now referred facetiously to such letters as "Dear Harold," "Dear Peter," and "Dear Hugh" letters. The President stated that he could "fully appreciate" the reasons for the resignation and expressed his appreciation for "the years of diligent service you have rendered with the Commission and for the constructive contributions to its work that you have made." Since this was very much the same formula followed in similar cases, it seemed to indicate a standard pattern devoid of any real understanding of the problems involved, lacking in any concern for the public interest, and without the slightest hint of reprimand for wrong doing.

The question as to whether Cross had been forced to resign was subject to debate. Although rumors of official pressure persisted, spokesmen for the Administration denied it. Presidential Press Secretary James Hagerty flatly rejected the contention that the case had been discussed by the White House.[54] His assistant,

[51] William S. White, "President Is Ready To Act in Inquiry on ICC Head," *New York Times,* November 19, 1955.
[52] Drury, *New York Times,* November 26, 1955.
[53] Both Cross's letter of resignation and Eisenhower's letter of acceptance are reproduced in full in *The New York Times,* November 26, 1955.
[54] Drury, *New York Times,* November 26, 1955.

Murray Snyder, told the press that, to the best of his knowledge, the President had not asked for Cross's resignation. Moreover, Sherman Adams insisted that he had never talked with Cross about his difficulties.[55] But later Snyder told reporters that while the Cross resignation was "not necessarily rushed," it had been "out of the usual course of events."[56] Such a statement hardly shed any light on the controversy. And the President was even more non-committal. He spent most of the day Cross resigned visiting with his grandchildren.

In all justice to the President, it should be noted that Cross was not an Eisenhower appointee. The former Illinois lieutenant governor had been appointed to the bipartisan commission by President Truman on April 8, 1949, to fill the unexpired term of one of the Republican members. On December 31, 1950, he was reappointed to a full seven-year term. Moreover, no special significance should be attached to the fact that Cross had become chairman under President Eisenhower, since the chairmanship is automatically rotated each year. Thus, Cross became chairman on July 1, 1955, simply because he was the most senior member of the commission who had not yet served as its chairman.[57]

The President, however, must accept much of the responsibility for the handling of the case following the disclosures of the Senate subcommittee. It is trite understatement to say that Cross's behavior hardly measured up to the standards of public morality so often referred to by the President. Though the executive session failed to prove that Cross had acted corruptly or illegally, it certainly revealed that he had acted with dubious propriety. When Cross talked with the rail executives the power and influence of his position were clearly in use, perhaps subtly and even unintentionally, but in use nevertheless. Under the circumstances, the President's "Dear Hugh" letter, somehow, seemed an inappropriate response.

Surprisingly, there seemed to be little enthusiasm anywhere to pursue the Cross investigation. The Justice Department apparently took no action as a result of its examination of the transcript of the executive session. And the members of the subcommittee, both Democrats and Republicans, appeared content to let the investigation lapse once Cross had tendered his resignation. The St. Louis Post-Dispatch asked bluntly if the subcommittee's apathy did not suggest "a cover-up of some kind."[58] Finally, it seems that Cross himself would have insisted on a public hearings if the

[55] St. Louis Post-Dispatch, November 25, 1955.
[56] New York Times, November 27, 1955.
[57] Drury, New York Times, November 26, 1955.
[58] St. Louis Post-Dispatch, November 27, 1955.

charges had been, as he said, "baseless." It does not seem natural, somehow, for an innocent man to resign his position in order to halt an investigation into his affairs. Though the casualties for questionable political behavior seemed by this time unusually high for the officials in a morally crusading administration, more and worse were yet to come.

Chapter 9

THE SNARE OF ILLUSION

Ladies and gentlemen, the purposes of those who are associated with me in this crusade—and my purposes—are simple and simply stated. . . . We want to substitute good government for bad government.

DWIGHT EISENHOWER

AN ARTICLE by Herbert Solow in the August, 1955, issue of *Fortune* charged that after three years of Republican control, the General Services Administration continued to be "Washington's most durable mess" and was guilty of "favoritism, factionalism, sloppiness, and waste." According to Solow, the plight of the agency was due, in no small measure, to what he termed "messy appointments" to top echelon positions by Presidents Truman and Eisenhower. He stated, none too subtly, that the agency's first three administrators, Major General Robert Littlejohn, Jess Larson, and Edmund Mansure were all less than competent administrators. He commented that it was especially ironical that the Eisenhower Administration, which had campaigned so vigorously against inefficiency and corruption in government service, had replaced Democrat Larson, an undistinguished Oklahoma politician, with Republican Mansure, a Chicago politician who was described by one of his Libertyville neighbors as a man who "could easily get over his head in very shallow water."[1]

The Solow article indicated that Mansure was, at the very least, administratively inept. He was pictured as a man engrossed in administrative trivia who encouraged subordinates to save paper clips from waste paper, who personally checked travel vouchers for his Washington staff and placed three-minute egg timers by the telephones in order to discourage prolonged conversations, but who failed to bring about long overdue reforms within his agency.

[1] Herbert Solow, "GSA: Washington's Most Durable Mess," *Fortune*, August, 1955, pp. 76–77.

115

By sheer coincidence, Mansure operated out of an office which had once been occupied by President Harding's Secretary of the Interior, Albert Fall, and took some delight in telling visitors that the Teapot Dome scandal had been contrived in that very room.[2]

The *Fortune* article did imply that Mansure was guilty of more than just administrative ineptness. Solow charged that William Balmer, vice chairman of the Cook County Executive Committee of the Republican party and the man responsible for Mansure's appointment to the government position, had continued to exert an unhealthy influence over Mansure after he had come to Washington. Solow revealed that shortly after the 1952 elections Balmer wrote to Herbert Brownell, one of Eisenhower's top campaign tacticians and later Attorney General, requesting Mansure's appointment to the GSA post. Information published subsequent to Solow's article, however, indicated that Balmer had asked the Administration to consider Mansure for a top government job, but did not specifically suggest that of administrator of the General Services Administration.[3] At any rate, the letter, written upon the stationery of the Cook County Republican organization, was forwarded to Sherman Adams for further consideration. Other messages were sent to Adams by the National Chairman of the Republican party, C. Wesley Roberts.[4] Interestingly, all of these figures, Roberts, Mansure, and Adams ultimately resigned under charges of conflict of interest.

Even before Mansure's appointment was official, rumors began circulating around Chicago to the effect that Balmer would soon be in a position to influence the awarding of GSA contracts. Such rumors seemed plausible, since Balmer, nicknamed the "Silver Fox" because of his white hair and innate shrewdness, had long been involved in Republican politics in Chicago. Indeed, it was Balmer who had managed the second "Big Bill" Thompson mayorality campaign. The Thompson administration will be remembered as unquestionably one of the most corrupt in Chicago's long history of dubious administrations. A mutual acquaintance of Balmer and Mansure reportedly told Solow that Balmer "has Mr. GSA [Mansure] in his pocket. Whenever Balmer walks in, Mr. GSA bows."[5]

This picture of Mansure was an amusing contrast with the image he attempted to convey at the Strobel hearings. Before the House Antitrust Subcommittee, Mansure stated that he considered

[2] *Ibid.*, pp. 76, 186.
[3] U.S., Congress, House, Special Government Activities Subcommittee of the Committee on Government Operations, *Hearings, Inquiry Into the Expansion and Operation by General Services Administration of the Government Nickel Plant at Nicaro, Cuba,* 84th Cong., 2d Sess., 1956, p. 294.
[4] Solow, *Fortune*, August, 1955, pp. 77, 188.
[5] *Ibid.*, pp. 77, 182.

the acceptance of a government post tantamount to the acceptance of a trusteeship on behalf of the people.[6] He opined that the actions of a public official must necessarily be guided by the general welfare of the people he serves rather than by the more narrow limits of his own private or personal interests. One could not serve two masters, one public and one private. "You have got to make up your mind who you are going to work for," he said. "I had to do that. It was hard for me to make the decision, and I made the decision, and I work for one master, the government, now."[7]

According to Solow, "the messiest single mess" involving the General Services Administration centered upon a United States government-owned nickel plant in Nicaro, Cuba.[8] The plant had been built during World War II after military mobilization brought on an acute nickel shortage. The comparatively low quality of the Nicaro ore, coupled with a decrease in the demand for nickel in the postwar period, placed it at a decided disadvantage with the rich Sudbury Basin in Canada, and Nicaro was shut down in 1947. Until 1951 the plant was listed as surplus property and, costing the government some $300,000 per year in maintenance, was regarded by the Administrator of GSA as a "costly white elephant." However, the Korean emergency affected the nation's stockpiling program to such an extent that the plant was reactivated in 1952, and the continuing nickel shortage caused the Office of Defense Mobilization to authorize a $43,000,000 expansion in 1953.[9]

The Frederick Snare Corporation had been awarded the contracts for both the construction and rehabilitation of the Nicaro plant. This was hardly surprising, for the company had established a reputation over the years for its construction work in Cuba. Indeed, Snare had long been one of the few American construction companies authorized under Cuban law to perform such work. From all reports, Snare did an excellent job at Nicaro in both 1942 and 1952, overcoming heat, insects, jungle, and wartime shortages to complete the projects on schedule, even if at a cost in excess of the original estimates.[10]

Yet, despite Snare's half century of solid accomplishments in the construction field in Cuba, and especially at Nicaro, the company did not get an exclusive contract for the plant expansion. Apparently with some reluctance, Snare accepted a fifty-fifty partner-

[6] U.S., Congress, House, Antitrust Subcommittee of the Committee on the Judiciary, *Hearings, Activities of Peter Strobel*, 84th Cong., 1st Sess., 1955, p. 185.

[7] *Ibid.*, p. 199.

[8] Solow, *Fortune*, August, 1955, p. 185.

[9] U.S., Congress, House, Committee on Government Operations, *Inquiry Into the Expansion and Operation by General Services Administration of the Government Nickel Plant at Nicaro, Cuba*, House Report No. 2390, 84th Cong., 2d Sess., 1956, pp. 3–7.

[10] *Ibid.*, pp. 4–5.

ship with Merritt, Chapman and Scott, a large construction firm, but one with virtually no experience in Cuba. Solow pointed out that the Merritt Company's single construction venture in Cuba, a water-supply project in 1952, had ended in a law suit. And in the supposedly joint operation at Nicaro, Solow found that the Snare Company had furnished all of the supervisory personnel. Following his investigation, journalist Solow concluded that Merritt, Chapman and Scott had been "at best, superfluous" to the partnership. Moreover, there seemed to be little doubt that factors other than competence had been decisive in the formulation of the Snare-Merritt partnership.[11]

It seems that National Lead Company had been chosen by the General Services Administration as the supervisory contractor for the Nicaro project. Such an arrangement gave National Lead the responsibility of choosing the operating subcontractors; that is, the companies which would do the actual construction work. Its choices would, of course, be subject to final approval by GSA. Since National Lead owned a majority of the stock in Nickel Processing Corporation, the company which had operated the Nicaro nickel refinery for the United States government since the early fifties, this meant, in effect, that the operator of the refinery had been retained by GSA to supervise plant expansion.[12] A congressional investigation would later reveal that such an arrangement was "without known precedent in government operations."[13] For some reason National Lead had thrown its support to the Merritt Company despite its inexperience in Cuba.

Solow suggested a variety of explanations for National Lead's position. First, the fact that National Lead sold a good deal of paint material to the company of Devoe and Raynolds, a Merritt subsidiary, may have influenced the company's decision. Moreover, Secretary of the Air Force Talbott admitted to Solow that he had contacted Mansure on Merritt's behalf, but insisted that it had been "casual, at a dinner party." Solow also discovered that Balmer, a friend of Merritt's executive Vice President Lewis Schott, had also spoken to Mansure about the Nicaro contract, but he, like Talbott, said the discussion was "casual, at a dinner party." Mansure insisted that the Merritt Company was made a partner to the venture primarily because of the size of the job. Such a statement is somewhat puzzling when one considers the fact that the expansion project was smaller than the initial construction of Nicaro. And in that instance the Snare Company, working alone and under

[11] Solow, *Fortune*, August, 1955, p. 185.
[12] *Ibid.*
[13] House Special Government Activities Subcommittee of the Committee on Government Operations, *Inquiry Into Nicaro*, 1956, p. 160.

far more difficult circumstances, had completed the project with efficiency and dispatch.[14]

Perhaps the most damaging evidence revealed by the Solow article concerned an insurance brokerage fee, which he estimated might run as high as $44,000, obtained by the firm of Balmer and Moore. Under Cuban law a broker automatically received ten percent of all workmen's compensation premiums. This was an unusually high percentage by United States standards, but apparently there was no legal alternative to it. Solow thought it was interesting, however, that the brokerage firm of Balmer and Moore had not even been registered in Illinois until May, 1954, just three months before it was selected as one of the Nicaro brokers. He thought the registration evinced "a nice sense of timing."[15] Actually, Illinois Department of Insurance records would later disclose that the firm of Balmer and Moore did not get a general brokerage license until August, 1955, although Balmer and Moore had been granted individual licenses in May, 1954, and September, 1953, respectively. This meant that the firm did not have a general brokerage license either at the time it solicited the Nicaro business or at the time it was officially appointed broker.[16]

As detailed as the Solow article was, it certainly raised as many questions as it answered. Indeed, it was Solow's opinion that nothing less than a congressional investigation could gather sufficient data to reveal fully all of the political machinations which were apparently involved in the Nicaro expansion. A few months after the August, 1955, article appeared, the House Special Government Activities Subcommittee, under Representative Jack Brooks of Texas, began an inquiry into the operation and expansion of the Nicaro plant, admittedly called in order to investigate the charges of impropriety raised by Solow. It is difficult to explain, however, why such an inquiry had not been initiated earlier. In at least two of Solow's many articles on Nicaro, one in April, 1952, and another in June, 1953, he had charged that there had been many instances of flagrant political influence and mismanagement at Nicaro.[17] Moreover, he had specifically charged that "the Larson crowd evades, stalls, falsifies, and even abuses security classification rules to suppress facts."[18]

Despite 600 pages of testimony taken by the House subcom-

[14] Solow, *Fortune,* August, 1955, p. 185.
[15] *Ibid.,* p. 182.
[16] House Special Government Activities Subcommittee of the Committee on Government Operations, *Inquiry Into Nicaro,* 1956, pp. 463–64.
[17] Herbert Solow, "The Struggle for Nicaro," *Fortune,* April, 1952, p. 97. See also Herbert Solow, "Who's Going To Clean up Nicaro?" *Fortune,* June, 1953, p. 108.
[18] *Ibid.,* p. 246.

mittee, the factors which contributed to National Lead's selection as supervisory contractor remained uncertain. One fact, however, was clear. Mansure's selection of National Lead had been made in flagrant disregard of the advice given him by his own technical staff. As early as May, 1953, W. C. Strecker, Industrial Engineer of Plant Operations for GSA, concluded that the cost of the supervision by National Lead would be "considerably in excess" of the cost of supervision by the Public Buildings Service.[19] In January, 1954, Colonel James Pinkley, chairman of GSA's Nickel-Graphite Committee, submitted a memorandum to Mansure in which he strongly recommended that the construction be negotiated directly between GSA and the construction contractor. Moreover, he thought it imperative to let the contract directly to Snare since it was the only American firm with demonstrated ability to perform major construction work in Cuba.[20] Finally, the engineering firm of Singmaster and Breyer, retained by GSA specifically to "make recommendations relative to ways and means for expediting and/or economizing on the Nicaro project," advised GSA to let the contract directly. It too recommended Snare. Based on its study, it felt that the selection of any other contractor would result in a delay of three months to a year and an additional cost of two to five million dollars.[21]

There is every reason to believe that Mansure himself initially had no plans for retaining National Lead as a supervisory contractor, but fully intended to let the construction contract directly. It also seems certain, despite some contradictory testimony by Mansure, that initially Snare was the only company seriously considered for the contract. Two factors substantiate this view. First, the memorandum in which Pinkley recommended direct negotiations with Snare had been O.K.'d and signed by the initials E.M.[22] Second, in a letter to Sherman Adams, Mansure stated that GSA was considering Snare for the construction because of its outstanding record in Cuba. Since no other construction firm was mentioned, it would seem that at the time only Snare was being considered. Moreover, there is no evidence that Mansure did not intend to let the contract directly to Snare. The last sentence in his letter to Adams was puzzling, however, and implied that GSA's plans might be subject to confirmation by Adams. "Knowing your very live interest in such matters," Mansure wrote, "I am making our tentative plans known to you before entering into any con-

[19] House Special Government Activities Subcommittee of the Committee on Government Operations, *Inquiry Into Nicaro,* 1956, pp. 159–60.
[20] *Ibid.,* pp. 162–63.
[21] *Ibid.,* pp. 54–55.
[22] *Ibid.,* pp. 162–63.

tractual commitments and shall appreciate any suggestions or comments you may care to give me."[23]

But whatever forces may have been at work, the fact remains that Mansure ultimately chose not to let the construction contract directly but instead to delegate the responsibility to National Lead. He made this decision despite the fact that he had been advised that it was "without known precedent in Government operations."[24] Mansure's principal defense seemed to be that he felt that the operator should let the construction contracts in order to assure coordination between plant operation and plant expansion. It will be recalled that National Lead controlled Nickel Processing Corporation, the operator of the Nicaro refinery.[25] The investigating subcommittee, however, was not particularly impressed by Mansure's rationale. Its report stressed that since the operator's fee was based on production, the natural inclination of the company would be to resist any interference with plant operation, even if such interference were in the best interest of the United States. Finally, the subcommittee thought the $530,000 allocated to National Lead—a half million for reimbursable expenses and the remainder as a fee—particularly generous.[26] Testimony revealed, for instance, that National Lead had once offered its services for a fee of ten dollars, but this had been rejected by GSA in favor of the more "equitable" fee of $30,000.[27]

This cost to the government is placed in an even more dubious light when one considers the nature of National Lead's recommendations for the expansion. In a letter to Mansure dated June 30, 1954, H. C. Wilder, vice president of National Lead and president of Nickel Processing Corporation, recommended selection of the Merritt, Chapman and Scott Corporation as sole contractor of the Nicaro expansion. National Lead had arrived at this recommendation, he said, only after careful investigation of the twenty-two companies which had indicated an interest in the contract. Wilder did suggest, however, that Merritt retain, "to the extent practicable," the Frederick Snare Corporation because of its previous experience at Nicaro. But since the letter explicitly recommended "sole responsibility" for Merritt, it can fairly well be deduced that Merritt alone was to determine to what extent, if any, Snare should participate in the expansion. The stated reason for the rejection of Snare as contractor was that the company was "not

[23] Ibid., pp. 179–80.
[24] Ibid., p. 160.
[25] Ibid., pp. 127–28.
[26] House Committee on Government Operations, Inquiry Into Nicaro, Report No. 2390, 1956, p. 9.
[27] House Special Government Activities Subcommittee of the Committee on Government Operations, Inquiry Into Nicaro, 1956, pp. 99, 214.

as adequately staffed at the supervisory, purchasing, and expediting level as Merritt, Chapman and Scott."[28] It should be said in Mansure's behalf that he flatly rejected this recommendation by National Lead.

At the time, Merritt, Chapman and Scott was not even authorized to do construction work in Cuba. Moreover, it did not receive this authorization from the Cuban government until four and one-half months after the expansion had begun.[29] Two vice presidents from National Lead testified that at the time of the recommendation they thought Merritt to be legally qualified to perform in Cuba.[30] At the very least, the ignorance of these executives was a dismal commentary on the thoroughness of National Lead's scrutiny of prospective contractors. Randall Cremer, executive vice president of Snare and later project manager of the Nicaro expansion for Snare-Merritt, testified that he told Mansure that Merritt did not have a Cuban permit and could not get one for several months. He reported that Mansure had not been particularly upset by the news; Mansure simply said that Snare could begin construction without Merritt.[31] The House committee report concluded that both National Lead and Mansure had "glossed over" Merritt's inability to perform work in Cuba and stated that their "indifference was appalling."[32]

Factors motivating the specific provisions of the Snare-Merritt partnership proved to be as confusing as those governing National Lead's selection as supervisory contractor. Cremer testified that in July, 1954, Vice President Wilder of National Lead proposed a joint venture between Merritt and Snare, but insisted that Merritt head the operation. Cremer said that he had been "shocked" by the proposition since it had been his understanding that Snare was then being considered as the primary contractor in a Snare-Merritt partnership. In conversation with Cremer later, Mansure confirmed this understanding and reiterated his view that Snare's unique qualifications for the Cuban venture entitled it to take the lead in the Nicaro operation.[33]

But in a few days, four vice presidents from Merritt informed Cremer that their company had already been awarded the Nicaro contract, but that they would be willing to sublet twenty percent to Snare. Upon inquiry by Cremer, Mansure denied that Merritt had been given the contract and, in addition, told Cremer that through this misrepresentation the Merritt officials had "disqualified them-

[28] *Ibid.*, pp. 165–66.
[29] *Ibid.*, p. 18.
[30] *Ibid.*, p. 101.
[31] *Ibid.*, p. 18.
[32] House Committee on Government Operations, *Inquiry Into Nicaro*, Report No. 2390, 1956, p. 9.
[33] House Special Government Activities Subcommittee of the Committee on Government Operations, *Inquiry Into Nicaro*, 1956, pp. 13–15.

selves." Mansure then suggested that he attempt to work out a partnership with the Raymond Pile Company. Yet, within a matter of days Mansure again reversed himself and told Cremer and the Merritt officials to work out an agreement. "I am sure you can, if you go at it in the right spirit," he said. "If you can't get together, we will just have to say goodbye and call in two other contractors."[34] As the committee report stated, "This indecision would seem to suggest that influential forces were finding expression."[35]

Throughout the hearings members of the subcommittee repeatedly expressed concern as to precisely what Merritt was doing to earn its half million dollar fee. The testimony suggested that the company was doing virtually nothing to earn the money. In the early stages of the construction, of course, Merritt was not even authorized to work in Cuba. Curiously, however, the company's role at the construction site did not increase appreciably once the permit was granted. Indeed, as late as January, 1956, one full year after the permit was granted, Merritt had yet to furnish any supervisory officials, e.g., foremen, superintendents, engineers, and technicians. Merritt's only contribution had been a single administrative official who had been assigned to supervise a small staff in the Havana office. His yearly income amounted to $12,000. On the other hand, the annual income of the 2,500 Snare employees, a figure that included several hundred Cuban laborers, amounted to roughly four million dollars. Furthermore, Cremer estimated that at least seventy-five percent of the purchasing had been done by Snare's chief purchasing agent.[36] This is a rather impressive record for a company which National Lead had said was "not as adequately staffed at the supervisory, purchasing, and expediting level as Merritt, Chapman and Scott."

Since Snare was performing most of the work at Nicaro, the question arose as to whether Snare would have accepted sole responsibility for the expansion for a half million dollar fee. Cremer stated that he personally thought this figure, which would have amounted to only one and one-fourth percent of the total value of the project, would be "a very low fee."[37] Yet, he admitted that his company "would have been willing to discuss it." He later went so far as to concede that, if the General Services Administration had been "hardboiled" about it, Snare would have accepted the fee, largely because the company felt it had a "moral obligation" at Nicaro.[38] The subcommittee uncovered one of Cremer's

[34] *Ibid.,* pp. 15–19.
[35] House Committee on Government Operations, *Inquiry Into Nicaro,* Report No. 2390, 1956, p. 12.
[36] House Special Government Activities Subcommittee of the Committee on Government Operations, *Inquiry Into Nicaro,* 1956, pp. 19–30.
[37] *Ibid.,* p. 28.
[38] *Ibid.,* pp. 32–34.

confidential memos, relating to one of his conversations with Pinkley and other GSA officials about a possible Snare-Raymond partnership for Nicaro, that supported such a view. Cremer told the officials that the Raymond people could not add anything to such a venture but suggested that if there were no other alternative they "could keep away and simply draw their fee—that would be better for the job."[39]

Under the terms of its construction contract with GSA, Snare had awarded the necessary insurance coverage at Nicaro on the basis of competitive bidding. However, the construction company was empowered to appoint a broker of its own choice. Cremer testified that common practice dictated that he select a broker "of high standing in the community and one who would be of service to the assured."[40] Yet, he chose to award two-thirds of the extremely lucrative brokerage contract to the tiny, inexperienced firm of Balmer and Moore. As late as February, 1956, Cremer could say that as far as he knew Balmer and Moore had performed "none" of the services normally expected of a broker.[41] But, in the last analysis, Cremer's choice may have been sound, for he had chosen Balmer and Moore, he said, solely because Mansure had told him to do so.[42] Obviously, Cremer decided that it would be much better to tolerate an inept broker than to alienate a man who held such influence over government contracts.

Very likely, had Cuban law not stipulated that a Cuban broker be retained, the firm of Balmer and Moore would have been awarded the whole brokerage contract. In order to overcome this legal obstacle, an arrangement was worked out whereby the Cuban firm of Porfirio Franca, Jr., would be associated with Balmer and Moore and share in the brokerage commission. Balmer reluctantly consented to give the Cuban firm one-third of the commission.[43] This reluctance is somewhat difficult to understand when one considers that, from the very outset, it was apparent that the Cuban firm was to do the work. Cremer said that the fee split had been based solely on "expediency," having nothing to do with the actual responsibility to be assumed by the two brokerage firms.[44]

Following Cremer's testimony, Mansure held a special news conference in which he denied categorically that he had ever requested Cremer to place the brokerage contract with "any specific firm." He told newsmen that at that stage of the negotiations he did not even know that Balmer intended to seek the contract. He had given Balmer's name to Cremer, he said, only because he

[39] *Ibid.*, p. 555.
[40] *Ibid.*, p. 41.
[41] *Ibid.*, p. 459.
[42] *Ibid.*, p. 43.
[43] *Ibid.*, pp. 41–43.
[44] *Ibid.*, p. 456.

thought Balmer would be familiar with midwestern brokerage firms which were "friendly to the [Republican] party." He wanted to place the brokerage contract with such a firm because he was "sick and tired" of all the brokerage business going to Democratic firms in the East, particularly in New York. He freely admitted that the fee was "a part of patronage," but said he could not see any reason why any firm which had supported the opposition should be rewarded with such a lush contract. Apparently with some pride, he pointed out that he "came from Chicago where all insurance is written on a political payoff basis. It's like fighting fire with fire," he said.[45]

The testimony established a strong inference that Mansure had been under heavy political pressure from the moment he accepted the government post. It seems that early in the Eisenhower Administration, members of Congress, as well as members of the Republican National Committee, had complained to the President that department and bureau heads were not displaying sufficient vigor in replacing Democratic with Republican personnel. Moreover, they said, in some instances when changes were made, department heads had not always consulted with members of Congress and the National Committee. Following these charges, many administrators were called into the White House and confronted with the political "facts of life" by leading Republican congressmen. President Eisenhower reportedly backed the congressmen and gave department heads explicit orders to "play the game accordingly."[46]

Pressure on the General Services Administration, long considered to be a "political" agency, seems to have been especially fierce. Mansure said that for thirty-four months he had been heckled steadily by congressmen and members of the National Committee to place loyal Republicans in his agency.[47] He told Eleanor Nadler, research associate for *Fortune,* that "half of the Cabinet made recommendations for the [Nicaro] job. Summerfield recommended somebody, Weeks somebody. Lots of people were pulling for somebody. Talbott mentioned Snare first then later recommended Merritt."[48] The name most frequently mentioned with regard to the Nicaro controversy, however, was that of the Republican National Chairman, Leonard Hall. Early in the Nicaro negotiations Mansure submitted a list of five or six construction firms to Hall for his approval. Although Mansure initially testified that

[45] C. P. Trussell, "Political Links in Nickel Hinted," *New York Times,* January 14, 1956. See also C. P. Trussell, "Politics Denied in Nickel Project," *New York Times,* January 17, 1956.
[46] House Special Government Activities Subcommittee of the Committee on Government Operations, *Inquiry Into Nicaro,* 1956, p. 551.
[47] *Ibid.,* pp. 600–601.
[48] *Ibid.,* p. 66.

this approval was not on "a political basis generally," it is difficult to imagine what other purpose would have interested Chairman Hall. Certainly Hall did not have the requisite training for assessing the companies' relative technical competencies.[49]

Subsequent testimony gathered by the subcommittee forced Mansure to concede that Hall had opposed giving the contract to anyone who, in his words, "had been at the Democratic trough for twenty years." There seems little doubt that most of Snare's difficulties had been caused by its reputation as a "New Deal" company, perhaps because it had been awarded government contracts under Democratic administrations. There was evidence, however, that the company had never been asked about its politics under the Roosevelt and Truman Administrations.[50] A. W. Buttenheim, chairman of the board at Snare, made this point quite clear in a letter to Mansure when he said that "these are the first negotiations we have ever entered into with our government in which we have been led to believe that it was necessary to qualify politically in order to get an award to which we would otherwise be entitled."[51]

A confidential memo obtained by the subcommittee pertaining to a meeting between Cremer and Hall indicated that the discussion between the two revolved almost exclusively around political matters. First, the chairman was assured that Snare was a good Republican firm. There were no Democrats whatsoever in the top positions at Snare, Cremer told him, and he believed there were few, if any, in the lower echelons. Hall reportedly stressed to Cremer the importance of electing a Republican Congress and inquired as to whether Snare would be willing to place bonds, insurance, etc., "where it would do the most good." Cremer told him that he would be willing to do "anything within reason." When asked whether the Snare company qualified, Hall supposedly responded "you certainly have."[52] Yet, Hall told newsmen that "I can't help what anyone writes in his personal diary. I never cleared any contractor, big or small, for work with the government. Any suggestion that I did is pure bunk."[53] It seems clear that someone was not telling the truth.

It was never proved conclusively that Hall, or any Republican for that matter, solicited financial or political aid from the companies seeking the Nicaro contract. But the behavior of the top Snare executives indicated fairly conclusively that they felt their chances for the contract would be enhanced if they contributed

[49] *Ibid.*, p. 131.
[50] *Ibid.*, p. 585.
[51] *Ibid.*, p. 563.
[52] *Ibid.*, p. 540.
[53] *New York Times*, September 15, 1956.

generously to the Republican campaign fund. The records of the Clerk of the House revealed that in the congressional elections of 1954 the top seven Snare officials suddenly decided to contribute $7,500 to the Republican coffer, or about 1,000 percent more than they had averaged in party contributions over the preceding fourteen years. It is difficult to believe that this spectacular increase in campaign contributions, coming at the very time of the Nicaro negotiations, was purely coincidental.[54]

Chairman Brooks of the House subcommittee felt that in all fairness to Chairman Hall, he should be given the opportunity to appear before the subcommittee to reply, under oath, to the testimony which suggested that contractors had to have Hall's political clearance in order to qualify for government contracts. Hall, however, rejected Brooks's invitation to appear, saying that he was then "completely devoted to urgent matters." He would, he said, be most happy to appear before the subcommittee immediately after the election. There could be no doubt that the chairman was busy, for the invitation came just a few weeks before the 1956 Presidential election. Yet, it is difficult to understand why he could not have spared an hour or two if, as he asserted, he could refute the rather serious charges made against him. In refusing to appear before the subcommittee, he had chosen to bear at least the suspicion of guilt which he never found occasion to dispel.[55]

Some attributed Hall's reluctance to appear before the subcommittee as simply an effort by him to avoid any situation which might prove embarrassing to the Eisenhower Administration. Actually Hall had a good deal more to fear than public embarrassment. If Cremer had not committed perjury, there was a very good chance that Hall had violated federal law in at least one, and possibly two, instances, an unusually embarrassing position for a national party chairman at election time. Section 600 of the United States Criminal Code, for example, prohibits an official from promising contracts, directly or indirectly, to anyone in return for his political support in an election.[56] And Section 601 prohibits an official from soliciting campaign contributions from a person or firm negotiating with the government for contracts.[57] Maximum penalty for conviction is five years in jail, a $5,000 fine, or both. Yet, despite the fact that Hall may have violated the Criminal Code, he was never to be subjected to any official questioning by the subcommitte nor, so far as is known, ever questioned or repri-

---

[54] House Special Government Activities Subcommittee of the Committee on Government Operations, *Inquiry Into Nicaro*, 1956, pp. 565–67.

[55] *Ibid.*, pp. 571, 574.

[56] 18 *U.S.C.* 600.

[57] 18 *U.S.C.* 601.

manded by Eisenhower.[58] In fact, there appeared to be a reluctance
on the part of even the Democratic members of the subcommittee
to ask any searching questions. Rumors persisted that the Democrats had played a similar game while in power and, consequently,
were fearful of digging too deeply.[59]

Democratic National Chairman Paul Butler argued, however,
that Hall should have been directed to appear before the subcommittee by President Eisenhower. Butler recalled that in the 1952
campaign candidate Eisenhower had styled himself as a moral
crusader and had promised the American people that his Administration would not even wait for "congressional prodding and investigations to kick out the crooks and their cronies."[60] The fact
that Butler's remarks were unquestionably motivated by partisan
considerations detracted little from their substance. Why the
President did not direct Hall to testify, if for no other reason than
to prove him as "clean as a hound's tooth," is a question remaining
unanswered. Perhaps the kindest thing to be said of the Presidential inaction is that at that time he did not seem to be particularly
well informed on the matter. In a September, 1956, press conference, Warren Unna of the *Washington Post* asked the President
what he thought of Hall's role in the controversy. "Well, I am
unable to answer the question, sir," he said, "because I am not familiar with the case or the instance to which you refer."[61] This
prompted Henry Reuss and Porter Hardy, Jr., both Democratic
members of the subcommittee, to insist that a transcript of the
proceedings be sent directly to the President, since they felt he
had not been kept informed by Attorney General Brownell.[62]

But if the Justice Department had not been of much service to
the President, there was precious little evidence to suggest that it
had lent any greater help to the investigating subcommittee. Early
in the investigation GSA officials had microfilmed some of the
confidential memos which Cremer had compiled on the Nicaro
negotiations. The Director of Security and Compliance at GSA
thought they contained information which, if corroborated, might
lead to criminal proceedings. Consequently, he forwarded the
microfilm to the Justice Department for its scrutiny. This action
very nearly proved fatal to the investigation. The original memos,

[58] Indeed, in accepting Hall's resignation "with regret" some four months
later, President Eisenhower said, "Leonard Hall has been a great Chairman. . . .
I sincerely hope that his wisdom and his long years of experience as a legislator,
judge, and Chairman, will continue to be available not only to the party but
to the nation in the years ahead." W. H. Lawrence, "Hall Quits as G.O.P.
Chairman," *New York Times*, January 12, 1957.
[59] *New York Times*, September 18, 1956.
[60] *Ibid.*, October 22, 1956.
[61] *Ibid.*, September 18, 1956.
[62] House Special Government Activities Subcommittee of the Committee on
Government Operations, *Inquiry Into Nicaro*, 1956, pp. 617–18.

for some unexplained reason, had mysteriously disappeared, and the GSA officials refused to testify as to the contents of the microfilm, claiming that it had become the sole property of the Justice Department.[63] The Justice Department bottled up the congressional investigation for nine months by refusing to release the microfilm to the subcommittee. In October, 1956, copies of the memos "turned up" in the hands of the Senate Government Operation Committee.[64] None of the newspapers seemed to know exactly what had transpired, and subcommittee Chairman Brooks would say only that it had been "without any cooperation from the Justice Department."[65]

It was interesting to note that in the final session of the congressional hearings it was Hall, rather than Mansure, who had assumed the leading role. But Mansure had not been completely forgotten. Rumors were circulating that he would be forced to resign after the Presidential election,[66] despite assurances of the President that, as far as he knew, "nothing actionable" against Mansure had been turned up.[67] Those who had followed the Talbott, Strobel, and Cross cases recognized these telltale signs and guessed that they could add up to but one thing, the "Hound's Tooth Club" was about to enroll a new member. Early in February, 1956, Mansure tendered his resignation, citing "personal obligations" as the motivating factor. In the President's letter of acceptance he told Mansure that he respected the reasons given for his resignation and hoped that he would be successful in future undertakings. It was interesting to note that neither Mansure's letter of resignation nor the President's letter of acceptance mentioned the Nicaro investigation.[68] Apparently, not even a most atrocious instance of public corruption could elicit a word of reprimand from the self-asserted paragon of public morality.

[63] *Ibid.*, pp. 507–18.
[64] C. P. Trussell, "Contract Linked to G.O.P. Loyalty," *New York Times*, October 19, 1956.
[65] House Special Government Activities Subcommittee of the Committee on Government Operations, *Inquiry Into Nicaro*, 1956, p. 525.
[66] "Ed and Mr. Mansure," *Time*, February 20, 1956, p. 16. "The Little Mansures," *Fortune*, April, 1956, p. 108.
[67] *New York Times*, February 12, 1956.
[68] C. P. Trussell, "Mansure Quits U.S. Post; Under Fire on Nickel Deal," *New York Times*, February 7, 1956.

Chapter 10

AN INSATIABLE HUNGER

I believe that corruption in government is not something to be shrugged off. I further believe that when corruption is discovered the faster and more firmly it is rooted out, the less likely it is to appear again.

DWIGHT EISENHOWER

HAD THE EISENHOWER ADMINISTRATION been as concerned about morality in government as it had so often asserted, surely seven scandals in four years would have been sufficient to produce a thorough house cleaning. For make no mistake about it, the Nixon, Roberts, Talbott, Wenzell, Strobel, Cross, and Mansure cases were clearly symptomatic of an ethically perverted administration. Eisenhower, as a candidate for the Presidency in 1952, had himself correctly observed that corruption "does not come by any process of spontaneous combustion; neither does it, like Topsy, just grow."[1] Still, no house cleaning ever came. Alas, hardly had the echoes of the Mansure case quieted when the now all too familiar round began again, this time involving the Assistant Secretary of Defense for Legislative and Public Affairs, Robert Tripp Ross.

Despite serving less than two years as assistant secretary, Ross managed to involve himself in no less than three public controversies. Shortly after Ross had assumed his duties in March, 1955, Secretary of Defense Charles Wilson had issued a departmental directive that only information which "would constitute a constructive contribution to the primary mission of the Department of Defense" was to be released.[2] *The New York Times* remarked that "a more knowing man" than Ross would have attempted to guide the obstreperous Wilson away from a statement so fraught with political danger, in spite of the fact that the secretary's memo

---

[1] *New York Times,* September 3, 1952.

[2] U.S., Congress, House, Committee on Government Operations, *Availability of Information From Federal Departments and Agencies,* House Report No. 2947, 84th Cong., 2d Sess., 1956, p. 34.

was, purportedly, intended only to prevent the many interservice controversies from gaining notoriety.[3] Ross, however, interpreted it in such a manner as to deny newsmen and congressmen all information which reflected unfavorably upon the Defense Department. In many instances this information appeared to have little, if anything, to do with national security.

An interim report of the House Government Operations Committee charged that the Defense Department's information policy was "the most restrictive—and at the same time the most confused—of any major branch of the federal government."[4] Ross, moreover, was singled out for special criticism. The report asserted that he had initially testified that his office was the sole agency responsible for the release of defense information. Later, however, he was forced to concede that the Army, Navy, and Air Force departments commonly withheld information from his agency. Thus, his office apparently exercised little more than rubber stamp authority over information the services decided to release. "Mr Ross's claims of authority," the report said, "his later denial of such authority, and his even later reassertions left the committee as confused about the functions of his office as Mr. Ross himself apparently is."[5] Ultimately, Special Subcommittee Chairman John Moss of California cancelled the final scheduled hearing due to what he termed Ross's "refusal to give the subcommittee cooperation."[6]

Before the repercussions from the investigation of the Department's information policies had died down, Ross became involved in a second controversy, again with members of Congress. Some Washington correspondents had discovered that a group of United States Senators had requested a government plane to fly them home from an European junket. When confronted by the reporters, Ross confirmed that three United States Senators had indeed requested that two Air Force planes be made available for their return trip from Europe. Discretion, it seems, is still the better part of valor for the bureaucrat dealing with influential members of Congress. No sooner had the Senators "hotly denied" the report than Ross extended his apologies, saying that the facts of the case had obviously been misrepresented.[7]

In less than three months, however, Ross again was the subject of congressional inquiry. *The New York Times* reported that

[3] *New York Times,* February 15, 1957.
[4] House Committee on Government Operations, *Availability of Information From Federal Departments and Agencies,* Report No. 2947, 1956, p. 88.
[5] *Ibid.*
[6] Katherine Johnsen, "Information Shroud Irks House Unit," *Aviation Week,* November 19, 1956, p. 30. See also Katherine Johnsen, "Moss Probe Would Abolish OSI, Says Ross Confused in His Job," *Aviation Week,* July 30, 1956, p. 30.
[7] *New York Times,* February 15, 1957. See also "Exit Under Fire," *Newsweek,* February 25, 1957, p. 38.

Senator McClellan's Senate Permanent Subcommittee on Investigations, Representative Holifield's House Government Operations Investigating Subcommittee, and Representative Hébert's House Armed Services Committee were conducting preliminary investigations of an $834,150 Army trouser contract awarded to Wynn Enterprises, a company headed by Claire Wynn Ross, wife of the assistant secretary. The initial bid had been submitted by Ross's brother-in-law, H. D. "Breezy" Wynn, at the time president of the company. Before the letting of the contract, however, his sister Claire had succeeded to the presidency. Ross told reporters that he was not embarrassed by his wife's connection with the company and pointed out that he was not connected with it in any manner—he owned no stock, drew no salary, and held no executive post with the firm. Moreover, he said, he made it a practice never to discuss business affairs with his wife.[8]

He admitted that he had not discussed his wife's connection with Wynn Enterprises with Secretary Wilson at the time of his appointment but insisted that he saw no reason to do so inasmuch as he had severed all connection with the firm in 1952 following his successful campaign for New York's Fifth Congressional District seat.[9] Certainly Wilson himself saw nothing improper in awarding a defense contract to Mrs. Ross if she had been, as she insisted, "the lowest responsible bidder." "There is no reason for criticism whatsoever," Wilson said. "I think it's bad enough to make a man sell everything he owns, but if he has to divorce his wife too, that's going pretty far."[10]

Commonweal, in a tongue in cheek editorial, pointed out to Secretary Wilson that there were alternatives other than divorce, a fact hardly in need of documentation. But in a more serious vein, the article opined that Wilson had simply failed to see that there was a very real ethical problem involved. For whereas a private businessman might, in good conscience, solicit business for a firm controlled by his spouse, such is not necessarily the case for a person holding a governmental position. Moreover, it has long been assumed that special safeguards might properly be erected in order to assure that public officials derive no personal benefit from such transactions. Wilson, it seems, was guilty of applying the so-called business ethic to a question involving the public sector, a dubious practice at best.[11]

Within weeks, the controversy received a new impetus when Jacob S. Potofsky, president of the 400,000 member Amalgamated

[8] Jack Raymond, "Ross' Wife Linked to Army Contract," *New York Times,* January 5, 1957.

[9] *New York Times,* January 6, 1957.

[10] *Ibid.,* January 10, 1957.

[11] "A Conflict of Interest," *Commonweal,* January 25, 1957, p. 422.

Clothing Workers Union, charged that the Southern Athletic Company, controlled by Ross's brother-in-law "Breezy" Wynn, had received $4,676,998 in government contracts in the preceding two years despite repeated violations of federal labor law. Specifically, he pointed out that the company's continuing violations of the minimum wage, overtime, sanitation, and record-keeping provisions of the Walsh-Healey Public Contracts Act had caused it to be blacklisted for government contracts by the Secretary of Labor, Lewis B. Schwellenbach, from December, 1946, until February, 1948. Moreover, he charged that the company had long obstructed the right of its workers to organize and had discriminated against union employees in direct violation of the Taft-Hartley Act. None of the Wynn companies were unionized at the time Potofsky made his charges.[12]

Potofsky told Secretary of Labor James P. Mitchell at his union's Miami meeting that he opposed the government's policy of awarding contracts to what he termed "unscrupulous employers intent on chiseling."[13] He also called on the McClellan subcommittee to determine why the government continued to let clothing contracts to "repeated violators of the law." Nonunion plants, he said, had an unfair advantage over "decent, enlightened manufacturers who attempted to meet reasonable costs and maintain a decent level of production and quality."[14] Both the McClellan and Holifield subcommittees announced that they were aware of the charges, and one spokesman for the Senate subcommittee told reporters that these revelations would play a "prominent" role in the investigation.[15]

On February 13, 1957, McClellan's subcommittee called Ross to testify before it in executive session. By that time, however, Ross had already taken an "indefinite leave of absence" from his Pentagon post, pending the final outcome of the inquiry. Inasmuch as executive sessions are closed to the public, it would be difficult to say what, if any, incriminating evidence was revealed. McClellan, who, coincidentally, was one of the three junketing Senators previously serviced by Ross, would say only that Ross had "answered all questions" and "had claimed no privileges." Yet, Ross appeared to be visibly shaken from his more than two hours before the subcommittee. One reporter commented that he had emerged from the executive session looking "grim and tense."[16] Moreover, rumors persisted that Ross had admitted that he had once telephoned a

[12] A.H. Raskin, "Potofsky Contends a Relative of Ross Broke Labor Laws," *New York Times*, January 23, 1957.
[13] *New York Times*, January 25, 1957.
[14] *Ibid.*, January 23, 1957.
[15] *Ibid.*, January 24, 1957.
[16] *Ibid.*, February 14, 1957.

Marine Corps general in order to arrange an appointment for "Breezy" Wynn, who wanted to discuss a Marine clothing contract. It was also reported that some members of the subcommittee, both Democrat and Republican, had advised Ross to resign.[17]

Less than twenty-four hours after his confrontation with the Senate subcommittee, Ross did, in fact, submit his resignation in a lengthy letter to President Eisenhower, who at that time was in Thomasville, Georgia, enjoying a golfing and quail hunting vacation with John Hay Whitney, ambassador to Great Britain; William E. Robinson, president of Coca Cola; and George E. Allen, Washington businessman and the Eisenhowers' Gettysburg neighbor.[18] In his letter to the President, Ross denied that he had violated what he termed "the historically recognized principles which have been applicable to government officials." It was his contention that "by practice, custom, and law" companies controlled by an official's immediate family could continue to do business with the government if the official did not exert any influence on behalf of the company, did not receive any remuneration from the company, and was not authorized by his official position to make decisions beneficial to the company. Ross contended that the Senate subcommittee had "brought nothing to [his] attention to indicate that [it] found any evidence of any wrongdoing, impropriety, or conflict of interest." His resignation, he said, had been submitted because the numerous news stories which had implied some impropriety on his part had "impaired his future effectiveness" as a public official.[19]

Despite the fact that *Time* magazine could still report that "the stern Eisenhower code forbad even the appearance of conflict of interest,"[20] there is little reason to believe that either the President or the Secretary of Defense had requested Ross's resignation. Publicly, at least, the Administration was citing a report by the Defense Department's general counsel which indicated that Ross had violated no federal law. Yet, the President did appear to accept the resignation with unusual dispatch. Within an hour and a half after he received Ross's letter, a brief and perfunctory note of acceptance was on its way to Washington. The President thanked Ross for his "contribution to the effective fulfillment of the Defense Department programs and mission," adding that he could "understand the reasons set forth for resigning." Everything considered, it had not been a particularly good day for the President, for he had failed to break ninety that morning on the golf course, had

[17] *Newsweek,* February 25, 1957, p. 38. See also *The New York Times,* March 10, 1957.

[18] *Ibid.,* February 15, 1957.

[19] The texts of Ross's letter of resignation and the President's letter of acceptance may be found in *The New York Times,* February 15, 1957.

[20] "The Administration: Pants Too Long?" *Time,* January 21, 1957, p. 14.

bagged only three quail on his afternoon hunt, and had been interrupted at dinner that evening in order to accept the Ross resignation.[21] Moreover, some columnists and cartoonists persisted in using the Ross episode as another indication of the general flabbiness of the "business ethic" guiding the Eisenhower Administration.

With Ross's resignation, McClellan and Hébert indicated that their investigations would be dropped. "Barring further developments," McClellan said, he saw no reason to pursue the question further. Hébert agreed that there was "nothing further to do." Their attitude fitted perfectly into the pattern clearly established in previous cases, i.e., that congressional committees would pursue a potential conflict of interest case with the utmost vigor only until the person in question submitted his resignation. Following the resignation, however, committee enthusiasm generally waned considerably. However, one member of the Senate subcommittee, Stuart Symington of Missouri, did dissent strongly, saying he was tired of the practice of discontinuing congressional investigations "because of resignations under fire." Representative Holifield told reporters that although his subcommittee had not officially closed its investigation, he was not in a position at that time to say definitely that it would pursue the matter further.[22]

Ross, apparently, could not have cared less. Through some strange and unreported machinations, he landed a $9,210 per year position as assistant commissioner of the Queens Borough Works less than one month after he submitted his resignation as Assistant Secretary of Defense. Most observers had assumed that he would either return to the chain drug store business, in which he had spent most of his life, or accept a position with one of the Wynn companies. The president of Queens Borough, James Lundy, announced that "the people of Queens and myself are fortunate in obtaining the services of a man possessed of such broad and invaluable experience."[23] His view of the appointment was something less than unanimous, however. Milton Bergerman, chairman of the Citizens Union, called Ross's appointment "of very doubtful wisdom, shocking, and without justification." And Acting Mayor Abe Stark argued that it was "both controversial and questionable" and stated that he "didn't think that the Republican party had the right to expect the City of New York to pull any chestnuts out of the fire."[24]

By April, 1957, the Holifield subcommittee had decided to hold public hearings on the Ross affair. It is not surprising that in the weeks preceding the hearings the conflict of interest charges against

[21] *New York Times*, February 15, 1957.
[22] John D. Morris, "McClellan Finds Ross in the Clear," *New York Times,* February 16, 1957.
[23] *New York Times*, March 12, 1957.
[24] *Ibid.,* March 13, 1957.

Ross had received the greatest public attention. Almost from the outset of the hearings, however, it became clear to the subcommittee that "Breezy" Wynn's conduct as a government contractor was of more significance to the country's military procurement program than any impropriety Ross may have committed.[25] Thus, the scope of the investigation was expanded to include all of the Wynn companies' contractual relations with the United States government. Although Wynn had long been engaged primarily in the manufacture of clothing, canvas goods, and athletic equipment, he had also been involved, at one time or another, in such diverse enterprises as gum manufacturing, trucking, real estate, a shopping center, and zinc production.

Wynn's zinc operation alone, the subcommittee discovered, cost the United States government more than $650,000, while failing to produce an ounce of zinc. In 1950, the Wynn-organized Appalachian Mining and Smelting Company received a loan of $400,000 from the Reconstruction Finance Corporation for plant development. In addition to the RFC loan, the company obtained a $3,500,000 contract from the General Services Administration in which GSA agreed to purchase up to 10,000 short tons, at a flat rate of seventeen and one-half cents per pound, all zinc not sold commercially. By the time the plant was completed, however, the Korean War had ended and the government had little need for the slab zinc. The government could have canceled the contract without liability inasmuch as the company had failed to produce on schedule. Instead GSA paid off the company's $400,000 RFC loan and paid Wynn, his family, and associates $269,000 for stock investments and company obligations.[26]

Moreover, the subcommittee's investigation of the fifty-eight government clothing contracts awarded to Wynn companies from 1951 through 1956 revealed that, with only five exceptions, the firms had been unable to meet the specified delivery schedules. It should be mentioned, however, that the government considered itself to be partly at fault in sixteen of these cases and wholly at fault in two others. Reasons given by the procurement officers included their failure to furnish material and patterns on the specified date, governmental changes in types of material to be used, and, finally, additional clarification of contractual specifications. Still, the government considered Wynn to be completely at fault no less than two-thirds of the time. Marine Corps letters incorporated into the official record were replete with charges that Wynn companies had been guilty of "serious delinquency," "extreme de-

[25] U.S., Congress, House, Committee on Government Operations, *Military Clothing Procurement*, House Report No. 1168, 85th Cong., 1st Sess., 1957, pp. 1–2.
[26] *Ibid.*, pp. 7–8.

linquency," "poor delivery," and "flagrant violation" of delivery terms.[27]

There is little doubt that these difficulties were at least partially due to what the committee report termed an "insatiable hunger" for government contracts.[28] Wynn, himself, admitted as much when he testified that "it is just like a man sitting down to eat a four-pound steak when he shouldn't eat but two. Sometimes I may have bitten off more than I could chew."[29] Yet, despite the fact that some of these deliveries were many months late, the military procurement officers never defaulted a single Wynn contract. Typically, these contracts authorized the government to cancel the contract, buy the materials elsewhere, and charge the additional costs to the defaulting company.[30] The report "severely criticized" the military authorities for continuing to reward defaulting companies with additional government contracts.[31]

But the Wynn companies were guilty of a good deal more than delinquent deliveries. Records of the Army Quartermaster also disclosed that in twenty of forty-nine clothing contracts awarded to Wynn firms, it had raised questions concerning the return of government-furnished material. These questions included such things as missing material, excess usage, and inconsistencies and inaccuracies in records. In most of these controversies the military had simply accepted the explanation offered by the Wynn firms and resolved the case in behalf of the company, generally at no cost to the contractor. Again the subcommittee accused the military of failure to exercise sufficient care in protecting government property and charged that clothing manufacturers "utilize every device and opportunity to gain some compensating profit advantage."[32]

It will be recalled that Ross, as well as his wife and brother-in-law, had repeatedly claimed that the awards to the Wynn companies had always been based on competitive bidding. "Breezy" Wynn, for example, had told the members of the subcommittee that "the Supreme Court can't help you get a contract, it [goes] to the lowest responsible bidder with capacity."[33] But the subcommittee discovered that ten of the seventy-five contracts awarded to Wynn firms between 1949 and June 30, 1957, had been negotiated. It also discovered that no less than half of the six contracts awarded specif-

[27] *Ibid.*, pp. 16–19.
[28] *Ibid.*, p. 20.
[29] U.S., Congress, House, Subcommittee of the Committee on Government Operations, *Hearings, Military Clothing Procurement*, 85th Cong., 1st Sess., 1957, p. 152.
[30] House Committee on Government Operations, *Military Clothing Procurement*, Report No. 1168, 1957, p. 26.
[31] *Ibid.*, p. 20.
[32] *Ibid.*, p. 30.
[33] House Subcommittee of the Committee on Government Operations, *Hearings, Military Clothing Procurement*, 1957, p. 134.

ically to Wynn Enterprises had been let on a negotiated rather than a competitive basis.[34] Ross insisted throughout the hearings that he knew nothing of these negotiated contracts even though his own signature appeared on two which had been awarded to Wynn Enterprises.[35] In each of these two contracts, moreover, the government had rejected four lower bidders.

Ross had also claimed on a number of occasions that Wynn Enterprises had been the "lowest responsible bidder" on the controversial Army trouser contract. But even this remark was found to be, at the very least, highly misleading. For although the Army had solicited bids from 178 concerns, only nine had responded. And of these nine bids, no less than seven were "conditional," i.e., any company submitting such a bid wished to be removed from consideration should it subsequently receive another contract. All seven companies were eventually eliminated, and the eighth bid on only 100,000 of the 249,000 pairs of trousers. Thus, in the last analysis, Wynn Enterprises was the sole bidder on the whole trouser contract. One Army witness conceded that "in the long run, we had no alternative. This man was the low bidder, and we had to go to him for supply."[36] It is particularly revealing that the accepted Wynn bid turned out to be a full thirty percent higher than the Army's cost estimate.[37]

The letting of this contract to Wynn Enterprises is even more surprising when one considers that a few weeks after Wynn Enterprises submitted its bid of $3.15 per unit on the 249,000 pairs of Army trousers, the Southern Athletic Company submitted a bid of $2.96 per unit on 234,480 pairs of the identical trousers. Had the Quartermaster Corps accepted the Southern Athletic offer on the second invitation, it would have saved the government over $40,000. For some reason, however, the Army cancelled the bids on the second invitation and awarded the contract to Wynn Enterprises. Captain James Caras, the contracting officer, testified that his reasons had been twofold. First, he had invested a good deal of time on the first invitation and thought that further delay in letting the contract would not be in the public interest. Second, he argued that the Southern Athletic Company "did not have the capacity or the facilities to perform."[38]

The report rejected both of Captain Caras' contentions, calling

[34] House Committee on Government Operations, *Military Clothing Procurement*, Report No. 1168, 1957, p. 11.

[35] House Subcommittee of the Committee on Government Operations, *Hearings, Military Clothing Procurement*, 1957, pp. 186, 346.

[36] *Ibid.*, pp. 259–60.

[37] House Committee on Government Operations, *Military Clothing Procurement*, Report No. 1168, 1957, p. 46.

[38] House Subcommittee of the Committee on Government Operations, *Hearings, Military Clothing Procurement*, 1957, pp. 223–24.

the first "specious" and the second "absurd." It was highly unlikely, it stated, that the procurement officers would have delayed awarding the contract for roughly eighty days had the need been so terribly urgent. It also found it inconceivable that Southern Athletic would have been disqualified because of a lack of capacity, when Wynn Enterprises had not been disqualified despite the fact that it had only two employees, Mrs. Ross and a typist,[39] and no manufacturing facilities at all.[40] In fact, Wynn Enterprises, as well as several other Wynn-controlled companies, were little more than "dummy corporations" created in order to expedite submission of multiple bids and qualify for contracts limited to "small business" concerns, i.e., concerns with less than 500 employees.[41] Since Wynn had always pooled the manufacturing facilities of his various companies, it was quite conceivable that the identical facilities would have been used had either Wynn Enterprises or Southern Athletic been awarded the trouser contract.[42]

Yet, Ross maintained that "political snipers" in New York had chosen to ignore the "known facts" when they continued to raise questions about his official conduct. "The implications of any impropriety on my part," he said, "had been entirely dispelled" long before he was called to testify before the House subcommittee. McClellan's decision not to pursue the case beyond the one executive session, he felt, constituted something of a *prima facie* case for his innocence, and he also claimed that "the publication of the certain facts relative to this matter" corroborated such a view. Ross also cited a letter from Acting Secretary of Defense Reuben Robertson, Jr., to President Eisenhower which stated, in part, that the Defense Department had uncovered no evidence to indicate that Ross had violated any federal statute, sought to influence the awarding of any defense contracts, or had received any personal profit from such contracts.[43]

Ross, of course, was free to draw any conclusion he desired as to the significance of the Senate subcommittee's decision to suspend its inquiry. There is evidence which suggests, however, that McClellan had been motivated in part by Holifield's decision to conduct full-scale public hearings.[44] It is a matter of record that the McClellan subcommittee cooperated with the House investigators by making all of its "pertinent records" available to them.[45]

[39] House Committee on Government Operations, *Military Clothing Procurement*, Report No. 1168, 1957, p. 15.
[40] *Ibid.*, pp. 47–48.
[41] *Ibid.*, pp. 34, 39.
[42] *Ibid.*, p. 47.
[43] House Subcommittee of the Committee on Government Operations, *Hearings, Military Clothing Procurement*, 1957, pp. 178–79.
[44] Morris, *New York Times*, February 16, 1957.
[45] House Committee on Government Operations, *Military Clothing Procurement*, Report No. 1168, 1957, p. 2.

Ross's reference to the published facts of the case is quite another thing, however, for the Senate subcommittee never published any formal report whatsoever.[46] The only record available appeared to be a series of remarks by McClellan to reporters following the Ross resignation. "Insofar as I know [Ross] is correct in saying he has done nothing illegal," he said. "Whether he did anything improper is a matter of opinion."[47] It is also interesting to note that in his letter to Eisenhower, Secretary Robertson had stated that "under the circumstances, however, I can only recommend that you accept Mr. Ross's resignation."[48]

Ross told the Holifield subcommittee, as he had told the President in his letter of resignation, that he had never violated the "historically recognized principles" which govern the ethical and legal conduct of public officials.[49] The subcommittee, however, was unable to accept such a view. For while it was technically true that no federal statute prohibited the awarding of government contracts to the spouse of a government employee, the subcommittee insisted that the term conflict of interest included not only the narrow interpretation of certain criminal statutes but also "considerations of public policy and self-imposed standards of conduct in public office." The facts of the Ross controversy, it insisted, were "more complicated and somewhat different than Mr. Ross would have it appear."[50]

It was quickly ascertained, for example, that Ross had not studied his "historically recognized principles" very carefully. Under questioning he conceded that he had neither checked his statement with the Defense Department's counsel nor solicited the legal advice of anyone outside the department. He rested his case, he said, on a "firm belief" gained in his seven years of legislative and executive experience in Washington, D.C.[51] Yet, he was unaware that cases similar to his, i.e., awarding of government contracts to close relatives of public officials, had already been litigated on the state level. And the state courts had repeatedly ruled that an unlawful conflict of interest might exist in spite of the absence of any specific statute prohibiting such awards.

The Michigan supreme court had ruled in Woodward v. Wakefield that a contract for the sale of real estate to a city by its mayor's wife was invalid in spite of the fact that no fraud had been

[46] *Ibid.*, p. 60.

[47] Morris, *New York Times*, February 16, 1957.

[48] House Subcommittee of the Committee on Government Operations, *Hearings, Military Clothing Procurement*, 1957, p. 178.

[49] *Ibid.*, pp. 179, 384.

[50] House Committee on Government Operations, *Military Clothing Procurement*, Report No. 1168, 1957, p. 62.

[51] House Subcommittee of the Committee on Government Operations, *Hearings, Military Clothing Procurement*, 1957, p. 188.

committed and that the price of the real estate was not excessive. The court reasoned that "the selfishness of human nature and the sentiment of the family" might conflict with the mayor's public responsibilities. It also rejected the notion that the mayor had received no profit from the transaction, an argument, it will be recalled, which was advanced quite forcibly by Ross. The husband and wife "live in the same home and their property interests are more or less a community interest," the court said.[52] But perhaps the most succinct statement concerning such cases came in the New Jersey case of Ames v. Board of Education: "Public servants shall not be interested, directly or indirectly, in any contract made with public agencies of which they are members. Public service demands an exclusive fidelity."[53]

The permissibility of granting contracts to the wives of public officials had never been litigated in the federal courts, however. But numerous decisions by the comptroller general did exist. A 1943 decision by that official, which also had not been brought to Ross's attention at the time he formulated his "historically recognized principles" letter, stated categorically that as a matter of public policy "contracts with wives of Government employees are open to criticism for possible favoritism and preferential treatment, and it has been held that such payments or contracts should not be made except for the most cogent reasons."[54] The subcommittee felt that in spite of the fact that Ross had apparently exerted little overt pressure on behalf of a Wynn company, "the fact that he occupied a high and influential post would not be lost upon military procurement officers."[55]

The subcommittee uncovered only one instance in which Ross clearly used his official position to aid a Wynn firm, or more specifically, to aid his brother-in-law, "Breezy" Wynn. Early in 1956, Ross arranged an appointment with Marine Corps General Robert O. Bare, so that Wynn might discuss the possibility of using a substitute material in fulfilling a Marine contract for baseball uniforms. It should be mentioned that the Marine procurement officer in Philadelphia had already rejected the substitute, even at a one dollar per uniform reduction. Major Thomas E. McCarthy testified that after "a whale of a lot of correspondence" between the Philadelphia depot and Wynn, the Marines became "weary of excuses; we wanted baseball uniforms for *that Spring*." After this

[52] Woodward v. Wakefield, 236 Mich. 417 (1926).
[53] Ames v. Board of Education, 97 N.J. Eq. 60 (1925). Related cases include Sturr v. Borough of Elmer, 75 N.J.L. 443 (1907). Nuckols v. Lyle, 8 Idaho 589 (1902). McElhinney v. Superior, 32 Neb. 744 (1891). Harrison v. Elizabeth, 70 N.J.L. 591 (1904).
[54] *Comp. Gen.* 944 (1943).
[55] House Committee on Government Operations, *Military Clothing Procurement*, Report No. 1168, 1957, p. 65.

failure to get what he termed "satisfaction," Wynn decided to take
the matter to a "higher authority."[56]

Wynn discounted the importance of Ross's phone call to General Bare. If he had not been on such a tight schedule, he said, he
could just as easily have called his Congressman or Senator to arrange such an interview.[57] Ross agreed. He viewed the phone call
as simply in the nature of a "courtesy appointment" similar to those
he often arranged for constituents of members of Congress.[58] But
whatever motivated the call, there is little doubt that Wynn was
not given any preferential treatment by the members of General
Bare's staff. Wynn himself testified that after twenty minutes "they
literally kicked me out of the office."[59] The substance of the discussion was that the general told Wynn that he "wouldn't use the
materials for a horse blanket."[60]

Thus, there was no reason to believe that General Bare—who
appeared to be the very epitome of the tough leatherneck—was influenced at all by Ross's telephone call. Quite to the contrary, the
testimony indicated that the general had been singularly "unimpressed" by it.[61] Yet, the fact remained that due to the importance
of Ross's position in the Pentagon, the possibility for influence
peddling in such a post was incalculable. Who could say, for example, that all of the officers involved in military procurement
would be made of such stern stuff as General Bare? In referring to
Ross's intervention, the committee report stated that "whatever
significance may be attributed to this episode, it indicated that Mr.
Ross was in a position to perform services for his brother-in-law."[62]
And this is the very point that Ross was never able, or refused, to
comprehend.

Such revelations are of even greater importance when one considers that the subcommittee had discovered that Ross's connection
with the Wynn companies had not been completely severed in
February, 1952, as he had reported. In the sworn annual report
of Southern Athletic to the Tennessee Secretary of State, Robert
Tripp Ross was listed as vice president from 1952 to 1956. In
Ross's defense, however, he appeared to be totally unaware of the
fact that he was an officer of the firm. Thus, he could hardly have
resigned from a position he did not know he held. The real villain,
if in fact there was a villain, appeared to be "Breezy" Wynn. For
the testimony indicated that Wynn probably never got around to

[56] House Subcommittee of the Committee on Government Operations, *Hearings, Military Clothing Procurement*, 1957, pp. 62–63. The emphasis is mine.
[57] *Ibid.*, p. 135.
[58] *Ibid.*, p. 189.
[59] *Ibid.*, p. 135.
[60] *Ibid.*, p. 63.
[61] *Ibid.*, p. 65.
[62] House Committee on Government Operations, *Military Clothing Procurement*, Report No. 1168, 1957, p. 66.

informing Ross that he had made him a vice president of Southern Athletic.[63] And Wynn explained that the listing of Ross's name on four successive annual reports had been simply an "auditor's error."[64]

Wynn also informed the subcommittee that Southern Athletic had owed Ross $1,500 in unpaid commissions since 1951, although he thought that Ross probably was not aware of it.[65] "Actually he has never asked for it," Wynn said, "and we are not ones to pay it unless someone asks for it. The statute of limitations has already run on it. I might not pay him."[66] Ross later confirmed Wynn's testimony, saying that he had learned of the $1,500 only a week or so prior to the public inquiry.[67] However, he told the subcommittee that even if he had known of the company's indebtedness to him, he still would have arranged Wynn's appointment with General Bare. It would not have been "improper," he insisted.[68]

Ross's guilt was not that he personally intervened on behalf of the Wynn companies. On the contrary, with the exception of this one phone call, Ross had not interested himself to any great extent in matters involving military procurement. Ross's weakness lay in his complete inability to grasp the fact that his high rank in the department, in and of itself, placed him in an extremely sensitive situation. The subcommittee's report, for example, stated that it was "incompatible with the highest standards of public conduct to maintain that position while his immediate family had business dealings with the Department."[69] The Comptroller General termed the awarding of government contracts to Wynn Enterprises "repugnant to public policy" and charged that Ross's position would "in itself tend to create a basis for favoritism in the making of the award or in the settlement of disputes on questions arising out of the contract."[70]

It is interesting to note that had Ross not first taken an "indefinite leave" and later tendered his resignation, he alone in his official position would have been responsible for forwarding to the investigating committees all of the pertinent information concerning his, and his immediate family's, activities on behalf of the Wynn companies. The committee report stated that the very fact that Ross felt compelled to take the leave, so as not to "hamper" the investigation, indicated how "untenable" his position really

[63] House Subcommittee of the Committee on Government Operations, *Hearings, Military Clothing Procurement,* 1957, pp. 136, 183–84.
[64] *Ibid.,* p. 442.
[65] *Ibid.,* p. 142.
[66] *Ibid.,* p. 160.
[67] *Ibid.,* p. 183.
[68] *Ibid.,* p. 187.
[69] House Committee on Governmental Operations, *Military Clothing Procurement,* Report No. 1168, 1957, p. 68.
[70] *Ibid.,* p. 69.

was. It charged that Ross could hardly discharge his public responsibilities if he had to take an indefinite leave every time a congressional committee inquired into the Defense Department's relations
with a Wynn company.[71] A cynic might even suggest that inasmuch
as three of Ross's assistants were wearing "Wynn-bilt" suits, secured
for them at the wholesale price of ten dollars, they too might not
be in a position to view such matters with complete objectivity.[72]

The congressional disclosures did not prove to be as detrimental to Wynn as one might expect, however. For some three
months after the conclusion of the hearings, the Department of Defense awarded Southern Athletic a $1,980,000 contract for Air Force
flight jackets. Jacob Potofsky again demanded to know why a firm
which had "achieved notoriety in connection with the conflict of
interest charges" had been awarded such a lush government contract. But Major General Webster Anderson, executive director of
the Army's Military Clothing and Textile Supply Agency in Philadelphia, reported that he "was unaware of any conditions or circumstances which would cast doubt" on the firm's ability to produce. Certainly, he saw no evidence, he said, that Wynn was guilty
of law violations "within the running of the statute of limitations."[73]
Such was the penalty for the Wynn empire, one termed by the
House subcommittee "a marginal operation magnified."[74]

The Ross case marked at least the eighth time in four years
that an official in the Eisenhower Administration had used his
public influence for private gain. All the landmarks of the now all
too familiar pattern were once more plainly visible. First, there
would be the loud protestations of high public morality. Next, the
private news media, or in some instances a congressional committee,
would charge that a public official had used his public office for
private gain. Then, following the predictable administrative denials, investigations would invariably prove the charges all too true.
The exposed official would then resign amid loud praise for his
great worth and sorrowful regret for the loss of his fine services. No
one would be charged by the Administration with wrongdoing, no
one would be dismissed, no one would be reprimanded. The peerless crusader for morality would then ride on to the next case, which,
as before, was not long in appearing.

[71] *Ibid.*, p. 66.
[72] House Subcommittee of the Committee on Government Operations, *Hearings, Military Clothing Procurement,* 1957, p. 188.
[73] *New York Times,* July 16, 1957.
[74] House Committee on Government Operations, *Military Clothing Procurement,* Report No. 1168, 1957, p. 19.

Chapter 11

MERELY AN OVERSIGHT

There I was, as recently as a month and a half ago, sitting in isolation in my academic ivory tower in New York, and lo, the call came to me to perform a great public service in Washington.

BERNARD SCHWARTZ

ON FEBRUARY 5, 1957, Sam Rayburn made one of his rare appearances on the floor of the House of Representatives to urge the establishment of a special subcommittee to investigate the independent regulatory commissions. The Speaker pointed out that all of the "big six" regulatory agencies other than the Interstate Commerce Commission had been established since he first came to the House in 1913—the Federal Trade Commission in 1914, the Federal Power Commission in 1920, the Federal Communications Commission and the Securities and Exchange Commission in 1934, and, finally, the Civil Aeronautics Board in 1938. An inquiry was needed, Rayburn said, in order to determine "whether or not the law as we intended it is being carried out or whether a great many of these laws are being repealed or revamped by those who administer them."[1]

Many Washington observers were, frankly, more than a little puzzled by the Speaker's rather vigorous endorsement of such an investigation. Few, of course, would argue that such an investigation was not needed. Rumors of both industry and White House influence over these agencies had been rampant for years.[2] "Carefully, steadily, and methodically," *The New Republic's* T.R.B. charged, "the regulatory commissions are being stacked against the consumer interest and for business." It was "here," he said, "here, that the foxes are being let in to guard the chickens."[3] Yet, Ray-

[1] U.S., *Congressional Record*, 85th Cong., 1st Sess., 103, Part 2, p. 1556.
[2] Louis L. Jaffe, "The Scandal in TV Licensing," *Harpers*, September, 1957, p. 77. See also Robert Bendiner, "The FCC—Who Will Regulate the Regulators?" *Reporter*, September 19, 1957, p. 26.
[3] T.R.B., "Washington Wire," *New Republic*, February 24, 1958, p. 2.

burn's own nephew, Robert T. Bartley, was at the time a member
of the Federal Communications Commission, toward which charges
of corruption had perhaps been strongest. Moreover, consumer-
oriented people had long complained that the Federal Power Commission had been remiss in regulating American gas producers, a
group dear to the hearts of most Texas politicians, including "Mr.
Sam."[4]

Two explanations were advanced for Rayburn's stand. First,
it was argued that the Speaker sincerely felt that repeated intervention by the White House and industry was corrupting the commissions. Inasmuch as Rayburn had personally helped draft the
legislation which created most of these agencies it may have been
especially disquieting to him to see the intentions of Congress being
so openly flouted. As one author so succinctly put it, "He had been
in on the 'borning' of all but one of the commissions; they were his
children and he wanted them to behave."[5] A second explanation,
equally plausible even if somewhat less altruistic, was that Rayburn
was motivated by purely partisan considerations. *Business Week,*
for example, thought that the Democrats could use the subcommittee to "mine campaign charges about Republican appointees
cozying up to businesses they were supposed to regulate."[6]

But regardless of what had motivated the Speaker, once he
lent his support to the proposed investigation the creation of an
investigatory subcommittee became a certainty. The House quickly
approved a quarter of a million dollars for the study, a most generous sum, and Oren Harris, Arkansas, chairman of the House
Committee on Interstate and Foreign Commerce, appointed a nine-
man subcommittee to conduct the inquiry. Harris chose Representative Morgan Moulder, a little known middle-of-the-road Democrat from Missouri, to be chairman of the new subcommittee.
Moulder had never chaired a subcommittee in his ten years in the
House; however, he had been the only member of the Missouri
delegation to support the Harris gas bill.[7] Reporters wondered
aloud whether this could have been a contributing factor in his
appointment. Still, an associate described Moulder as a man who
could be "very mulish about his convictions."[8] The next few months
would certainly prove that the chairman was, to say the very least,
"mulish."

The newly constituted subcommittee was termed officially "The
Special Subcommittee on Legislative Oversight," a name which
would be alternately described in the press as "curious," "humor-

[4] Roland W. May, "The FCC Inquiry," *Nation,* February 15, 1958, p. 138.
[5] *Ibid.*
[6] "Mack's Exit Just Starts the Story," *Business Week,* March 8, 1958, p. 29.
[7] May, *Nation,* February 15, 1958, p. 138.
[8] Jay Walz, "Schwartz Ousted After He Charges Whitewash," *New York Times,* February 11, 1958.

ous," "quaint," and "strange." It was obvious that the term "oversight" was taken from the verb "to see," rather than from the verb "to overlook," and was intended to convey the meaning "supervision or watchful care." But the dictionary also lists alternative definitions of "failure to notice or consider" and "an omission or error due to inadvertence."[9] And the political pundits were ultimately to produce a good deal of copy from this duality of meaning. From the very outset the more astute political observers recognized certain telltale signs which suggested that a majority of the subcommittee members were more interested in "overlooking" than they were "overseeing" the regulatory agencies. *The Nation,* for example, referred to the subcommittee as one "that tried hard not to succeed."[10]

Anyone slightly familiar with Representative Oren Harris' background would have had serious doubts about the proposed investigation from the outset. Harris was, at the time, cosponsor of the controversial Harris-O'Hara natural gas bill, one designed to remove federal price controls over natural gas at the wellhead, and one which was opposed vigorously by consumer-oriented people throughout the country. Moreover, it was common knowledge that Harris had obtained a quarter interest in the El Dorado, Arkansas, television station KRBB shortly after he became chairman of the House Committe on Interstate and Foreign Commerce in January, 1957. He had obtained his interest in the station for only $500 in cash and a $4,500 promissory note, which was never paid. He disposed of his interest in January, 1958, he said, "because of constant and continuous harassment in certain press circles, accompanied by accusations, implications, insinuations and innuendoes."[11]

Harris arranged for both him and the ranking Republican member of the parent committee to be *ex officio* members of the subcommittee with voting privileges, a very unusual arrangement. In effect, this meant that the conservative Dixiecrat-Republican coalition, a group which promised to be less than enthusiastic about any searching probe of the commissions, could muster eight of the eleven subcommittee votes. Harris also refused to delegate to the subcommittee the power to subpoena witnesses and/or documents, as is customarily done when an investigatory subcommittee is created. Finally, before Harris would even consider the appointment of a general counsel, he insisted on filling most of the subcommittee's staff positions.[12]

It was Representative John Moss, Democrat of California, who suggested that the subcommittee approach Dr. Bernard Schwartz,

[9] *The American College Dictionary* (New York: Random House, 1962), *s.v.* "oversight."

[10] May, *Nation,* February 15, 1958, p. 138.

[11] Anthony Lewis, "Three FCC Members Deny Wrongdoing," *New York Times,* January 25, 1958.

[12] "Oversight?" *Newsweek,* February 3, 1958, p. 22.

a scholarly young professor of Administrative Law at New York University, about the $14,700 position of chief counsel. Schwartz had earlier made quite a favorable impression on the California congressman while testifying before his Government Operations Subcommittee on freedom of information. Other subcommittee members were reported to be impressed by the fact that Schwartz had once been retained by the Second Hoover Commission. As one congressman put it, "He came from the Hoover Commission—how much safer can you get?"[13] In other words, a quiet academician would probably not attempt to conduct any "runaway" investigation, something that always struck fear in the hearts of congressmen. Later Schwartz admitted that he had been retained "as a harmless, academic type who could be trusted not to upset the congressional apple cart by an unduly vigorous investigation."[14] Still Rayburn was reported to be dubious about Schwartz's scholarly background and stressed to Chairman Moulder the need for "riding herd" on the counsel at all times.[15]

During his earlier interviews with members of the subcommittee, however, Schwartz seemed to be perfectly willing to accept their individual assurances that the investigation would not become embroiled in politics. It seems not unfair to assume that anyone who had had "Political Science I" would have realized the impossibility of avoiding politics in such an investigation, and Dr. Schwartz held degrees from New York University, Harvard, and Cambridge. The professor should have realized the political implications of the investigation, for example, when he was informed that fourteen of his seventeen-member staff had already been selected. Those chosen, moreover, included a former aide to Harris, the son of Republican subcommittee member Joseph O'Hara, and a seventy-year old blind consultant.[16] As a counsel of another committee put it, "Only a magician or a simpleton could have avoided politics in this investigation." Schwartz's wife—who was an attorney!—insisted, however, that "we were naive. We were so naive we were dumb."[17]

New York Governor Al Smith once observed that academicians who left their ivory towers for the helter-skelter of the political world were likely to fall in one of two categories. The "timid," he said, were frequently reduced to ineffectiveness by their confrontation with the "political realities." The rigidity of the "crusaders," on the other hand, generally prevented the fulfillment of their

[13] Bernard Schwartz, *The Professor and the Commissions* (New York: Alfred A. Knopf, 1959), p. 3.
[14] *Ibid.*
[15] Walz, *New York Times*, February 11, 1958.
[16] *Newsweek*, February 3, 1958, p. 22.
[17] William S. Fairfield, "Dr. Schwartz Goes to Washington," *Reporter*, March 20, 1958, pp. 24–25.

idealistic goals, for they never seemed to be able to comprehend that "politics is a matter of the second best."[18] There is little doubt that Dr. Schwartz was no timid Casper Milquetoast. It was not long, in fact, until the slight, bespectacled scholar's investigatory zeal had forced some to conclude that he was nothing short of a liberal counterpart to Senator Joseph McCarthy. *The New Republic* stated editorially, for instance, that Schwartz's conduct of the inquiry had been "unprincipled." "Dr. Schwartz did what McCarthy used to do," it said. "This is a hard thing to say, but it is the exact truth."[19]

The chief counsel's first *faux pas* came less than two months after accepting the government post. In a September speech before the Federal Bar Association, he asked the lawyers employed by the "big six" to submit leads which might prove useful to the investigation. Schwartz promised to treat all such information with confidence. His appeal was met with a stony silence, for most of those present felt that, in essence, they were being asked "to become secret informers against their bosses." About the same time Schwartz sent a similar request to all lawyers practicing before the Federal Communications Commission. And again, he promised to treat all such information with confidence. One of the lawyers contacted told a reporter that the letter was "just plain silly." They were being asked to involve themselves in "a sort of mutual throat-cutting competition."[20]

Early in October, the chief counsel drafted still another letter. This one was dispatched to all the commissioners and their top staff in the "big six." Specifically, it asked whether they, or any member of their immediate families, had ever received any "gifts, honorariums, loans, fees or other payments" from any person or company under their agency's regulation.[21] Several of the commissioners were furious and stated so publicly. And despite the fact that the questionnaire had been approved, and signed, by Chairman Moulder, most of the subcommittee members seemed to agree with the commissioners. In a closed meeting of the subcommittee on October 17, 1957, a majority voted to prohibit Schwartz and his staff from examining any of the returned questionnaires. The sending of the questionnaires was "a lousy thing to do," subcommittee member O'Hara said. "Never before has any congressional investigating group started out by assuming everyone was crooked."[22] The subcommittee had administered its first official rebuff to its chief counsel. More were to come.

[18] Lindsay Rogers, "Professor-at-Large," *Reporter,* April 16, 1959, p. 42.
[19] "Dirty Business," *New Republic,* March 3, 1958, p. 3.
[20] Fairfield, *Reporter,* March 20, 1958, p. 25.
[21] Jay Walz, "House Unit Split Over Its Counsel," *New York Times,* January 10, 1958.
[22] Fairfield, *Reporter,* March 20, 1958, p. 26.

On January 8, 1958, the subcommittee attempted to administer the *coup de grâce* to both Schwartz and the investigation. On that day Schwartz submitted a twenty-eight page secret memorandum containing the results of his nearly six months' investigation of the Federal Communications Commission. The report was replete with examples of "constant fraternization" between commissioners and individuals who appeared as litigants before their agency. The report indicated, for example, that the regulated industries generally picked up the tab for all hotel, entertainment, cafe, valet, and golf outlays by the commissioners and their wives while attending industry conventions. It related one instance in which a commissioner and his wife had been reimbursed by both the government and the television industry for delivering a convention speech. All of the commissioners' homes, moreover, had been equipped with new color television sets free of charge. An attached opinion of the comptroller general took a "strong position" against the propriety of these things.[23] Indeed, United States statutes prohibited a paid public official or employee from receiving "any salary in connection with his services as such an official or employee from any source other than the Government of the United States."[24]

Schwartz recommended a searching investigation of this industry influence over the commissioners. He wanted especially to determine whether this influence might not explain the FCC's vacillating standards in granting television licenses. The report had indicated that one of the commission's few consistencies in granting such licenses had been its fairly uniform practice of favoring the larger, more established firms over the smaller ones.[25] "Dr. Schwartz charges conduct which involves criminal charges, or at least, or at the very least, grounds for resignation," one Republican member of the subcommittee exclaimed. "I am shocked. I had no idea when I voted to set up this subcommittee and agreed to serve on it that we would go into this sort of thing."[26] Such an attitude carried the day. For over the strong objections of Moulder and Moss, a majority of the subcommittee rejected the type of probe outlined by its chief counsel and voted instead for a "general survey" of the "bix six." The "general survey" would be nothing but "general baloney," snorted one observer.[27] And it was.

Representative Moss's reasons for opposing the subcommittee's decision had been twofold. "First, I felt that the memorandum outlined a valid investigation," he said. "And second, the fact that

[23] Jay Walz, "FCC Members Accepted Gifts, House Group Told," *New York Times,* January 23, 1958.
[24] 18 *U.S.C.* 1914.
[25] Walz, *New York Times,* January 23, 1958.
[26] Fairfield, *Reporter,* March 20, 1958, p. 26.
[27] James Deakin, "Moulder Tells of Harassment," *St. Louis Post-Dispatch,* January 26, 1958.

the memorandum was already in the hands of both the subcommittee members and the staff made it almost certain that its contents would be 'leaked' to the press."[28] Anyone who had observed the Washington political scene over the previous decade could appreciate the significance of such a statement. He would have known that leaking secret documents to the press had become a way of life for many individuals in both the legislative and executive branches. On occasion these revelations had led to the discovery of real scoundrels in the public service, while at other times, the true villain seems to have been the one responsible for the leak.

It was not surprising that Drew Pearson was the first columnist to get wind of the memorandum. In his column of January 17, 1958, he revealed that the House Special Subcommittee on Legislative Oversight had voted to side-step its inquiry into the Federal Communications Commission because "the facts were too hot to handle." Pearson thought it ironical that the Republican members of the subcommittee, especially representatives Joseph O'Hara of Minnesota and John Heselton of Massachusetts, had fought so hard "to keep the public in the dark." The Republicans opposed a thorough probe of the regulatory agencies, according to Pearson, because they knew that White House calls to various commission members had become commonplace over the years. Apparently the Republican position on corruption in government had experienced something of a transformation since the days of the sugar-cured hams and deep freezers. It looked like the subcommittee's whole $250,000 would be "wasted," Pearson lamented.

Most of Pearson's first column dealt with the circumstances surrounding the awarding of the Channel Ten television license in Miami, Florida. After a prolonged debate, the FCC had awarded it to National Airlines, thus making it the first American airline in history to be granted such a license. Moreover, the FCC had overruled its own examiner, Herbert Swarfman, who had favored Miami civic leader Frank Katzentine. Pearson observed that President Eisenhower's brother-in-law, Colonel Gordon Moore, was a very close friend of National's President George "Ted" Baker and had, in fact, frequently visited with him in Miami during and shortly after the examiner's preliminary investigation of the Channel Ten applicants. Rumors persisted, moreover, that commission member Richard Mack, appointed to the FCC in 1955, had promised Thurman Whiteside, a Miami attorney "close" to National Airlines, that he would support its application in the Channel Ten struggle.

In a phone conversation with Pearson's associate, Jack Anderson, Mack admitted that he and Whiteside were close friends. In

---

[28] Fairfield, *Reporter*, March 20, 1958, p. 26.

fact, Mack's personal assistant, Earl "Buzz" Barber, had come from Whiteside's law firm. However, Mack insisted quite adamantly that "I have never committed my vote to anybody." Anderson told the commissioner that he had obtained phone company records which revealed a series of phone calls between Mack's office and Whiteside's office just prior to the Channel Ten award. These calls, moreover, had ceased rather abruptly after National was granted the license. Mack said that Whiteside was his lawyer and that the calls involved "a personal matter" and "had nothing to do with the FCC." The fact that the calls had ceased after the award of the license had been "purely a coincidence." However, it was never made clear just why these "personal" phone calls were charged to the FCC.

Mack also conceded that he had borrowed money from Whiteside over the years but "only in small amounts." He "didn't remember," he said, whether he had borrowed any money from Whiteside while the Miami television license was under review by the commission, but could say that he still owed the lawyer some money, "a couple hundred dollars," he thought. "After all," he said, "this fellow I have known since grammar school." Still, the commissioner could not see any reason why he should have abstained in the Miami case and pointed out that his vote had not been a deciding vote anyway. But he had to admit that as the commissioner with the least tenure he had been required to vote first on the case in question, and that at the time he cast his vote he had "no idea how those fellows were going to vote."[29]

A second Pearson column, this one released on January 22, also involved alleged irregularities on the Federal Communications Commission. Specifically, Pearson charged that Chairman John Doerfer had allowed both the government and the television industry to pay for one of his junkets to the West in 1954. He reported that station KWTV in Oklahoma City, Oklahoma, had reimbursed Doerfer for the first leg of his trip from Washington. Doerfer was reimbursed for the second part of his journey, from Oklahoma City to Spokane, Washington, by the National Association of Radio and Television Broadcasters. Yet, according to Pearson, the chairman had turned in travel vouchers to the government for his trip from Oklahoma City to Spokane and back to Washington, D.C., plus expense vouchers for twelve dollars per diem allowances. Edgar Bell, manager of KWTV, told Pearson over the phone that "I will tell you the same thing I told the congressional committee. This is none of your business. I consider it to be a matter between the station and Mr. Doerfer." Doerfer's secretary, when told of the

[29] Drew Pearson, "The Washington Merry-Go-Round," *Harrisburg* (Ill.) *Daily Register,* January 17, 1958.

nature of Pearson's column, made it clear that "the FCC Chairman did not wish to comment."[30]

This charge of corruption in high places was, of course, exactly the kind of thing which so excited and delighted the American press during the Truman Administration. Yet, the American news media virtually ignored the Pearson stories the week following their initial publication. Warren Unna wrote a single article for the *Washington Post* on the Schwartz memorandum but nothing followed. The wire services contributed nothing at all during these first few days. Finally, on January 23, 1958, *The New York Times* gave the memorandum the "full treatment." It devoted a column on the front page to the "secret" memo and reprinted the pertinent portions of the text on page fourteen.[31] As Miles McMillin pointed out in *The Progressive*, following the *Times* coverage "the flood gates opened. The wire services, which had kept a stony silence through the Pearson chirping, awoke to the majestic fog horn of *The New York Times*."[32]

Doerfer told the *Times* that he had received twelve dollars per diem expenses on his western trip and had, in addition, received an "honorarium" for addressing the convention. He insisted that the twelve dollars paid "only a part of the expense involved" and that the acceptance of an honorarium in such an instance was "permitted by law."[33] He referred to Section 4 (b) of the Communications Act which provided that "Commissioners shall not engage in any other business, vocation, profession, or employment; but this shall not apply to the presentation or delivery of publications or papers for which a reasonable honorarium or compensation may be accepted."[34] He also told the *Times* that the commissioners, including himself, had allowed the television industry to place color television sets in their homes. "To us," he said, "it's no luxury. It's part of our job to know how it works. We look at television shows, not for fun, but to learn what's going on."[35] One could almost envisage the chairman dutifully at work before his color television set each evening.

Following the *Times* release, the subcommittee met in a stormy five and one-half hour session in an attempt to discover who had been responsible for leaking the confidential memo to the press. In what *Time* magazine described as "one of history's silliest con-

[30] Drew Pearson, "The Washington Merry-Go-Round," *Harrisburg* (Ill.) *Daily Register*, January 22, 1958.

[31] Walz, *New York Times*, January 23, 1958.

[32] Miles McMillin, "Congress and the FCC Shenanigans," *Progressive*, April, 1958, p. 12.

[33] Walz, *New York Times*, January 23, 1958.

[34] 47 *U.S.C.* 154.

[35] Walz, *New York Times*, January 23, 1958.

gressional scenes," Schwartz managed somehow to maneuver each subcommittee member into swearing, under oath, that he had not given Pearson a copy of the secret report.[36] Schwartz himself freely admitted to the subcommittee that he had given his friend William Blair of the *Times* his copy of the memo, but insisted that he had done so only after the Pearson column of January 22 displayed verbatim extractions from it. Later the chief counsel would argue that his motive in giving Blair the memo had been "to vindicate the public's right to know the facts about these vital agencies," and would contend that this was the only way he "could counter the Congressmen's decision to bury the results of the investigation."[37]

By this time the chief counsel was being subjected to heavy criticism for his alleged "McCarthyite" tactics. Some of these defenders of procedural due process sprang surprisingly from places like the Republican "Old Guard," a group which had distinguished itself only by its silence during McCarthy's heyday. Suddenly, they became intensely aware of the potential for abuses inherent in all congressional investigations. At a Lincoln Day dinner in Elkhart, Indiana, for example, Senator Homer Capehart made a vigorous attack on the methods employed by the Subcommittee on Legislative Oversight. Chairman Moulder, the Senator said, "was trying to turn a congressional committee room into a medieval torture chamber," and Chief Counsel Schwartz "was acting [like] a paranoiac prosecutor who is setting out after his first hanging."[38] It was small wonder, he lamented, that it was so hard to get good men to come to Washington. This, of course, was the liberal lament of the early fifties. It seemed to make a good deal of difference whose ox was gored.

An editorial in the *Chicago Tribune* charged "McSchwartzism." It was not intended to attack Schwartz for his alleged acceptance of the odious doctrine that "the end justifies the means," however. Quite to the contrary, it used the Schwartz controversy to make something of a retroactive defense of the Senator from Wisconsin. The analogy was something like this. Schwartz was attempting to root out corruption in the public service. McCarthy had attempted to prevent the insidious doctrine of Communism from undermining the Republic. Both Schwartz and McCarthy, therefore, had quite commendable goals. But both were thwarted, to one degree or another, by public officials in high places. Thus, they were literally forced to revert to such tactics as "leaking" information to the press, taking license with "confidential" government documents, and "bending" committee rules of procedure. It concluded that

---

[36] "Lo, The Investigator," *Time,* February 24, 1958, p. 15.
[37] Schwartz, *The Professor and the Commissions,* p. 87.
[38] *St. Louis Post-Dispatch,* February 8, 1958.

Schwartz's behavior simply proved that McCarthy's techniques had not been, as the liberals had always contended, "unspeakably wicked."[39]

The radio and television industries, not surprisingly, presented a united front against both Schwartz and the investigation throughout the controversy. Early in the investigation, the "voice" of the communications industry, the periodical *Broadcasting-Telecasting*, attacked the investigation with sarcasm. In an editoral entitled "The Great Free Lunch Inquiry," it informed its readers, "If you have ever taken an FCC commissioner to lunch or picked up a bar check for a party of which a commissioner happened to be a member, chances are you're headed for a congressional investigation." "We cannot predict what the Moulder committee will find at the FCC," it continued, "but we doubt it will find anything approaching corruption." In fact, the editors expressed their personal view that there was less political pressure on the FCC under the Eisenhower Administration than there had been under any other administration since the commission's creation in 1934.[40]

As the inquiry progressed, however, the periodical's editorial page became noticeably more bitter. In its December 2, 1957, issue it charged that the "machinations" of the Subcommittee on Legislative Oversight had given FCC members their worst case of jitters in the nearly twenty-five year history of the commission. It was also fairly obvious that the editors of *Broadcasting-Telecasting* had developed a case of jitters since their October editorial on "The Great Free Lunch Inquiry." Now they thought "it reasonable to assume that administrative agencies have lost sight of their assigned functions and have deviated from the Congressional intent." They protested, however, to the subcommittee's mode of inquiry which they charged was "more akin to a criminal inquisition than a legislative study." They also complained that the subcommittee seemed to operate on the assumption that a commissioner's vote could be "bought" for a "free lunch or a case of Florida grapefruit."[41]

The executive branch gave Schwartz no more support than did Congress or the communications industry. Even after the chief counsel had revealed that Doerfer had accepted expense payments from both the government and industry, President Eisenhower's ethical sensibilities did not seem to be particularly upset. In one of his press conferences, for instance, he told the reporters that "one of my law group brought in the law which says [commissioners] are entitled to reasonable honorariums. Now that is the limit of my thought on that."[42] Nothing was ever said about the color

[39] "McSchwartzism," *Chicago Sunday Tribune*, February 16, 1958.
[40] "The Great Free Lunch Inquiry," *Broadcasting-Telecasting*, October 14, 1957, p. 130.
[41] "Case of Nerves," *Broadcasting-Telecasting*, December 2, 1957, p. 106.
[42] *New York Times*, February 9, 1958.

television sets. Jack Gould, television critic for *The New York Times*, suggested that this silence could be readily explained. The White House, it seemed, had also accepted a color television set.[43] Harris even admitted to Schwartz that he had cleared his appointment as chief counsel with the President's legal counsel, Gerald Morgan.[44] Since one of the main objectives of the proposed investigation was to check out the persistent rumors of undue White House influence over the regulatory commissions, Morgan should have been one of the last persons in Washington to be consulted on such an appointment.

Early in February an article in the *Tulsa Tribune* intimated that at the very time Schwartz was maligning the commissioners for doubling up on their expense accounts, he had been padding his own travel vouchers as chief counsel for the subcommittee.[45] Schwartz told reporters that the ridiculous charge had been dreamed up simply as "an excuse to get rid of" him.[46] "The powerful interests who are afraid of what we are uncovering," he said, "will stop at nothing to stop this investigation."[47] Actually all the evidence appeared to favor Schwartz. The author of the column in question, for example, was a social friend of Oren Harris, and many people, including Schwartz, thought that Harris himself had planted the story to embarrass the counsel.[48] Moreover, the vouchers, which amounted to roughly four hundred dollars, had all been approved and signed by both Harris and Moulder. And at any rate it hardly seemed likely that Schwartz had accepted the $14,700 position because of a desire for monetary gain. He had made more teaching. He probably took the position for the reason he gave, i.e., he saw an opportunity "to do a real job."[49] At the time, however, it looked very much like the subcommittee was about "to do a real job" on its chief counsel.

On February 10, 1958, following a long and bitter secret session of the subcommittee, one in which such emotionally charged epithets as "liar," "smear," and "whitewash" had been freely bandied about, Schwartz was dismissed as its counsel. The vote had been seven to four, with only New Jersey Republican Charles Walverton and the three northern Democrats, Moulder, Moss, and Mack, opposing. Three southern Democrats had joined four Republicans for dismissal. Harris told reporters that Schwartz had

---

[43] Jack Gould, "T.V.: Why All the Fuss?" *New York Times*, January 24, 1958.

[44] Schwartz, *The Professor and the Commissions*, p. 10.

[45] *Tulsa Tribune*, February 8, 1958.

[46] William Blair, "Battle in House Due if Schwartz Loses Job Today," *New York Times*, February 10, 1958.

[47] *New York Times*, February 9, 1958.

[48] Schwartz, *The Professor and the Commissions*, p. 99.

[49] Walz, *New York Times*, February 11, 1958.

long exhibited an "improper attitude." "He was vitriolic and indignant," he said, "because the committee did not agree to go ahead with his memorandum." Moulder disagreed and termed the counsel "the most courageous man I have ever known" and "a lawyer of the highest caliber."[50] The following day Moulder resigned as chairman of the subcommittee. He had been subjected to "constant harassment" in his efforts to conduct a "clean, thorough investigation," he said.[51] "My resignation speaks for itself."[52]

At 12:35 A.M. on the day following Schwartz's ouster, a deputy United States marshall presented the chief counsel with a subcommittee subpoena. It ordered Schwartz to appear before it, at 10:00 A.M. the very same day, with all of the evidence, records, and documents he had collected in his six months of investigation.[53] It was not surprising that Schwartz failed to deliver this information to the subcommittee at the designated time. Indeed, it may have been a physical impossibility. What was surprising, however, was the ex-counsel's announcement that he had turned over all of his "personal working files," which consisted of a suitcase and two cardboard boxes full of material, to Senator Wayne Morse of Oregon. He had, he said, also shown his files to Senator John Williams of Delaware, a Republican who had established something of a reputation over the years for his investigatory zeal. Harris termed these revelations by Schwartz "shocking" but told reporters that "knowing Senator Morse as I do, I assume he will voluntarily return the papers."[54] The Senator did, in fact, return the files the next day, but only after having received a phone call from Speaker Rayburn about the "stolen property" in his possession. Morse said he had kept the files in his home solely for safekeeping.[55]

As *Newsweek* magazine pointed out, "By all rules of the Washington game, young Dr. Bernard Schwartz should have packed up his law books and gone discreetly back to New York University. Instead, he was sticking to his guns and firing in all directions."[56] He had been a victim, he said, of a "Kangaroo Court" that made the "Star Chamber itself the very paragon of justice." The only crime he had committed was to pursue an "honest investigation" rather than the "bipartisan whitewash" desired by a majority of the subcommittee. "I accuse the majority of this subcommittee,"

[50] *Ibid.*
[51] James Deakin, "Moulder Tells of Harassment," *St. Louis Post-Dispatch,* January 26, 1958.
[52] Walz, *New York Times,* February 11, 1958.
[53] *Ibid.*
[54] Jay Walz, "Schwartz Gives Morse Big Part of Inquiry Files," *New York Times,* February 12, 1958.
[55] Jay Walz, "Harris Promises Thorough Inquiry On U.S. Agencies," *New York Times,* February 13, 1958.
[56] "The Accuser," *Newsweek,* February 24, 1958, p. 25.

he said, "of joining an unholy alliance between big business and the White House to obtain a whitewash." "I accuse Mr. Harris," he said, "of hypocritically posing publicly as a supporter of an investigation which he has done everything in his power to suppress."[57]

A few days before, Schwartz was reported to have told one member of his staff that "they could convict me of contempt of Congress—I have nothing but contempt for most members of this committee.[58] But it was soon to become apparent that the beleaguered professor's fortunes had already fallen as low as they were destined to go. He was not to be cited for contempt of Congress, either then or in the future. Indeed, in the next few months Schwartz would win, and unquestionably deserve, the plaudits of a good many members of the Congress he initially found so contemptuous. For the evidence which he had uncovered in his brief services as the subcommittee's chief counsel would ultimately bring about the resignations of two members of the Federal Communications Commission, including its chairman, and the assistant to the President of the United States.

[57] Walz, *New York Times,* February 12, 1958.
[58] *Ibid.,* February 11, 1958.

Chapter 12

BUGGED!

This Washington mess did not come to pass by any process of spontaneous combustion; neither did it, like Topsy, just grow. This mess is the inevitable and sure-fire result of an Administration by too many men who are too small for their jobs, too big for their breeches, and too long in power.

DWIGHT EISENHOWER

MOST WASHINGTON OBSERVERS thought that Professor Schwartz's spectacular statement to the press following his dismissal by the subcommittee would prove to be his "swan song." They were as firmly convinced, moreover, that it would signal the end of the eighth abortive investigation of the FCC.[1] But the Schwartz news release had specifically accused "the majority of the subcommittee of firing me knowing that I have secured evidence of the payment of money to a Federal Communications Commissioner in a comparative television case."[2] Such a public charge prompted Representative Oren Harris, who had by this time formally assumed the chairmanship of the subcommittee, to subpoena Schwartz as a witness. He told reporters that he wanted to know "who the Commissioner was, how much money was paid, and what for."[23] If Harris was, as many had charged, interested in conducting only a friendly inquiry, his decision to subpoena the former chief counsel was a disastrous miscalculation.

The day after he was subpoenaed Schwartz appeared before a hostile subcommittee in the New House Office Building. Though Harris had obtained use of the spacious hearings room of the House Ways and Means Committee, some 500 interested spectators

[1] Miles McMillin, "Congress and the FCC Shenanigans," *Progressive*, April, 1958, p. 12.
[2] *New York Times*, February 12, 1958.
[3] Jay Walz, "Harris Promises Thorough Inquiry on U.S. Agencies," *New York Times*, February 13, 1958.

and seventy-odd reporters filled it to overflowing.[4] According to *Newsweek* magazine, the Capital had not evinced such curiosity about the affairs of a congressional committee since the infamous Army-McCarthy hearings of 1954.[5] In a prepared statement, Harris denounced the "dirty accusations by the press" which had suggested that he wanted something less than a searching probe of the commissions, and promised the American people "the most thorough investigation" Capital Hill had ever seen. "Whoever gets caught," he said, "must suffer the consequences," and added, "I will stand or fall on the success of this investigation."[6]

When Schwartz was being sworn in the clerk inadvertently asked, "Do you solemnly swear that the *truth* you are to give will be the truth, the whole truth, and nothing but the truth so help you God?"[7] Some of the subcommittee members appeared to be visibly upset as the audience rocked with laughter at a phrase so pregnant with Freudian implications. But the chamber was quickly brought to order, and the corrected oath administered. It was the moment of truth for the former chief counsel. As one of his reporter friends told him at the time, "So far as you're concerned, this is put up or shut up."[8] And having been stripped of his authority and barred access to his files, there was every reason to believe that he would be unable to "put up." T.R.B. reported in *The New Republic* that at that crucial moment Harris "sat back smiling."[9]

But Harris' smile soon faded as Schwartz coldly and methodically reeled off testimony which suggested gross improprieties on the part of FCC Commissioner Richard Mack. Reporters noticed too that Schwartz was far more effective as a witness than he had ever been as chief counsel of the subcommittee. "The Congressmen," Schwartz would later write, "had not counted on my being able to tick off the details of the Mack case by rote, so familiar with it I had become before my discharge."[10] Schwartz's forceful presentation of his case before the subcommittee reminded T.R.B. of a heretic who "suddenly leaped off the pyre of fagots and began chasing the grand inquisitors." In all his years of reporting the Washington political scene, he said, he had never seen a committee "so taken aback" by the testimony of a witness.[11]

[4] Walz, "Schwartz Says Mack Got $2,650 in Miami T.V. Case," *New York Times,* February 14, 1958.
[5] "The Accuser," *Newsweek,* February 24, 1958, p. 26.
[6] U.S., Congress, House, Special Subcommittee on Legislative Oversight, *Hearings, Investigation of Regulatory Commissions and Agencies,* Part 2, 85th Cong., 2d Sess., 1958, pp. 417–20.
[7] *Ibid.,* p. 421. The emphasis is mine.
[8] Bernard Schwartz, *The Professor and the Commissions* (New York: Alfred A. Knopf, 1959), p. 75.
[9] T.R.B., "Washington Wire," *New Republic,* February 24, 1958, p. 2.
[10] Schwartz, *The Professor and the Commissions,* p. 110.
[11] T.R.B., *New Republic,* February 24, 1958, p. 2.

Specifically, Schwartz produced cancelled checks amounting to $2,650 which Commissioner Mack had received from Miami attorney Thurmond Whiteside. He also pointed out that Whiteside, regarded as something of a "fixer" in Florida political circles, had supported the successful applicant in the Miami television controversy. Schwartz said that Mack had admitted to his staff investigators that he received the money, but insisted that the checks represented loans from a lifelong friend. "We were like brothers," he said.[12] Still, Mack had been forced to concede that he had "no specific recollection" of ever having repaid any of the $2,650 and thought that a portion had undoubtedly been "forgiven" by Mr. Whiteside. Schwartz told the subcommittee members that he had "no way of knowing" whether the commissioner was involved in any other dubious financial transactions. Mack had refused to volunteer his financial records to staff investigators, and Harris had never issued the requested subpoena which would have forced the commissioner to do so.[13]

In a dramatic moment, Schwartz revealed that, unknown to Mack, his second interview with the subcommittee staff members had been secretly recorded on a "Miniphone" in investigator Herbert Wachtell's briefcase. It was in this second interview, moreover, that Mack made his most damaging admissions, i.e., that he received the "loans" from Whiteside, that he had not repaid any of the "loans," and that he knew that the Miami attorney was associated with one of the applicants in the Miami television case. Until that very moment, not a single member of the subcommittee had any idea that such a recording existed. Solely on his own initiative Schwartz had requested his assistant to tape the interview as a precaution against the commissioner's subsequently changing his testimony. The tape was "insurance," Schwartz said. And like his other insurance policies, it had been stored in a safe place, namely his wife's bank vault. The value of such insurance could well be judged by the fact that Mack at one point had told the investigators, "I am going to tell you this, but I certainly wouldn't tell it to the subcommittee if they asked me."[14]

Of course, the "bugging" episode touched off new charges of "McCarthyism." "If it isn't [illegal], it surely ought to be," editorialized *The New Republic.* "Jimmy Hoffa isn't being prosecuted for anything much worse. This is dirty business."[15] And Wayne Morse, to whom Schwartz's wife eventually delivered the controversial tape, denounced on the Senate floor the use of hidden recording devices

[12] House Special Subcommittee on Legislative Oversight, *Regulatory Commission Hearings,* Part 2, 1958, p. 449.
[13] *Ibid.,* pp. 457–58.
[14] *Ibid.,* pp. 461–75.
[15] "Dirty Business," *New Republic,* March 3, 1958, p. 4.

and called for legislation to prohibit their future use by government investigators.[16] It is certainly not difficult to understand why such unauthorized recordings would shock the sense of justice and fair play of many persons. However, there was actually little doubt about the legality of such activity. In a similar case in 1952, the Supreme Court had ruled that the use of mechanical or electronic devices to obtain evidence was not an unreasonable search and seizure under the Fourth Amendment as long as access to the "listening post" was not obtained by illegal methods.[17]

Finally Schwartz produced a sworn affidavit by Colonel A. Frank Katzentine, which his staff had uncovered in the files of Senator Kefauver's antitrust subcommittee. It suggested that politics rather than merit may have governed the Channel Ten award. It should be noted, however, that Katzentine was anything but an impartial observer. He was president, director, and sole stockholder of the Miami AM radio station WKAT, Inc., the Channel Ten applicant which had received the strong endorsement of FCC examiner Herbert Sharfman. Moreover, he was a personal friend of Senator Kefauver. Many people suspected that Katzentine's association with the Tennessee Senator may have been his greatest liability. To be a Democratic applicant for a television license in 1958 was bad enough, but to be a Kefauver Democrat was simply too much for the industry-oriented commissioners.[18]

According to the Katzentine memorandum, a phone call from a "trusted friend" in the late summer or early fall of 1955 gave him his first indication that the FCC would overrule its examiner and award the Channel Ten license to National Airlines. Katzentine's confident, it seems, had picked up his information from two of George Baker's "best friends" the previous evening. Since Colonel Gordon Moore was handling National's application, they said, it was "sure to win." Katzentine's quick check of the Miami newspapers revealed that Colonel and Mrs. Moore had indeed been house guests of the Bakers, and he later learned that Colonel Moore and one of the directors of National Airlines were associated in a business venture in the Dominican Republic. Finally, newspaper publisher John Knight told him that an attorney for National Airlines had stated in his presence that the Channel Ten license was "in the bag."[19]

Eventually both Katzentine and a friend, Perrine Palmer, contacted Thurmond "Whitey" Whiteside who was rumored to be connected with National Airlines and known to be a close friend

[16] U.S., *Congressional Record*, 85th Cong., 2d Sess., 104, Part 2, pp. 2067-68.
[17] On Lee v. United States, 43 U.S. 747 (1952). For a more recent case see Lopez v. United States, 373 U.S. 427 (1963).
[18] House Special Subcommittee on Legislative Oversight, *Regulatory Commission Hearings*, Part 2, 1958, pp. 699, 756.
[19] *Ibid.*, pp. 498–500.

of Commissioner Mack. According to the affidavit, Whiteside admitted that he had contacted Mack and that, as a result, he considered the commissioner to be "pledged" to vote for National Airlines in the Channel Ten case. He had been asked to talk with the commissioner by another Miami attorney, Robert Anderson, at the time a counsel for National Airlines and later a judge of the Dade County circuit court. I would give Mr. Anderson "the shirt off my back," Whiteside said. Palmer and Jerry Carter, chairman of the Florida Railroad and Public Utilities Commission, then contacted Mack in Washington to see if he could secure a release from his "pledge." The commissioner was reported to have told the two men that he "was over a barrel."[20]

Schwartz's appearance before the subcommittee opened a Pandora's box. Shortly after Schwartz completed his testimony, Attorney General William P. Rogers announced that he had sent the FBI into the case.[21] All charges would be investigated "fully," he said. Speaker Rayburn was reported to have concluded that only thorough, public hearings could recapture the House's lost prestige.[22] This was especially revealing when one considered that, in arguing for closed hearings a few days earlier, Harris had cited an often ignored House rule which provided for executive sessions to take "evidence or testimony that may tend to defame, degrade or incriminate any person."[23] The editors of *The Nation* charged that the chairman had literally "ransacked" the rule book to come up with this "lost rule."[24] But the Schwartz performance necessarily changed the whole scope of the investigation. "There can no longer be any doubt," *The New York Times* said, "that Bernard Schwartz has started something that must be carried through to an uncompromising conclusion."[25]

Testimony given by FCC examiner Herbert Sharfman, who was regarded by Washingtonians as a man of "impeccable integrity," raised even more serious doubts as to the wisdom of the FCC's decision on behalf of National Airlines.[26] Of the four applicants for the Miami television license, he said, he regarded WKAT, Inc., as clearly the "best qualified." Moreover, since National Airlines had not placed first in any of the individual rating categories, he thought that a "fair analysis" of his report would make National Airlines the "least qualified" of the four applicants. Sharfman conceded that an examiner was seldom free of doubts in such cases, but stated that "I felt more sure in [the Channel Ten]

[20] *Ibid.*, p. 499.
[21] *New York Times*, February 14, 1958.
[22] *Newsweek*, February 24, 1958, p. 26.
[23] U.S., *House Rules*, Number 11, Section 25, Paragraph m.
[24] "The Lost Rule," *Nation*, February 22, 1958, p. 149.
[25] *New York Times*, February 15, 1958.
[26] "Poet in the FCC," *New York Times*, February 19, 1958.

case than I had in other cases" and was, therefore, "surprised" when
the commission awarded the license to National Airlines.[27]

Such testimony again raised the question as to whether technical competence or political influence had been of primary importance in the license award. Certainly the subcommittee uncovered fairly conclusive evidence that both National Airlines and WKAT, Inc., had, throughout the controversy, attempted to exert political pressure on the commissioners. Of course, each insisted that the other had made the initial contact and that it had been forced to resort to such tactics purely as a "defensive" move. But ignoring the question as to which applicant played offensively and which defensively, each certainly played the influence game with vigor. In addition to contacting his friend Senator Kefauver, for example, Katzentine attempted to solicit the aid of Florida Senators Spessard Holland and George Smathers, chairman of the Senate Interstate and Foreign Commerce Committee Warren Magnuson, former mayor of Miami Perrine "Gootsie" Palmer, Democratic national committeeman from Florida Jerry Carter, and vice president of the Florida Light and Power Company Ben H. Fuqua.[28]

Harris even produced letters from Downey Rice, a Katzentine supporter, which suggested that his friend "cry wolf as high up in the circle of Eisenhower associates as possible." With luck, Rice said, they might be able to reach as high as Vice President Nixon through his administrative assistant Bob King. "Obviously the Republicans cannot afford to risk exposure by Democrats of an 'influence' deal." The threat of such a "hot potato" in their laps, he thought, would force the Republicans to "pass the word" to the FCC commissioners. Apparently Rice had, at one point, considered contacting Republican Senator Alexander Wiley of Wisconsin. In one of his letters he said, "I feel so happy and confident about the Nixon arrangement that I would recommend forgetting Wiley. Action by Nixon compared with action by Wiley would be like comparing an atomic cannon with a popgun."[29]

With some 3,000 Miami attorneys from which it might choose additional legal talent for the Channel Ten case, the law firm representing National Airlines had solicited only the services of Commissioner Mack's good friend Whiteside.[30] Moreover, testimony by two of National's top attorneys, Robert H. Anderson and Paul R. Scott, made it abundantly clear that Whiteside had been approached solely because of his close personal relationship with Mack and not because of his ability. Anderson admitted, for example, that his firm had never before had occasion to go beyond

[27] House Special Subcommittee on Legislative Oversight, *Regulatory Commission Hearings*, Part 2, 1958, pp. 557–70.
[28] *Ibid.*, pp. 682, 702, 752, 791, 817.
[29] *Ibid.*, pp. 673–75, 691, 699.
[30] *Ibid.*, p. 643.

its own staff, much less to Whiteside, in cases dating back some
fifteen years.[31] In the Channel Ten case Anderson had seen fit to
offer Whiteside a fee of $10,000, an extremely generous retainer, it
would seem, for an attorney who had had virtually no previous
experience in such cases and who was not, at the time, even authorized to practice before the Federal Communications Commission.[32]

At one point in the hearings, Representative John J. Flynt
of Georgia asked Anderson quite bluntly whether the warm friendship known to exist between Whiteside and Mack had not been
of the utmost importance in his decision to solicit Whiteside's
services. "Well, let's put it this way," Anderson said, "it was a fact
that was not completely overlooked."[33] Under further questioning, Anderson conceded that in his discussion with Whiteside he
had probably mentioned the possibility of his speaking directly to
Mack. Scott too testified that an "important consideration" in
Whiteside's selection had been his past association with Mack.[34] It
was important, he said, for National to have a lawyer in whom
Mack would have "confidence." "Whether [Mack] participated or
not," Scott said, "it seemed to me probable that his fellow commissioners would say, 'Well now, here, Mr. Mack, you live in Miami.
What about these people?' "[35]

Whiteside, however, appeared to be singularly unimpressed by
such testimony. The brusque and argumentative attorney told the
subcommittee that its former chief counsel was simply an "un-
mitigated liar."[36] "Bernard Schwartz," he said, "through his use
of half-truths, innuendoes, distortions, omissions, and deliberate
misrepresentation, has created, produced and published a scandalous lie."[37] First, Whiteside insisted that he had not been "retained"
as an attorney for National Airlines. He never considered himself
"retained" in any case, he said, unless "there was an agreement or
an expectation of receiving compensation for the services rendered."[38] Secondly, he insisted that he had not solicited a "pledge"
from Mack in the Miami television case. Mack, he said, "has never
been pledged to me for any person or corporation at any time or
for any purpose." He argued, moreover, that Schwartz's charges to
the contrary had been based at best on "secondhand hearsay"
evidence.[39] Finally, he insisted that he had not earned a reputation
as a "fixer" in Florida political circles and specifically challenged

[31] *Ibid.*, p. 616.
[32] *Ibid.*, p. 599.
[33] *Ibid.*, p. 601.
[34] *Ibid.*, pp. 635, 643.
[35] *Ibid.*, p. 624.
[36] *Ibid.*, Part 3, p. 837.
[37] *Ibid.*, p. 841.
[38] *Ibid.*, p. 843.
[39] *Ibid.*, p. 839.

Schwartz to produce evidence that he had ever "fixed so much as a parking ticket."[40]

Actually the question as to whether Whiteside was literally "retained" by National Airlines was never completely resolved. Judge Anderson's testimony indicated that he was of the opinion that Whiteside's services had been secured in spite of his refusal to accept the traditional fee.[41] Actually Whiteside's view of the whole affair was pretty much the same as that of Judge Anderson if one ignored his semantical struggle with the word "retained." He testified, for example, that he told the Judge that "I was not available for employment, but that I would be as helpful to him as I could be."[42] In other words, he had agreed to work in his capacity as a "human being" rather than in his capacity as a "member of the bar and an attorney at law."[43]

Actually, whether Whiteside was or was not retained in the traditional sense would seem to be of relatively little importance to an understanding of the case. For the testimony presented before the subcommittee made it quite clear that Whiteside had offered to do what he could for National Airlines, even if on something of a personal basis. And it would not seem unfair to say that this was about all that the company had ever wanted from Whiteside anyway. The firm had been fully prepared to give Whiteside $10,000 for his service, but in the end got it for nothing. Indeed, Whiteside freely admitted to the members of the subcommittee that he had approached Mack, not once or twice, but "several" times on behalf of National Airlines. "I advised [Mack] of my opinion of the high character, integrity, and reputation in the community of the individuals involved in the National Airlines application, and of my friendship for Robert H. Anderson," Whiteside said. "And all things being equal, I would appreciate his giving National his consideration."[44]

Whiteside also admitted, quite candidly, that he had lent Mack a good deal of money both before and after his appointment to the FCC. And Mack was equally candid in confirming Whiteside's testimony. "I was having a hard time making ends meet," the commissioner said.[45] "I must confess that throughout my career I have not been what may be called a money maker. There have been many times in my life when I have been in need of financial assistance."[46] But neither Whiteside nor Mack saw anything unethical or improper about these "ordinary loan transactions."[47] Both stressed

[40] *Ibid.*, p. 840.
[41] *Ibid.*, p. 846.
[42] *Ibid.*, pp. 844–46.
[43] *Ibid.*, p. 848.
[44] *Ibid.*, pp. 848–49.
[45] *Ibid.*, part 4, p. 1279.
[46] *Ibid.*, Part 3, p. 1190.
[47] *Ibid.*, p. 839.

the fact that they had been friends for over forty years and that Whiteside had lent his friend money since they had been fellow students at the University of Florida, some twenty years before.[48] "Money has never been a requisite of friendship between us or a tool with which to secure favors," Whiteside asserted. "I did not cease to regard him as a member of the human race when he was appointed to public office. Only the night crawlers of this world . . . can so twist and distort a decent human relationship."[49]

Whiteside said that he had given Mack $7,830 in interest-free loans since 1950, and that $2,650 of that figure represented loans made after Mack's appointment to the FCC.[50] He insisted, however, that none of the loans had ever been "forgiven" and that the balance due was only $250. According to Whiteside's testimony, he had always received promissory notes from Mack marked "payable on demand." He maintained, moreover, that seven of these promissory notes, all of which were supposedly marked "paid and satisfied," had been subpoenaed by the subcommittee.[51] However, the subcommittee was never able to locate them, and Whiteside's own inventory of the subpoenaed documents made no mention of them at all.[52] Equally puzzling, however, was the lender's contention that he had retained notes which had been paid in full. Representative John Williams thought that this was, at the very least, "irregular." For this meant, in fact, that Commissioner Mack was left with no proof that his financial obligations to Whiteside had been satisfied. Even Whiteside was forced to concede that under such an arrangement Mack had only "his confidence in me and my good faith."[53]

The subcommittee found that the funds for the repayment of Mack's loans had come almost exclusively from his earnings in two Florida corporations, Stembler-Shelden of Miami and Andar Incorporated of Coral Gables. But of particular interest to the subcommittee was its discovery that Mack's interest in the two firms had been obtained from Whiteside. As trustee and sole stockholder in the Stembler-Shelden insurance agency, for example, Whiteside had simply "orally declared" a one-sixth interest for Mack in 1953. At the time of this "declaration" of ownership, Mack was a member of the Florida Railroad and Public Utilities Commission, and Stembler-Shelden insured trucking firms under its jurisdiction.[54] Though Mack had not been obliged to pay anything for his interest in the firm, he reported "earned income" of $9,896.58 from Stembler-Shelden between 1954 and 1956.[55]

[48] *Ibid.*, pp. 843, 1190.
[49] *Ibid.*, pp. 840–41.
[50] *Ibid.*, pp. 837, 959.
[51] *Ibid.*, p. 851.
[52] *Ibid.*, pp. 864, 895.
[53] *Ibid.*, pp. 886–87.
[54] *Ibid.*, pp. 898–99.
[55] *Ibid.*, p. 927.

Whiteside was of the opinion that the firm's payments to Mack had been based upon the number of insurance "leads" he had provided.[56] Yet, Mack himself could not recall a single lead that he had ever given the company and, as a matter of fact, could not recall that he had ever assisted the firm in any manner whatsoever from 1954 to 1956.[57] Actually, there was precious little evidence to show that Mack was in any way connected with Stembler-Shelden. That he performed no service for it was fairly evident, but he also conceded that he had never received, or even requested, a yearly accounting from the firm in which he ostensibly owned a one-sixth interest.[58] Finally, the subcommittee discovered that Mack's name did not appear on the stock certificates. Thus, it had only the word of Whiteside and Mack that an "orally declared" agreement had ever been consumated.[59]

What made Mack's connection with the insurance firm especially awkward was the disclosure that it had sold the National Airline's television subsidiary some $20,328.41 in insurance shortly after it had been awarded the Miami television license.[60] Whereas previous revelations had raised questions of impropriety, this one brought forward some rather serious problems of legality. Indeed, the Federal Communications Act of 1934 specifically provided that "no member of the commission . . . shall be financially interested . . . in any company furnishing services . . . to any company engaged in communication by wire or radio."[61] Whiteside testified that he had first learned of the controversial insurance policy two or three months earlier when he made one of his "rare excursions" into the agency's office.[62] Mack testified that he first learned of the policy's existence while reading his evening newspaper only three days before.[63] One might well have wondered, at this point, whether anyone was tending the store at Stembler-Shelden.

In 1957 Whiteside made Mack the sole stockholder in Andar Incorporated, which he described as an "inactive" holding company. Throughout his testimony before the subcommittee, Whiteside stressed the fact that the Andar Corporation had "no assets of any kind" and that its stock had absolutely "no value." Initially, Andar had been a holding company for the Coral Gables Checker Cab Company and, although it had conducted no business for the previous two or three years, it was, in 1957, still authorized to borrow and lend money, buy and sell personal property, and en-

[56] Ibid., p. 929.
[57] Ibid., p. 1210, Part 4, p. 1270.
[58] Ibid., Part 3, p. 1229.
[59] Ibid., pp. 927, 943, 986.
[60] Ibid., p. 948.
[61] 47 U.S.C. 154.
[62] House Special Subcommittee on Legislative Oversight, Regulatory Commission Hearings, Part 3, 1958, p. 934.
[63] Ibid., pp. 938–39.

gage in the insurance business. The transfer of Andar's stock to
the commissioner had been motivated, Whiteside said, by a "change
or criticism in the bookeeping in Stembler-Shelden" which made
it inconvenient to continue payments to Mack from the insurance
company.[64]

But whatever Whiteside's motive for the stock transfer had
been, beginning in 1957 the commissioner received income from
Andar Inc. and not from Stembler-Shelden. And Whiteside testified
that in slightly over one year Mack received, either directly or indirectly, some $4,350 from this second corporation.[65] This figure
would, at first glance, appear to be a rather substantial return from
stocks which had "no value," but it became even more impressive
after the commissioner conceded that he had done nothing to earn
his yearly dividends. As in the case of Stembler-Shelden, Mack had
never actually received any stock certificates evincing his ownership in Andar. Yet, he was "certain" that he owned the company,
he said, because Whiteside had told him so. "I have absolute trust
in Mr. Whiteside, and I do not think he would tell me that unless
it were true."[66]

Stripped of all facade, it looked very much like Whiteside had
simply given Mack $14,246.58. "As far as I am concerned," Rep-
resentative Moss said, "the moral and ethical question is not one
whit different in this instance than had you sat down and done one
of two things, forgiven the indebtedness or given Mr. Mack a check
to use for the purpose of repaying the indebtedness." It was obvious that Mack had done nothing for Stembler-Shelden or Andar
Inc., and Whiteside, or someone in his office, had perhaps spent a
few minutes on such things as "declaring" trusts, transferring stock
certificates, and writing dividend checks. But one thing was clear:
at the end of 1957 Mack was $14,246.58 richer and Whiteside was
$14,246.58 poorer. Whiteside, of course, disagreed. "There is a vast
difference between a gift and placing a lifelong friend in a position
where he can earn money on an income basis," he asserted.[67] Such
subtle distinctions were unappreciated by most members of the
subcommittee.

The frankness of the testimony given by Whiteside and Mack
was most striking, as was their total inability to see the ethical
questions involved. Neither, for example, saw anything improper
about Whiteside's playing the role of financial angel to Mack. "If
Mr. Whiteside had given me $20,000 on which he paid the income
tax," Mack said, "I think I would have taken it."[68] Whiteside,
if anything, was more imperceptive than the commissioner. "I

[64] *Ibid.*, p. 937.
[65] *Ibid.*, p. 1012.
[66] *Ibid.*, pp. 1248–49.
[67] *Ibid.*, p. 973.
[68] *Ibid.*, p. 1202.

know of no offense when a man has the milk of human kindness in his heart and tries to help one of his oldest friends," he said. "I do not know why he should be condemned for such actions."[69] Neither, apparently, saw anything wrong in Whiteside's direct appeal to Mack on behalf of National Airlines. It was, after all, only a "recommendation." Yet, it would be difficult to imagine the analogous situation of a politician making a similar "recommendation" to a judge about a case pending before his court.

After these admissions by Whiteside and Mack, it became apparent to everyone, except perhaps the commissioner himself, that Mack would have to submit his resignation.[70] On February 28, 1958, Chairman Harris told Mack that the hearings had uncovered "one of the most fantastic operations" in his congressional experience. Although he conceded that Mack may well have been used as a "tool" in the unfortunate affair, he told him that "the best possible service you could render now as a member of the Federal Communications Commission would be to submit your resignation." After Harris finished reading his prepared statement, a prolonged silence fell over the huge chamber. Finally, a badly shaken commissioner, with palms clasped together as if in prayer, whispered "I will certainly most seriously consider your remarks."[71] "Only seven hours of testimony," *Newsweek* reported, "had reduced Mack from an urbane, self-confident, 'bright young man' of Florida Democratic politics to a broken and weary man."[72]

In his statement to Mack, Harris had also remarked that President Eisenhower "should unhesitatingly under the circumstances revealed during these hearings, make a direct request to you for your resignation."[73] But the President had remained conspicuously silent about such a possibility throughout the controversy. Indeed, only the day before, *The New York Times* had quoted the President as saying "Well, I have no judgment at this time [about Mack's resignation or dismissal] because the evidence, so far as I know, is in the process of being concentrated." He was of the opinion, however, that no member of a regulatory commission could be removed without "a trial of some kind."[74] In all fairness to the President, the constitutional question involved was, at best, uncertain.

Of course, the Supreme Court had ruled in Humphrey's Exec-

[69] *Ibid.*, pp. 1055–56.
[70] Jay Walz, "Mack Won't Quit; Denies Pressure," *New York Times,* February 28, 1958.
[71] House Special Subcommittee on Legislative Oversight, *Regulatory Commission Hearings,* Part 4, 1958, p. 1287.
[72] "Step Down," *Newsweek,* March 10, 1958, p. 38.
[73] House Special Subcommittee on Legislative Oversight, *Regulatory Commission Hearings,* Part 4, 1958, p. 1287.
[74] *New York Times,* February 27, 1958. See also Anthony Lewis, "Could President Discharge Mack?" *New York Times,* February 28, 1958.

utor v. United States that the President could remove a member of
the Federal Trade Commission only after a hearing and only for
specific cause.[75] However, the statute which created the Federal
Trade Commission, as well as those which created the Interstate
Commerce Commission and the Federal Tariff Commission, had
made the commissioners removable "for inefficiency, neglect of
duty, or malfeasance in office." The implication was clear, therefore, that the President could not remove on any other grounds.
But the statutes which created the Federal Power Commission, the
Federal Communications Commission, and the Securities Exchange
Commission placed no such limitation on the President's power to
remove. Thus, there was some question whether the principle set
down in the Humphrey case was applicable to a member of the
Federal Communications Commission.

On at least one previous occasion, however, the President had
not exhibited such sensitivity to subtle points of constitutional
law. Shortly after he took office in 1953, for example, he asked
the two remaining Democratic members of the War Claims Commission to submit their resignations solely because he wanted personnel of his own choosing, that is Republicans, to administer the
provisions of the War Claims Act of 1948. When the two commissioners refused, Eisenhower summarily discharged them. The
constitutional question was ultimately resolved, but not until the
Mack controversy had ended. On June 30, 1958, a unanimous
Supreme Court ruled that President Eisenhower had exceeded his
authority in removing the two commissioners. Moreover, the fact
that the War Claims Act had placed no specific limitations on the
President's removal power was held to be of no importance.[76]
Thus, it would appear in retrospect that the President did indeed
lack authority for the summary discharge of Commissioner Mack.

Although rumors were rampant that the Administration had
passed the word to the commissioner that his "usefulness" had
ended, its official policy in the controversy continued to be cloaked
in silence. When questioned specifically about these rumors, the
White House issued a terse "no comment." The few Republicans
who did comment on the affair, and the group included National
Chairman Meade Alcorn, went out of their way to stress the fact
that Mack was, after all, a Democrat and had been sponsored
by the "highest Democrats in Florida."[77] None mentioned, of
course, that the man who appointed Mack to the Federal Communications Commission was, after all, a Republican, and none
mentioned that these same "highest Democrats in Florida" had
sponsored Mack for both the Federal Power Commission and the

[75] Humphrey's Executor v. United States, 295 U.S. 602 (1935).
[76] Wiener v. United States, 357 U.S. 349 (1958).
[77] New York Times, February 23, 1958.

Interstate Commerce Commission under President Truman and had been singularly unsuccessful.[78]

Although the Administration never broke its official silence in the affair, there was reason to believe that Mack submitted his resignation only after being specifically ordered to do so by Presidential Assistant Sherman Adams and Presidential Counsel Gerald Morgan. They reportedly phoned the commissioner and ordered him to resign by nightfall or face immediate discharge. Philip Warden, political columnist for the *Chicago Tribune,* quoted Adams as saying, "The President was willing to let Mack take the easy way out, to resign rather than be fired."[79] Mack was told that he should not expect any help from the White House in drafting his letter of resignation. What he chose to put in it was his "own business," Adams said. In the middle of the commissioner's protestations of his innocence, Adams reportedly hung up. It was obvious that the Administration planned no parade, no award, no congratulatory letter in its then current conflict of interest case.[80]

Following Adams' phone call, Mack went into seclusion with his lawyer, William A. Porter, to draft his letter of resignation. When the letter was released, however, one might have found it hard to understand why he had thought it necessary to spend several hours in isolation to compose a letter which was, in many respects, identical to those already submitted by Talbott, Strobel, Cross, Mansure, and Ross. A quick reading of these letters in *The New York Times* would undoubtedly have saved the commissioner a good deal of time. Mack insisted, as had all of his predecessors, "I feel in my heart that I have done no wrong and my conscience is clear." Although he thought that his "character and good name had been sacrificed to political expediency," he also knew that his "usefulness as a member of the Federal Communications Commission had been brought into question." Therefore, he thought it wise to submit his resignation, "to take effect at [the President's] pleasure."[81]

The commissioner's letter of resignation was delivered to the White House at 5:00 P.M. on March 3, 1958. A little over an hour later Mack received the President's letter of acceptance. "Without attempting to pass judgment upon the questions you have raised in your letter," Eisenhower said, "I, nevertheless, agree with you that your usefulness as a member of the commission is so seriously

[78] House Special Subcommittee on Legislative Oversight, *Regulatory Commission Hearings,* Part 3, 1958, p. 1234.

[79] Philip Warden, "Ike Ousts Mack From the FCC," *Chicago Tribune,* March 2, 1958.

[80] Allen Drury, "Mack Drafting FCC Resignation on Adams' Orders," *New York Times,* March 3, 1958.

[81] Jay Walz, "Mack Quits FCC," *New York Times,* February 4, 1958. The texts of the Mack and Eisenhower letters are reproduced on another page of the *Times.*

impaired that you are wise to tender your resignation." It was quite obvious, moreover, that Eisenhower was very anxious to remove this latest albatross from the Administration's neck, for he made the resignation effective at the close of business that very day. Thus, unless the commissioner had worked into the early evening in front of his color television set, the resignation was made retroactive. Still, as in all the other conflict of interest cases, if the President had any moral scruples about corruption in his Administration, he made no public statement to that effect.

No discussion of the Schwartz-Mack controversy should be concluded, however, without a special reference to the particularly inept reporting of it by *Time* magazine. Early articles, for example, called Schwartz the "most unlovable congressional investigation counsel since Roy Cohn" and implied that he was something of a light-weight Joe McCarthy.[82] And use of such emotionally loaded phrases as "flinging his innuendoes high, wide and handsome," "under Schwartz's taunting," "shrieked Schwartz," "cocky law professor," etc., was hardly designed to earn the self-styled nation's leading news magazine any awards for objective reporting. Its article of February 24, 1958, would concede only that Schwartz had made, in his appearance before the subcommittee, "something of a plausible case against Richard Mack." And even this minor concession was followed by a *tour de force:* "Not before [Mack's appearance before the subcommittee] could anyone tell whether Bernard Schwartz had performed any public service other than proving that a cocky law professor can sling more half-truths and innuendoes in less time than a skilled politician."[83]

In reporting Mack's forced resignation two weeks later, however, *Time* referred to Schwartz as the "contentious New York law professor."[84] It appeared that *Time* followed the sage advice given by Satchel Paige, i.e., "never look back." Still, it was not difficult to understand why *Time* proved to be one of Schwartz's more intemperate critics. Henry Luce, who controlled the *Time-Life-Fortune* empire, also owned a number of television stations throughout the United States. Thus, this automatically made him a member of the group least enthused about a probe of the FCC. As Schwartz would later write, "It was more than mere coincidence that *Time-Life* itself had, under the Eisenhower Administration, built up a TV and radio empire with approval of the FCC, and that at least one of its TV acquisitions had been slated for inquiry in my projected investigation schedule."[85]

[82] "The Unlovable Counsel," *Time*, February 17, 1958, p. 26. See also "Lo, the Investigator," *Time*, February 24, 1958, pp. 14–15.
[83] *Time*, February 24, 1958, p. 15.
[84] "Investigations: You Are To Be Pitied," *Time*, March 10, 1958, p. 16.
[85] Schwartz, *The Professor and the Commissions*, p. 250.

Chapter 13

THE CONVIVIAL COMMISSIONER

I came to Washington a man of modest means. I am still a man of modest means. I followed my conscience in deciding every matter that came before me. I have done the best I know how and I am willing to subject my record to the sharpest scrutiny.

JOHN C. DOERFER

RICHARD MACK was not the only member of the Federal Communications Commission to suffer a well-earned embarrassment at the hands of the subcommittee and Bernard Schwartz. In 1958, the commission's junketing chairman, John C. Doerfer, also came in for a share of questioning and considerable criticism for his close fraternization with members of the regulated industry. Due to President Eisenhower's beneficence, or perhaps it was his imperceptiveness, Doerfer was not forced to submit his resignation at that time. However, two years later, after a second subcommittee hearing disclosed that the chairman had continued to elicit industry favors in the intervening period, Doerfer was compelled to tender his resignation.

According to an old Scottish proverb, "Experience makes even fools wise."[1] Yet, there is precious little evidence to suggest that Doerfer, member of the Federal Communications Commission from 1953 to 1960 and its chairman after 1957, learned anything at all from his experiences before the House Special Subcommittee on Legislative Oversight in 1958. It was this subcommittee which established the fact that Commissioner Doerfer had repeatedly accepted honorariums from the broadcasting industry, as well as hotel and travel expenses for both himself and his wife while traveling at government expense to various trade conventions. It was this same subcommittee, moreover, which publicized the fact that

[1] Sir Gurney Benham, *Benham's Book of Quotations* (London: George G. Harrap and Company, Ltd., 1948), p. 807.

Doerfer had allowed the television industry to place a costly color television set in his home.[2]

The subcommittee, influenced no doubt by the revelations in Drew Pearson's column of January 22, 1958,[3] discussed previously, spent most of its time questioning Doerfer about his junket into the states of Oklahoma and Washington in the fall of 1954. The commissioner readily admitted to the subcommittee that, for the first leg of his western trip, i.e., from Washington, D.C., to Oklahoma City, Oklahoma, Station KWTV furnished plane tickets in the value of $165.12 for him and his wife and, in addition, paid all of their $34.47 hotel bill for their one-night stay in the city. Of course, most of this information, minus the specific details and the concrete documentation, had already been outlined in the Pearson column which appeared some five days before the subcommittee opened its hearings.[4]

The subcommittee, however, also discovered that Station KWTV had later sent a check to Doerfer for an additional $165.12. "It was our intention that a round-trip ticket be delivered to you," the station's promotion manager explained to the commissioner in a letter which accompanied the check, "and since this was not possible because of your extended trip [to Spokane, Washington], we wish to reimburse you for the return portion of the ticket." On the day Doerfer deposited this check in his personal account, he signed government travel forms which included the entire cost of plane tickets for his return trip from Spokane.[5] Thus, on the last leg of this return trip, i.e., from Oklahoma City to Washington, D.C., Doerfer was doubly reimbursed for his transportation expenses, once by Station KWTV and once by the Federal Government.

When confronted with such evidence as the endorsed check for $165.12, the letter from the promotion manager at Station KWTV, and the signed government travel voucher, Doerfer had, of course, no alternative but to concede that he had indeed been doubly compensated on a portion of his journey. However, he insisted that he had taken the check by mistake. "I was under the impression," he said, "that I paid transportation for Mr. and Mrs. Doerfer from Washington to Oklahoma City."[6] He told the members of the subcommittee, moreover, that he had signed a blank check about this time for his personal secretary, who always handled

[2] U.S., Congress, House, Special Subcommittee on Legislative Oversight, *Hearings, Investigation of Regulatory Commissions and Agencies*, Part 1, 85th Cong., 2d Sess., 1958, pp. 265–79.

[3] Drew Pearson, "The Washington Merry-Go-Round," *Harrisburg* (Ill.) *Daily Register*, January 22, 1958.

[4] House Special Subcommittee on Legislative Oversight, *Regulatory Commission Hearings*, Part 1, 1958, pp. 226–27.

[5] *Ibid.*, p. 228.

[6] *Ibid.*, p. 320.

his travel arrangements, and he had assumed that she had used it to purchase two plane tickets. "When I discovered, around January 20, that this was an error, I did what any honest man would do. I returned the money to the Oklahoma television company."[7]

It should be made clear, however, that the commissioner's discovery date of January 20 was not in 1955, but instead 1958, some three years after he received the check from the television company, at the time of the Pearson exposé, and only one week prior to his appearance before the subcommittee. Chief Counsel Schwartz observed that the most cursory examination of the letter accompanying the check would certainly have precluded Doerfer's view that it was reimbursement for a personal outlay of money. First, Schwartz cited a portion of the letter which stated that "American Airlines advises me that you and Mrs. Doerfer used only the Washington, D.C., to Oklahoma City portion of the tickets we asked the airline to deliver to you." He then cited the portion of the letter, previously noted, in which the promotion manager said categorically, "It was our intention that a round-trip ticket be delivered to you, and since this was not possible because of your extended trip, we wish to reimburse you for the return portion of the ticket."[8] Doerfer told the chief counsel that he could not recall having ever read the letter. "I, perhaps, didn't read the letter," he said. "And if I read it I read it very superficially."[9]

An examination of the transcript of the hearings made it quite clear, however, that the chief counsel was skeptical of Doerfer's explanation of the double payment. Schwartz's questioning of Doerfer on his blank check story, for example, suggested that he believed that there was at least a possibility that the commissioner created the story retrospectively. "You never bothered to see what your check was for," Schwartz taunted, "you never asked your secretary, you received this windfall out of the blue from Mr. Bell, but you assumed he was reimbursing you?" The commissioner coldly informed the chief counsel, "This was no windfall, Dr. Schwartz. This was a misunderstanding."[10] There was, of course, no way to prove or disprove Doerfer's contention. In the last analysis, one was left with only a rather subjective, intuitive opinion of it.

The commissioner's trip to Spokane raised additional questions of propriety. It was established, for example, that the National Association of Radio and Television Broadcasters paid all of the Doerfer's $141.16 hotel bill, where the couple spent two nights in a $50 suite of rooms, and later sent the commissioner a check for

[7] *Ibid.,* p. 321.
[8] *Ibid.,* p. 322.
[9] *Ibid.,* p. 325.
[10] *Ibid.,* p. 321.

$575.[11] Doerfer termed $300 of this figure an "honorarium or compensation"[12] and cited as justification for his acceptance of it a 1952 amendment to the Federal Communications Act which provided, "Commissioners shall not engage in any other business, vocation, profession, or employment; but this shall not apply to the presentation or delivery of publications or papers for which a reasonable honorarium or compensation may be accepted."[13] He termed the remaining $275 a reimbursement for his wife's expenses. Yet, Mr. R. K. Richards, vice president of NARTB and the official who negotiated with Doerfer on his fee, testified that he thought the $575 was for the commissioner's "out-of-pocket expenses." He hastened to add, however, that he was not complaining about the fee. Regardless of what it was for, he thought the figure was, under the circumstances, "quite reasonable."[14]

Even the association's arrangement for paying Doerfer the $575 was unusual, if not irregular. The association sent its check, not directly to the commissioner as one might have expected, but to R. M. Brown, general manager of Station KPOJ in Portland, Oregon. Brown, in turn, endorsed the check and forwarded it to Burl G. Hagedone, president and general manager of Station KNEW in Spokane, Washington. Hagedone then deposited the check in his own bank account, waited a period of several days, and sent Doerfer one of his personal checks for $575.[15] Baron Shacklette, chief investigator for the subcommittee, managed to obtain a copy of a letter from Hagedone to Brown which shed some light on these strange machinations, however. "In reading between the lines, the check in the amount of $575 is to pay the travel expense of the commissioner and his wife, plus incidental expenses other than hotel," Hagedone had written. "I suggest that the check be deposited to my personal account and I will issue a check to the commissioner in the same amount. . . . This is going a long way around, but should achieve the desired results."[16] Such a "roundabout way devised for the receipt of money," Schwartz charged, "can only be construed as an attempt to conceal the payment [to Doerfer]."[17]

The fact that the commissioner had received benefits from the broadcasting industry which totaled $1,080.87 during his five-day western sojourn did not deter him from submitting travel and ex-

[11] Ibid., pp. 232–34.
[12] Ibid., p. 271.
[13] 47 U.S.C. 154.
[14] House Special Subcommittee on Legislative Oversight, Regulatory Commission Hearings, Part 1, 1958, p. 234.
[15] Ibid., pp. 240–47.
[16] Ibid., p. 263.
[17] William M. Blair, "Inquiry Accuses Chairman of FCC on Expense Funds," New York Times, February 3, 1958.

pense vouchers to the government which amounted to an additional
$296.15. Specifically, Doerfer charged the government $240.65 for
his travel from Oklahoma City to Spokane and return to Washington, D.C. In addition, he claimed five days of per diem in lieu of
subsistence, at nine dollars per day, plus another $10.50 for miscel-
laneous expenses such as taxi fare and tip from the airport to the
hotel and vice versa.[18] Thus, the commissioner ultimately claimed
and received, from both private and public sources, money and
services to the value of $1,377.02. For the sake of accuracy, how-
ever, it should again be pointed out that some three years later the
commissioner returned $165.12 to Station KWTV and, consequently,
lowered this total to $1,211.90. Even this reduced amount was an
impressive return on a trip of less than one week.

Doerfer justified his acceptance of government reimbursement
for travel and per diem expenses on the grounds that much of his
time on such trips was expended on matters of official government
concern. He conceded that had he simply "made a speech, grabbed
the check and flown back again" it would have been improper to
have charged such expenses to the government.[19] But, he argued,
this was not the case. On his trip to Oklahoma City, for example,
he told the members of the subcommittee that he had stopped
in Tulsa to inspect television stations, flown by private plane to
Muskogee to inspect antenna towers, as well as studio and micro-
wave facilities, and, finally, flown to Oklahoma City to observe
studios and antenna towers. Indeed, he insisted that, on the whole,
he had had "not one moment of recreation" during his 1954
western trip. Schwartz remarked, facetiously, that the $24.13 in
"cafe" charges to the commissioner's Spokane hotel bill seemed to
suggest that Doerfer might have had at least "one moment" of
recreation.[20]

On the commissioner's final day of testimony he described,
with some prodding by the chief counsel, the details of other trips
which had been financed by various industry groups. A nine-day
junket to St. Simon Island, Georgia, and White Sulphur Springs,
West Virginia, in August, 1954, where he spoke to broadcasting
groups, undoubtedly raised the most serious questions of propriety.
The hearings established, for example, that Commissioner and
Mrs. Doerfer's hotel bills, including room, board, golf fees, and
restaurant charges, were paid by the broadcasting associations, and
at both St. Simon Island and White Sulphur Springs Doerfer received an additional $100 in cash.[21]

The commissioner chose to regard these two $100 gifts as

[18] House Special Subcommittee on Legislative Oversight, *Regulatory Commission Hearings*, Part 1, 1958, pp. 316, 407–8.
[19] *Ibid.*, p. 275.
[20] *Ibid.*, pp. 274–75.
[21] *Ibid.*, pp. 351–53.

honorariums despite the fact that the secretary-treasurer of the Georgia association insisted that its payment was for "out-of-pocket expenses during [Doerfer's] trip." Later, the commissioner claimed and received an additional $168.14 from the Federal Government for travel, per diem, and miscellaneous expenses purportedly incurred on this trip to the South. Such charges were justified, he told the subcommittee, because the primary purpose of his trip had been "to gather as much information as I could . . . with respect to the propagation and reception of the various signals in that area.[22] Actually Doerfer had no alternative but to insist that he had performed official duties on those trips for which he had submitted expense vouchers to the government inasmuch as it was a criminal offense to make knowingly a "false, fictitious, or fraudulent" claim against the Federal Government.[23]

The subcommittee also discovered that in August, 1955, Doerfer and his wife had flown to Miami, Florida, in a private plane and, from there, to the Bimini Islands some forty or fifty miles out into the straits. It developed that the plane transporting the Doerfers was owned by George B. Storer, president of the Storer Broadcasting Company which controlled a number of radio and television stations throughout the United States. Doerfer conceded, moreover, that while in Miami he and his wife had been personal guests in the Storer home and that while on the Bimini trip all of their expenses had been paid by the broadcasting magnate. Despite such admissions, however, Doerfer insisted that the six-day junket was not a pleasure trip since he had flown to Florida primarily to observe the operation of Storer's UHF station in Miami and to investigate the feasibility of licensing another VHF channel there. "I wouldn't consider that much of a rest," the commissioner said. "That was a postman's holiday. To me, it was work."[24]

The only other trip of any particular consequence uncovered by the 1958 hearings involved a 1956 excursion to the famous Pinehurst golf center in North Carolina. The invitation had been extended by an undisclosed airline company which underwrote all of the commissioner's travel, hotel, and other expenses on the three-day golfing vacation. Remarkably, there was no indication that Mrs. Doerfer accompanied her husband on that particular junket. Perhaps she did not play golf. Doerfer told the members of the subcommittee that there were "several" public officials, a general or an ex-general, he was not sure which, and at least one other member of a regulatory commission, Civil Aeronautics Board member James Durfee, who also accepted the hospitality of the airline. In

[22] *Ibid.,* p. 340.
[23] 18 *U.S.C.* 287.
[24] House Special Subcommittee on Legislative Oversight, *Regulatory Commission Hearings,* Part 1, 1958, pp. 396–98.

this instance, according to the commissioner, there was absolutely no question of impropriety involved. "I didn't charge the government for any of that," he said, as though this were the only and the ultimate test of propriety.[25]

Considering the nature of the subcommittee revelations, one might have expected Doerfer to be, at the very least, apologetic about his acceptance of these industry favors. Such, however, was not the case. Except for his "honest mistake" in accepting the $165.12 check from Station KWTV, the commissioner relentlessly maintained throughout the hearings that his behavior was neither illegal nor improper. "These things are accepted today as American amenities," he said.[26] "Hell, if I'd gone out to Spokane and accepted $10,000 there'd be something to investigate."[27]

What Doerfer did do, however, was to direct an extremely sharp attack upon Chief Counsel Schwartz and upon those newspapers which had been critical of his fraternization with industry officials. "I have undergone a good deal of annoyance, to put it mildly, by various of the twelve-hundred-odd newspapers in this country," he said, "and trial by ordeal and torture in medieval times is but nothing compared to trial by innuendo by some of the newspapers."[28] Doerfer's testimony indicated, quite clearly, that he questioned both the motives and the intelligence of the subcommittee's chief counsel. At one point in the hearings, for example, he termed the Schwartz memorandum "the work of a man who either does not understand or does not wish to understand the responsibilities of the Federal Communications Commission."[29]

Later, the commissioner pointed out, obviously for the chief counsel's edification, that it had been the practice, rather than the exception, "for almost all of the regulatory agencies to meet freely with the people whom it regulates and to discuss the problems of the industry with them." A full ninety percent of his time, Doerfer argued, was spent in a quasi-legislative capacity searching for solutions to the great variety of complex problems which face the communications industry. While acting in this capacity, moreover, Doerfer told the members of the subcommittee, "I will talk to [an industry representative] on the steps of the Capital, or at lunch with him at any public restaurant in this city."[30] He was convinced, he said, that Congress had not intended "to push [the commissioners]

[25] *Ibid.*, pp. 394–95.
[26] *Ibid.*, p. 414.
[27] *New York Times*, February 5, 1958.
[28] House Special Subcommittee on Legislative Oversight, *Regulatory Commission Hearings*, Part 1, 1958, p. 218.
[29] *Ibid.*, p. 266.
[30] *Ibid.*, p. 267. The commissioner cited, as justification for his association with members of the regulated industry, U.S., Congress, Senate, *Administrative Procedures in Government Agencies*, The Attorney General's Report of the Committee on Administrative Procedures, 77th Cong., 1st Sess., Senate Doc. 8, 1941.

behind a glass panel where they see nothing, hear nothing, and speak nothing but get their expertise by some metaphysical way."[31]

"Your counsel assumes that a public official could be improperly influenced by a luncheon, a dinner, or a stay at a hotel where he is attending a public function," Doerfer bluntly informed the members of the subcommittee. "If the public officials of America could be so easily influenced, then God save the Republic."[32] In fact, however, the commissioner's position was not as impregnable as he would have had the subcommittee believe. Indeed, a few days later it discovered that another member of the FCC, T. A. M. Craven, had a strikingly different view on the matter. He once returned a check to an industry group, to which he had previously delivered an address, for precisely the reason that he had already received per diem and travel expenses from the government. In a strong letter, moreover, he advised the group that he thought it would be "grossly improper" for him to accept the second reimbursement.[33]

In all fairness to Doerfer, neither the question of legality nor the question of propriety was clearly established by the 1958 hearings. The difficulty lay primarily in the uncertainty of congressional intention in its 1952 amendment to the Federal Communications Act. Specifically, it was unclear what Congress meant by the words "honorarium" and "compensation." Certainly there was some truth in the commissioner's contention, "If I did wrong, and I deny it—that is a mousetrap statute."[34] Moreover, the statements by the Comptroller General of the United States, Joseph Campbell, were hardly designed to clarify the situation. After much indecision, he finally decided that if the word "compensation" were given a "broad interpretation" it might include the expenses for which Doerfer had been reimbursed. Even then, though, he was forced to concede that in the past both the federal courts and the Comptroller General had frequently ruled that expenses, especially travel expenses, were not included within the meaning of the term "compensation."[35]

The Comptroller General reported to Subcommittee Chairman Moulder that the question of acceptance of favors, gifts, and gratuities by public officials was also anything but clear. Indeed, other than those statutes dealing specifically with bribery, Federal law was completely silent. Campbell was of the opinion that the acceptance of an occasional luncheon by a public official would hardly con-

---

[31] House Special Subcommittee on Legislative Oversight, *Regulatory Commission Hearings*, Part 1, 1958, p. 413.

[32] *Ibid.*, p. 267.

[33] *Ibid.*, Part 2, p. 536.

[34] *Ibid.*, Part 1, p. 271.

[35] *Ibid.*, p. 306. For a radically different view by the Comptroller General see *ibid.*, pp. 281–84.

stitute inappropriate behavior inasmuch as it was generally regarded by both the giver and the receiver as simply a "courteous
gesture." However, if an official accepted what Campbell termed
"lavish or frequent entertainment, gifts, paying of hotel bills, or
travel costs, and allowances in purchasing" he would clearly be
guilty of improper conduct.[36]

There were, in 1958, a variety of factors which worked to
Doerfer's advantage and, consequently, prevented his forced resignation from the Federal Communications Commission. Certainly, the
charges of "McCarthyism" leveled at Chief Counsel Schwartz relieved a good deal of the pressure from the commissioner. Much of
the subcommittee's time on Doerfer's last day of testimony was
taken up by acid exchanges between Schwartz and various members
of the subcommittee, and especially between Schwartz and John B.
Bennett, Republican congressman from Michigan. The latter
charged vehemently and repeatedly that the chief counsel was conducting the hearings as if it were a criminal proceedings but, at the
same time, denying the witness those procedural rights he would
enjoy in a regular court of law.[37] Such a contention was not without merit. Indeed, the rumors of Schwartz's bullying tactics had
received sufficient credence to elicit a letter of protest from Patrick
Murphy, executive director of the American Civil Liberties
Union.[38]

Doerfer's case at this time was also strengthened immeasurably
by President Eisenhower's inability to perceive anything improper,
much less illegal, in the commissioner's acceptance of these industry gratuities. In a Presidential press conference of February 5,
1958, Carleton Kent of the *Chicago Sun-Times* asked the President
specifically if he thought that the acceptance of such honorariums
by a member of a regulatory commission was in the public interest.
"Well, I don't know much about it," the President answered. "But
this morning one of my lawyer group brought in the law which says
specifically that . . . [members of the FCC] are entitled to take
reasonable honorariums. Now, that is the limit of my thought on
that."[39] And that one statement was also the limit of the President's
public utterance on the Doerfer affair, 1958 version.

Not only was Doerfer supported by his chief, he was not especially abused by the news media. Actually, the nation's newspapers

[36] *Ibid.*, p. 283. The Comptroller's views were taken largely from U.S., Congress, Senate, Report of the Subcommittee of the Committee on Labor and Public
Welfare, *Ethical Standards in Government*, 82d Cong., 1st Sess., 1951. See also
U.S., Congress, Senate, Subcommittee To Study Senate Concurrent Resolution 21
of the Committee on Labor and Public Welfare, *Hearings, Establishment of a
Commission on Ethics in Government*, 82d Cong., 1st Sess., 1951.
[37] House Special Subcommittee on Legislative Oversight, *Regulatory Commission Hearings*, Part 1, 1958, pp. 356–57.
[38] The letter from Murphy is reproduced in *ibid.*, pp. 341–42.
[39] *New York Times*, February 6, 1958.

and periodicals, as in previous conflict of interest cases under Ike, gave scant attention to the Doerfer controversy. Two of the nation's leading news magazines, for example, tended to play down the significance of the whole affair. *Time,* which again managed to maintain its almost unblemished record for less than objective reporting of the improprieties of members of the Eisenhower Administration, reported that Doerfer had indeed accepted these honorariums but hastened to add that they were "not very lavish." Besides, it said, "Schwartz behaved as if accepting $100 honorariums was a crime ranking close to arson."[40]   Even *Newsweek,* which presented a much better balanced account of the subcommittee investigation than did its competitor, was of the opinion that Commissioner Doerfer's misdeeds were "small potatoes."[41]

Nevertheless, there were enough critical comments by members of the subcommittee, a few editorial writers, and some disgruntled Republican congressmen facing off-year campaigns to have made it abundantly clear to the commissioner that his close fraternization with members of the regulated industry was not universally approved. The subcommittee's report, moreover, recommended specifically that the section dealing with honorariums and compensations be deleted from the Federal Communications Act.[42] Finally, a number of people had become convinced that the atmosphere created by such close proximity between the commissioners and those they are supposed to regulate made it, as one writer observed, "harder and harder for the commissioners to distinguish between their own honest convictions and their friendly inclinations."[43] Thus, by all the rules of logic and common sense, Doerfer should have rejoiced in his good fortune and immediately severed all of his social, and one might have even hoped financial, relationships with members of the broadcasting industry. He did not.

On March 3, 1960, the *New York Herald Tribune* reported that FCC Chairman John C. Doerfer had, while on vacation in Fort Lauderdale, Florida, the previous month, spent a good portion of his time aboard a yacht owned by broadcasting magnate George B. Storer.[44] This was, of course, the same Storer who had financed the commissioner's junket to Miami and the Bimini Islands in the fall of 1955 and who, by 1960, controlled thirteen radio and television stations in the United States. On the same day that the story broke, however, Doerfer told reporters that he had not, in fact, vacationed on any such yacht and insisted, moreover, that

[40] "The Unlovable Counsel," *Time,* February 17, 1958, p. 26.
[41] "Accuser Accused," *Newsweek,* February 17, 1958, p. 30.
[42] U.S., Congress, House, Special Subcommittee on Legislative Oversight, *Independent Regulatory Commissions,* Report No. 2711, 85th Cong., 2d Sess., 1959, p. 12.
[43] "The Reporter's Notes," *Reporter,* February 20, 1958, p. 2.
[44] *New York Herald Tribune,* March 3, 1960.

while in Fort Lauderdale he had stayed with some home-state Wisconsin friends who had no interest whatsoever in the broadcasting industry.[45]

Doerfer admitted to the reporters only that he had once taken a "two-hour cruise" to Miami on the Storer craft to play a few rounds of golf.[46] He had been, he contended, only one member of a party of eight, which had included a bishop and a priest. (One wonders if he felt that such presences would guarantee the purity of the occasion.) No business whatsoever was discussed, Doerfer said, and besides, Storer "had nothing before the FCC and [I] hoped he never would."[47] This, however, was true only in the most narrow sense, for the Federal Communications Act required renewal of all radio and television licenses every three years.[48] Thus, Storer would have, in no less than three years, thirteen cases pending before the FCC. Still, the story, that first day, did not have much of an impact on the journalistic world. Even the conscientious *New York Times,* for example, thought the item rated no better than a brief account on page fifty-nine.[49]

By the following day, however, Doerfer's recollection of the Florida trip had undergone a remarkable transformation. The commissioner's "two-hour cruise" aboard the Storer cabin cruiser, for example, had grown to "one or two nights," and in addition, Doerfer revealed to reporters that inclement weather had caused the Miami golfing party to return to Fort Lauderdale in Storer's private plane. Nevertheless, the commissioner was adamant in his insistence that "it wasn't a junket and just wasn't a cruise." We "shared expenses" on both fishing and golfing, he said. "I am not obligated to Mr. Storer in any way and have nothing to hide." However, if the Special Subcommittee on Legislative Oversight wanted to inquire into his Florida trip, as had been reported in the newspapers, he would, he said, be "available at any time."[50]

Actually, members of the subcommittee had already indicated that they fully intended to question Doerfer about his most recent excursion into Florida. They were, they said, especially interested in knowing more about the extent of his relationship with Storer because the subcommittee's report which followed its investigation in 1958 had specifically warned the commissioners against "excessive fraternization" with representatives of the regulated industry. Representative John Moss, Democrat from California and a subcommittee member, told reporters that the relationship between

[45] *New York Times,* March 3, 1960.
[46] "The President," *Facts on File Yearbook,* March 10, 1960, p. 87.
[47] *New York Times,* March 3, 1960.
[48] 47 *U.S.C.* 154.
[49] *New York Times,* March 3, 1960.
[50] William M. Blair, "Inquiry To Hear Head of the F.C.C.," *New York Times,* March 4, 1960.

Doerfer and Storer which had been indicated by some of the newspaper accounts was "very much the thing we had in mind when we
cautioned against it in our report of last year."[51]

Consequently, on March 4, 1960, Doerfer appeared for a second
time before the Special Subcommittee on Legislative Oversight.
Despite the fact that his testimony concerning the Fort Lauderdale
vacation comprised less than eight pages, the commissioner managed to give a third distinct version as to what had transpired there.
He had taken, it now seemed, neither a "two-hour cruise" nor spent
"one or two nights" on the Storer craft, the "Lazy Girl." Rather,
he had been aboard for a full six days and nights. Still, he argued,
there was nothing wrong with his vacationing aboard the "Lazy
Girl" as long as its owner did not have anything pending before the
commission of an "adjudicatory nature." Even a commissioner had
a "right to pick his friends," he said. "I do not think that a commissioner should be a second class citizen."[52]

The subcommittee also discovered that Doerfer had flown
from Washington to his Fort Lauderdale vacation quarters in
Storer's private plane. The commissioner testified that after he had
already secured round-trip tickets from Northeast Airlines for both
himself and his wife, he was offered, and subsequently accepted, a
ride with Storer who happened to be "passing through" Washington. Apparently, Storer likewise just happened to be going back
to Washington at an appropriate time, for Doerfer said he returned
"under the same circumstances." However, the commissioner told
the subcommittee that he had accepted the business official's invitation only with the understanding that Storer would take the price
of his two round-trip tickets from Northeast Airlines as payment.
According to Doerfer, Storer had agreed to the proposition and intended to turn the money over to a heart fund or an eye foundation.[53]

The Administration's first reaction to these newest revelations
was, as it had been in the past, to say as little as possible. "High administration officials" were quoted as saying, however, that they
hoped that the case would "blow over."[54] When it did not, Doerfer
was summoned to the White House to confer privately with the
President. Even here the commissioner justified his free association
with industry representatives, including the acceptance of Storer's
rather lavish hospitality, and insisted that such fraternization was

[51] New York Times, March 4, 1960. See also House Special Subcommittee on
Legislative Oversight, Report No. 2711, 1959.
[52] U.S., Congress, House, Special Subcommittee on Legislative Oversight,
Hearings, Responsibilities of Broadcasting Licensees and Station Personnel, Part
1, 86th Cong., 2d Sess., 1960, p. 720.
[53] Ibid., p. 721.
[54] William M. Blair, "F.C.C. Head Admits He Got Yacht Trip," New York
Times, March 5, 1960.

necessary in order for the commissioners to become, and remain, knowledgeable about the intricacies of the broadcasting media. The President, who had said little throughout the twenty-minute session, concluded the meeting by quietly informing the deeply tanned Doerfer, "If you want to offer your resignation, it will be accepted."[55] The commissioner, of course, had no alternative but to accept the President's suggestion and promised to deliver his letter of resignation the following day.

The next morning, however, a White House aide received a call from Doerfer informing him that he would be unable to deliver his letter of resignation on schedule. A six-inch snow had fallen the previous evening and marooned the commissioner in his Bethesda, Maryland, home. But the White House was, by that time, so eager to rid itself of its latest conflict of interest case that it had not the patience to await a thaw. The aide told the commissioner to have his resignation ready to be picked up by an official car which he would dispatch. Only a few hours after this telephone conversation a White House limousine, specially equipped with snow chains, pulled into the driveway of Doerfer's suburban home. The "Hound's Tooth Club" was about to enroll a new member.[56]

Even in Doerfer's letter of resignation he never wavered from his position that contact with industry officials was both necessary and desirable. "The mandate from Congress which requires a Commissioner to study new uses for radio and generally encourage the larger and more effective use thereof," the commissioner told the President, "requires day-to-day contact with many industry people." He also pointed out that "a number of these contacts eventually ripen into social acquaintances and sometimes friendships, which despite appearances, do not imperil the integrity of either the Government official or the member of industry." He was submitting his resignation, he said, only "to avoid possible embarrassment to you and your Administration."[57]

As was to be expected, the style and content of the President's letter of acceptance followed the pattern of those written in previous conflict of interest cases. First, he told the commissioner that he "regretted the circumstances which have led you to your conclusion, but they do, in my opinion, indicate your decision to be a wise one." Despite the fact that William Blair of *The New York Times* termed the President's letter "unusually curt," one might well argue that Eisenhower was, if anything, overly generous with the junketing Doerfer. There was, for example, a very real question as to whether the commissioner had, as the President's letter stated, "earned the

[55] "Sunset Cruise," *Time*, March 21, 1960, p. 15.
[56] "Stormy Weather," *Newsweek*, March 21, 1960, p. 41.
[57] The text of Doerfer's letter of resignation appears in *The New York Times*, March 11, 1960.

appreciation of his fellow citizens and of the Administration."[58]

Doerfer, a man described by Representative Moss as the "reluctant regulator of the broadcasting industry"[59] and by *Time* magazine as "a notable friend of the broadcasting industry,"[60] had seldom in his seven years on the commission aligned himself with the public interest. The amiable commissioner's pro-industry bias can be judged reasonably well by the fact that he had continued to insist upon the right of the broadcasting industry to police itself even after rigged television quiz shows and payola scandals had revealed its lack of enthusiasm for such a task.[61] On another occasion the commissioner had opposed a television license application of William T. Evjue, the fighting liberal editor of the *Madison* (Wis.) *Capital Times* and militant anti-McCarthyite, solely because, he said, "I don't like him and I don't like his views."[62]

Various newspaper accounts had already revealed that certain unnamed cabinet members and other high administrative officials had specifically expressed their disapproval of Doerfer's latest indiscretions. They were reported to be angered, and apparently amazed, by the commissioner's complete inability to see anything wrong with his conduct despite the fact that he had been criticized for precisely the same behavior in 1958.[63] Moreover, when it is recalled how the Democrats used the Sherman Adams–Richard Mack controversies in the congressional campaigns of 1958, it is easy to suspect that these high Republican officials were doubly distraught that Doerfer had again suffered the misfortune to be caught in an election year.

It would probably be unfair to criticize President Eisenhower for Doerfer's initial appointment to the Federal Communications Commission even though his experience lay almost exclusively in the field of public utility regulation. Indeed, at the time of his confirmation hearings, Doerfer admitted that he was "totally unfamiliar" with educational television and had never, in fact, even owned a television set.[64] However, he was strongly endorsed by Senators Wiley and McCarthy, Governor Kohler, and virtually every major newspaper in the state of Wisconsin. "Mr. Doerfer has shown keen concern for the public interest," said the *Milwaukee*

---

[58] The text of President Eisenhower's letter of acceptance appears in *The New York Times*, March 11, 1960.

[59] William M. Blair, "Doerfer Resigns as F.C.C. Chairman at President's Bid," *New York Times*, March 11, 1960.

[60] *Time*, March 21, 1960, p. 15.

[61] *Newsweek*, March 21, 1960, p. 41.

[62] "Doerfer's Resignation," *New Republic*, March 21, 1960, p. 6.

[63] William M. Blair, "Conduct of F.C.C. Chief Is Studied by White House," *New York Times*, March 10, 1960.

[64] U.S., Congress, Senate, Committee on Interstate and Foreign Commerce, *Hearings, Nomination of John C. Doerfer To Be a Member of the F.C.C.*, 83d Cong., 1st Sess., 1953, p. 8.

Journal; "It is only in the name of patriotism that Wisconsin lets him go without a stiff fight," said the *Wisconsin State Journal;* "The United States of America will be richer for the choice [Eisenhower] has made," said the *Milwaukee Sentinel;* and "We are pleased to see that [Doerfer's] abilities are recognized nationally," said the *Sheboygan Press.*[65]

But if the commissioner's acceptance of industry favors was unacceptable to the Eisenhower Administration in 1960, which seems a reasonable conclusion since the President asked for his resignation, the question remains as to why his identical activities, revealed some two years earlier, were not equally unacceptable. The President's indulgent position in 1958 was especially remarkable when one considered that as a candidate in 1952 Eisenhower had advertised himself, not as a man with an ordinary sense of propriety and ethics, but as a veritable crusader for morality in government. He was a man who told the American people that "when corruption is discovered the faster and more firmly it is rooted out, the less likely it is to appear again."[66] Again, it seemed, the standards of propriety established by the candidate Dwight Eisenhower were quite different from those applied by him as President.

[65] *Ibid.,* pp. 2–4. On the second confirmation hearings, however, Edward Lamb did appear before the Senate Committee to oppose Doerfer's appointment to a full term. U.S., Congress, Senate, Committee on Interstate and Foreign Commerce, *Hearings, Nomination of John C. Doerfer to F.C.C.,* 83d Cong., 2d Sess., 1954. His testimony was to no avail, however, as the commissioner was confirmed for a full term without objection. U.S., *Congressional Record,* 83d Cong., 2d Sess., 1954, 100, Part 7, p. 9127.

[66] *Ibid.,* 83d Cong., 1st Sess., 1953, 99, Part 3, p. 3095.

Chapter 14

AS MAINE GOES . . .

As I look back, I was not sufficiently aware of the added impor-
tance that I might be giving to these inquiries by handling them
myself. A call or inquiry from the Assistant to the President was
much more liable to cause suspicion of interference than a call
from a less prominent White House staff executive, but I was not
alert to the fact at the time. If I had been, I might have saved
myself later embarrassment.

SHERMAN ADAMS

FOR NEARLY SIX YEARS—from Richard Nixon's secret political fund
through John Doerfer's expense account peccadillos—the Eisenhower Administration had been embroiled almost continuously
with conflict of interest cases. Significantly, it was against this
lurid background of repeated administrative improprieties that
the House Special Subcommittee on Legislative Oversight first became interested in Presidential Assistant Sherman Adams. It is
remarkable that a man of Adams' background and experience had
not been made aware of the fact that the Administration would be
placed in an exceedingly awkward position should his various dealings with Bernard Goldfine ever become public knowledge. Adams'
imperceptivity is especially amazing when one considers the fact that
many of the offending officials who had been forced to submit their
resignations had been guilty of misbehavior very similar to that
with which the Presidential Assistant was charged. President Eisenhower's initial reaction to *l'affaire Adams*, i.e., "I need him," was
perhaps less remarkable. Indeed, in the light of the previous cases,
his position might well have been anticipated. And now, to complete the drama.

Shortly after Adams' appearance before the subcommittee,
newsmen asked its chairman, Oren Harris, if he thought that the
Presidential Assistant should resign. "Mr. Adams will have to
search his own conscience and Mr. Eisenhower should do likewise,"

he answered. Only a few hours after Harris' remark, presumably with conscience thoroughly searched, Eisenhower responded. Predictably, the President gave his aide his complete and unqualified support. "The President still has full confidence in Adams," Hagerty told reporters.[1] "The Governor . . . is back at his desk at work at White House business."[2] Reaction within the Republican party to Adams' testimony, however, was mixed. Senate Minority Leader William Knowland said that most of the party leaders were still reserving judgment. John J. Williams, Republican Senator from Delaware, asserted that he could see little difference between the deep freezers under Truman and vicuña coats under Eisenhower. "Adams' resignation is in order," he concluded.[3]

And the *New York Herald Tribune*, long regarded as the official voice of the Republican party, also made herculean efforts to save Adams. Shortly after the first charges of impropriety were leveled against the Presidential Assistant, for example, the *Tribune* termed the whole affair nothing more than a "teapot tempest." What was incontestable, it editorialized, was the fact that Adams was "as flinty and incorruptible as a piece of New Hampshire granite."[4] A few days later the newspaper even attempted to transfer the innate righteousness of President Eisenhower to his assistant, a difficult and hazardous task in any case. "The heart of the matter is that Dwight Eisenhower had the faith, trust and affection of the American people," it said. "If the American people place such faith and trust in the President, he is entitled to ask them to place equal faith and trust in those whom he chooses. . . . No more needs to be said."[5]

Despite the editorial inanities of the *Tribune*, a good deal more was destined to be said about the "flinty and incorruptible" New Englander. Approximately two months after the *Tribune*'s ringing endorsement of the Presidential Assistant, a House armed services subcommittee released the transcript of its executive hearings of the previous month, held to investigate charges that Adams had intervened in an Army contract case.[6] The matter in question involved Raylaine Worsteds, Inc., a New Hampshire clothing manufacturer which had been penalized $50,000 for late delivery of 250,000 yards of olive-drab material to the Army in 1941. The company's appeal for a rebate, which initially amounted to $25,000 but

[1] William M. Blair, "Adams Denies Using His Influence," *New York Times*, June 18, 1958.

[2] "The Administration," *Time*, June 30, 1958, p. 12.

[3] Blair, *New York Times*, June 18, 1958.

[4] *New York Herald Tribune*, June 13, 1958.

[5] *Ibid.*, June 19, 1958.

[6] U.S., Congress, House, Subcommittee for Special Investigations of the Committee on Armed Services, *Report and Hearings, Raylaine Worsteds, Inc., Case Before Armed Services Board of Contract Appeals, No. 1842*, 85th Cong., 2d Sess., 1958.

was later raised to $40,000, was, over the years, rejected by the Comptroller General, the United States Court of Claims, and twice by the Armed Services Board of Contract Appeals. In a mood of final desperation, apparently, officers of the firm, including President Leo Wolff, Vice President George C. Lincoln, and Office Manager Allen Crew, wrote at least seven letters directly to Adams soliciting his aid. The letters, five of which began "Dear Sherm," variously requested Adams' "good offices," "interest," "intercession," and "weight" in the Raylaine case.[7]

In his responses—which incidentally began "Dear George"— to the earlier letters from Lincoln, Adams drafted rather routine replies giving the status of the case and assuring the Raylaine official that the Board of Contract Appeals would give his case careful consideration. A later letter to Adams, this one from Office Manager Crew, was not answered directly but was channeled through General Maxwell D. Taylor, Army Chief of Staff, to Colonel Robert C. Bard, a member of the Contract Appeals Board. Accompanying the Crew letter was a cover letter from Adams inquiring about the details of the Raylaine case. When the matter was brought to the attention of Bard's fellow board member Rosewell M. Austin, he, in his own words, "just blew up."[8]

Austin admitted to the members of the subcommittee that he had a low boiling point,[9] but was still of the opinion that the letter was highly improper. "The inference to me was," he said, "Look, Mr. Board of Contract Appeals, here is a letter I have gotten from my constituent who wants my help with you. Now what can I say to him?"[10] At that point Austin had dashed off a memorandum to fellow board members which stated, "Because of [the] intervention of Mr. Adams from the White House, and some congressmen, I understand that sentiment is growing to grant another oral hearing. Tho I deeply resent the intrusion, which I think is highly unethical, I am willing to 'go along' with another hearing."[11]

In April of 1957, the Contract Appeals Board reconsidered the Raylaine case and awarded the firm $40,382. Strangely, Austin, who was no longer a member of the board at the time of the reversal, insisted that Adams' intervention had had no effect on the board's final decision. "I think every member understood by that time what all of the issues were and what all of the pressures were," he testified, "and they acted, I think, independently and correctly."[12]

[7] "The Administration: More Imprudence?" *Newsweek*, August 18, 1958, pp. 26–27. See also Anthony Lewis, "House Unit Finds No Adams' Intent To Sway U.S. Board," *New York Times*, August 11, 1958.

[8] House Subcommittee for Special Investigations of the Committee on Armed Services, *Raylaine Worsteds, Inc., Report and Hearings*, 1958, p. 53.

[9] *Ibid.*, pp. 71, 79.

[10] *Ibid.*, p. 71.

[11] *Ibid.*, p. ix.

[12] *Ibid.*, p. 76.

Whether there was any intention on the part of Adams to influence the board's decision, however, was never completely resolved. The subcommittee's report, actually a rather brief and innocuous document, tended to give the assistant the benefit of the doubt. There was "no evidence," it reported, which indicated an "intent" on the part of Adams to use improper influence.[13] However, Chairman Hébert told reporters, "I'd say it's a Scotch verdict: not proven. We couldn't pass judgment on Mr. Adams' intent because Mr. Adams refused to testify."[14]

A number of factors combined, however, to take the pressure off Adams. From the outset of the controversy, of course, the President gave his aide his unqualified support. For example, when things seemed stickiest for Adams, he was given a prominent role in a White House ceremony in which retiring Atomic Energy Chairman Lewis Strauss was awarded the Medal of Freedom. Newsmen reported that such a move was calculated to evince the President's support of his assistant and, hopefully, to silence some of the criticism of Adams.[15] And quite by coincidence, the continuing crises in the Middle East, especially in Lebanon, and the intermittent bombardment of Quemoy and Matsu by the Chinese Communists in the Straits of Formosa, served to take much of the publicity away from the embattled Adams.

At the height of the controversy, it was discovered that in November, 1956, Eisenhower himself had accepted several yards of vicuña material from Goldfine and had, in fact, acknowledged the receipt of the gift in the form of a "thank you" letter to the Boston industrialist. Presidential Press Secretary James Hagerty conceded as much to a group of assembled newsmen on June 17, but insisted that the material had been given to a "friend" of the President. It had never been made up into a coat. However, the somewhat embarrassed Hagerty was unable to give the eager reporters the friend's name. It had, he said, slipped Eisenhower's mind. "But we're trying to find out."[16] By ordinary rules of politics, this revelation should have had a devastating impact upon the Republican Administration. But in this case it didn't. Apparently, most Americans regarded Eisenhower as a thoroughly moral man, a man incapable of misconduct. Thus, the very fact that he accepted a bit of vicuña cloth from Goldfine meant that it was perfectly proper to do so, and perhaps correct for Adams to receive other favors from the same source.

Even the activities of the Subcommittee on Legislative Oversight, which some charged had grown into something of a Franken-

[13] *Ibid.*, p. iii.
[14] Lewis, *New York Times,* August 11, 1958.
[15] *New York Times,* July 15, 1958.
[16] W. H. Lawrence, "Goldfine Sent Eisenhower a Gift of Vicuna Material," *New York Times,* June 18, 1958.

steinian monster, seemed designed at times to aid rather than to indict the Presidential Assistant. First, Chairman Harris decided to ignore the rule of the House which provided for executive sessions to take testimony which might "tend to defame, degrade, or incriminate any person,"[17] and to allow John Fox to testify publicly. He reached this decision, moreover, despite the fact that Goldfine's attorneys had revealed, in a letter to Harris, that Fox had been arrested in Pittsburgh, Pennsylvania, only two days previously on a criminal libel charge. The letter also charged that the same man had, in April, 1958, charged in open court that Goldfine had once admitted embezzling millions of dollars from the Boston Port Development Company. Yet, the attorneys stated that Fox was unable to produce a "scintilla of evidence" to substantiate his charge at a later hearing. "It is apparent that John Fox is an irresponsible and malicious individual who is bent upon maligning and defaming Mr. Goldfine by false and reckless accusations," the letter asserted.[18]

Fox was, to say the very least, an extremely controversial figure. He first began to gain national attention in 1952 when he purchased the *Boston Post*. He decided to purchase the long-time Democratic newspaper, he said, in order "to get the Communists, to the extent that I could help, out of the White House."[19] A few days before the elections that same fall, the *Post* scrapped its neutral position in the United States senatorial race in Massachusetts and came out strongly in support of John F. Kennedy, the Democratic candidate. Fox testified that he had been motivated solely by the fact that the incumbent, Republican Senator Henry Cabot Lodge, Jr., had been "soft on Communists for at least the past two or three years."[20] It was an established fact, however, that Fox received a loan of one-half million dollars from Joseph P. Kennedy, the candidate's father, shortly after the paper made its rather spectacular switch. Of course, many observers suspected that the two events were not completely unrelated.

Fox proved to be as flamboyant a witness as Goldfine's attorneys had feared. He charged, for example, that Goldfine had once told him that "those so-and-so's at the Federal Trade Commission are giving one of my mills and my son and some other people a hard time, and Governor Adams is going to take care of that for me."[21] On another occasion, Fox testified, Goldfine had told him that he "had nothing to worry about as far as the Securities Exchange Commission was concerned because Mr. Adams would make sure that nothing happened to him."[22] In the course of his three days of

[17] U.S., *House Rules*, Number 11, Section 25, Paragraph m.
[18] House Special Subcommittee on Legislative Oversight, *Regulatory Commission Hearings*, Part 11, 1958, p. 4090.
[19] *Ibid.*, p. 4131.
[20] *Ibid.*, pp. 4131–32.
[21] *Ibid.*, p. 4103.
[22] *Ibid.*, p. 4109.

testimony Fox also quoted Goldfine as saying that he had "helped Mr. Adams financially and very materially, especially when the Adams children were going to school,"[23] and, "he had bought interests in various ventures for Mr. Adams."[24] Still, virtually all of Fox's testimony was unsubstantiated, i.e., he simply quoted Goldfine as having said such and such about Adams. It was pure and simple hearsay and as such could not have been admitted as evidence against Adams in any court of law. In the last analysis, Fox's appearance seemed to bring discredit to both himself and the subcommittee and probably did Adams more good than harm.

Finally, early in July members of Goldfine's staff discovered that the subcommittee's chief investigator, Baron I. Shacklette, and columnist Drew Pearson's assistant, Jack Anderson, had placed a recording device in Goldfine's hotel suite. Later, Goldfine's secretary and bookkeeper, Mildred Paperman, charged that the hotel room had been burglarized and that various papers and records had been stolen.[25] The subcommittee quickly condemned Shacklette's tactics and forced his resignation. Still, the unfavorable publicity brought further discredit to the subcommittee and undoubtedly weakened its case against the Presidential Assistant. As one reporter put it, the bugging episode was "like the impact of the Marx brothers on a Shakespearian tragedy."[26]

But all hopes that Adams would be able to ride out the storm were dashed by the September general elections in Maine. It was uncontestable, of course, that the Republican party suffered a disastrous defeat there. For in the race for United States Senator, Edmund Muskie's victory over Republican incumbent Frederick Payne was so overwhelming that the Democratic gubernatorial candidate and two of the three Democratic candidates for the House of Representatives were swept in by the tide.[27] Moreover, the election had a very special bearing on the Adams controversy because the Presidentially endorsed Payne, like Adams, had allowed Goldfine to pay his hotel bills, lend him money, and give him a vicuña coat. Only a few weeks before the election, Payne had completely discounted the significance of his relationship with the Boston textile magnate. Indeed, he had once quipped to reporters that he had no idea what his vicuña coat was worth but said he found it "ideal" for the harsh New England winters.[28]

Since Maine held its election some two months before any of the other states, it had long been regarded as something of a polit-

[23] *Ibid.*, p. 4105.
[24] *Ibid.*, p. 4112.
[25] William M. Blair, "House Investigator Quits Inquiry," *New York Times,* July 8, 1958.
[26] *New York Times,* July 13, 1958.
[27] John H. Fenton, "Muskie Is Elected Maine Senator; Democrats Score," *New York Times,* September 9, 1958.
[28] Blair, *New York Times,* June 14, 1958.

ical barometer in the United States, although, in fact, Maine had long been a veritable bastion of Republican strength. Still, over the years Republicans had observed that if the party polled less than sixty percent of the Maine vote, it had little chance of winning control of Congress.[29] Thus, after the Grand Old Party received less than half of the Maine vote, no Republican candidate in the country could afford to take a cavalier attitude toward vicuña coats, oriental rugs, or hotel bills marked "Paid." Beleaguered Republican candidates from coast to coast renewed their demands for Adams' ouster.[30]

On the morning of September 22, an "unsmiling" Adams flew to Newport, Rhode Island, where he conferred for an hour and a quarter with the vacationing President Eisenhower. Significantly, upon leaving the President's chambers, the Presidential Assistant went directly to Hagerty's quarters where he conferred for an additional twenty-five minutes with the Presidential press secretary. The reporters, who had been rather hastily assembled and told to "be ready for anything," suspected that circumstances had finally forced the President's trusted aide to submit his resignation. Still, Hagerty flatly refused all that day to confirm their suspicions. "I have asked the radio and television networks to furnish time this evening for Sherman Adams to make a statement in connection with the controversy surrounding himself," Hagerty said. "Has he resigned, Jim?" shouted one anxious newsman. "All I have is the statement I have just read you," he answered.[31]

All doubts as to Adams' fate, however, were quickly dispelled by his radio and television address that evening. Speaking from a mock executive office which had been set up in one of the Washington studios of the Columbia Broadcasting Company, the stern Adams told the American people that he had tendered his resignation as Presidential Assistant. His decision was, he said, "final and unqualified" and was "not open to reconsideration." The resignation was to become effective, he said, "as soon as an orderly transition can be arranged for the assumption of my duties and responsibilities." Significantly, only moments before Adams went on the air Hagerty had discreetly removed one of the props, a copy of the book *The Happiest Man In The World,* which had been placed upon the huge desk by one of the studio technicians. Obviously, the President's alter ego, that evening, was anything but the happiest man in the world.[32]

[29] W. H. Lawrence, "G.O.P. Is Stunned by the Maine Result," *New York Times,* September 10, 1958.

[30] Lawrence, "Adams Must Go Move Renewed by Election," *New York Times,* September 14, 1958.

[31] *New York Times,* September 23, 1958.

[32] Russell Baker, "Sherman Adams Resigns," *New York Times,* September 23, 1958. For the text of Adams' address see *The New York Times* of that date.

It is particularly interesting to note that Adams refused that
evening to admit to the slightest impropriety. "I have done no
wrong," he stated categorically. Just why Adams chose at this
point to insist so adamantly upon his complete innocence is difficult to ascertain. Unquestionably, he was not without fault. He
had already conceded as much to the subcommittee, e.g., "If I had
the decisions now before me to make I believe I would have acted
a little more prudently."[33] In his memoirs he would admit, "As I
look back, I was not sufficiently aware of the added importance that
I might be giving to these inquiries by handling them myself."[34]
But on the evening of September 22, 1958, apparently by some
strange metamorphosis, the Presidential Assistant had become the
innocent victim of a "calculated and contrived effort" to discredit
him.

Adams insisted that his testimony before the subcommittee,
plus the testimony of what he termed "every responsible official"
called before it, had "clearly established" that he had "never influenced nor attempted to influence any case, decision or matter
whatsover." He argued, moreover, that in the subcommittee's attempt to make something of a plausible case against him, it had
chosen to receive "completely irresponsible testimony and, without
conscience, gave ear to rumor, innuendo and even unsubstantiated
gossip." Despite this proclaimed innocence, however, Adams conceded that his continuance in office might prove to be a serious
burden to President Eisenhower and the Republican party, especially in the coming congressional elections.

The reasons Adams gave for not resigning earlier were twofold.
First, he pointed out that it was against his very nature to run "in
the face of adversity." He had never done so, he said, in some
twenty years of public service. Second, and in a style slightly reminiscent of Vice President Nixon's "Checkers" speech, he pointed out
that he hated to sever his relationship with his beloved President.
"When a man has been afforded the privilege that has been mine
of serving a great American, a great humanitarian, and a great
President," the somber assistant told his radio and television lis-
teners, "when a man has come to understand the selflessness and the
dedication with which that President has served all of our people,
regardless of race, religious or political persuasion, it poses a decision . . . which is difficult in the extreme to make."[35]

The Presidential Assistant conveniently ignored the fact that
most of the "calculated and contrived effort" to dispose of him had

[33] House Special Subcommittee on Legislative Oversight, *Regulatory Commission Hearings*, Part 10, 1958, p. 3738.
[34] Sherman Adams, *First-Hand Report: The Story of the Eisenhower Administration* (New York: Harper and Brothers, 1961), p. 436.
[35] For a comparison between the Nixon and the Adams television perform-
ances see "The Teapot (Dome?) Tempest," *Nation*, June 28, 1958, p. 573.

come from within his own party.[36] In the last analysis, the Democrats would have been most pleased if Adams had remained, for he would have made a better campaign issue on the job than off. The various public utterances of the nation's leading Democrats indicated quite clearly, moreover, that they were thoroughly enjoying their unexpected opportunity to castigate the keeper of the Republican conscience. Their revenge was particularly sweet because Adams, perhaps more than any other administrative spokesman, had repeatedly made slashing attacks against corruption in the Truman Administration. Typical of these was his "Augean Stables" speech in 1952. According to Greek legend, it will be recalled, King Augeas kept 3,000 oxen in a stable which purportedly had not been cleaned in thirty years. Ultimately, however, Hercules cleaned the stable in a single day by diverting the Alpheus and Peneus rivers through it. Eisenhower, Adams implied in his speech, was to be the Hercules of the twentieth century; he would clean the Truman stable. "Here is the man to do it," Adams told the American people. "The kind of people with whom he has surrounded himself is answer enough to that."[37]

Thus, to discover that the New England moralist himself had committed a number of ethical peccadillos was comparable, as one New York newspaper put it, to witnessing "a prohibitionist falling on his face in the corner saloon." Ralph Yarborough, Democratic Senator from Texas, told reporters that Adams had not come to Washington on the "Goodship Mayflower." He had come on the "gravy train."[38] National Democratic Chairman Paul Butler could hardly conceal his delight when he suggested that the Republican party might initiate a television program called "The Price is Right."[39] But the ultimate in insults came from Major General Harry Vaughn, long regarded as the very symbol of corruption and decadence in the Truman Administration. Shortly after the Adams controversy began, Vaughn offered the Presidential Assistant the loan of his famous deep freezer so that he might protect his equally famous vicuña coat from the moths during the summer months.[40] Finally, former President Truman added a "sad" note. The government would be "in a bad fix," should Adams be forced to resign, he said. "He's running it, you know."[41]

Ultimately, however, Republicans rather than Democrats were responsible for Adams' fall from grace. In fact, this Republican

[36] "Exit Adams," *Time,* September 29, 1958, p. 12.
[37] *Time,* June 23, 1958, p. 13.
[38] Phillip Benjamin, "Adams Gifts Set Cliché Pot Aboil," *New York Times,* June 19, 1958.
[39] "More Furor Over Influence: What Adams Case Stirred Up," *U.S. News and World Report,* July 4, 1958, p. 50.
[40] Benjamin, *New York Times,* June 19, 1958.
[41] "The Ordeal of Sherman Adams," *Newsweek,* July 21, 1958, p. 18.

hostility toward Adams became so pronounced that it prompted Vice President Nixon to remark to a group of GOP state chairmen, "The trouble with Republicans is that when they get in trouble they start acting like a bunch of cannibals."[42] Some Republicans, of course, had simply insisted that Adams be governed by precisely the same rules of conduct that he himself had espoused for nearly half a dozen years. Admittedly, the ethical sensibilities of other Republicans had not been particularly upset until they had perused the Maine election returns, but whatever the motivation, following the fiasco there virtually all Republicans realized that the Presidential Assistant represented too great a burden for the party to carry. "I wish Adams would be booted out," asserted James Short, the Republican state chairman from Oregon. "It would make [the coming elections] easier for us." Glen Rhodes, Republican state chairman from South Dakota, told reporters sadly, "I've been going around for years making speeches about mink coats and deep freezes. Now I'm going to have to change my speeches. That [mess in Washington] issue is dead."[43]

The animosity toward Adams within the Republican party was particularly intensive among the Old Guard members, most of whom had never forgiven the Presidential Assistant for his anti-Taft activities both before and during the 1952 convention. "That sonofabitch [Adams]," complained one embittered conservative. "He was one of those who went down to Texas and planted that flag—'Thou Shalt Not Steal'—on Taft in the delegate vote fight in 1952. Now that he's got the same thing coming his way, nobody's going to defend him. He's got it coming to him."[44] In some respects these right-wing Republicans were the contemporary counterparts of the old French Bourbons, who reportedly "never forgot anything and never learned anything." Unquestionably their opposition to Adams was always unfailing and, in some instances, thoroughly vituperative. Emmet John Hughes was moved to remark to Adams the day the latter left the White House, "Well, the vultures of the Grand Old Party finally descended." Adams only shrugged and answered, "That's the great game of politics."[45]

Admittedly, however, not all of the enmity toward Adams came from the Right. A good deal of the Republican ill will could be traced, no doubt, to the assistant's rather cold, austere personality. Frequently, he dispersed with such formalities as "hello" and "goodby," and it was not uncommon for him to hang up on a telephone caller as soon as he had finished his remarks.[46] A story re-

[42] *Newsweek,* June 30, 1958, p. 19.
[43] *Ibid.,* p. 19.
[44] *Time,* June 30, 1958, p. 13.
[45] Emmet John Hughes, *The Ordeal of Power: A Political Memoir of the Eisenhower Years* (New York: Atheneum, 1963), p. 269.
[46] *Time,* June 30, 1958, p. 12.

lated by Representative John Saylor, a Pennsylvania congressman and a Republican, was typical. He told reporters that when he called upon Adams about a project in his district, the assistant announced in a curt fashion, "I'll give you just fifteen minutes." Adams then proceeded to turn his back on the bewildered congressman and stare out the window. "I walked out on him and I haven't been back since," Saylor said.[47]

Then, too, the nature of Adams' duties was hardly designed to ingratiate the assistant with his fellow Republicans in any case. Adams served, as one journalist so perceptively observed, as the President's "abominable no-man."[48] Furthermore, the assistant's area of responsibility was extremely broad. When a newsman once asked Eisenhower to describe his assistant's duties, he said, "If you will take the Constitution and all the laws of America and find out exactly what my duties are, you will find that, in some form, minor or major, he is involved in assisting me—that's his whole task."[49] Virtually all matters, both large and small, were first channeled through Adams. If the President were, by chance, personally contacted by some Republican favor-seeker, his response was invariably the same—"Clear it with Sherm." "Adams is the only man around here with status enough to say no and make it stick," one White House aide told reporters. "Every time I say no to a Senator, he says the hell with it and goes to Adams. When Adams says no, it does not get appealed."[50]

The magnitude of Adams' lack of support within the Republican ranks can fairly well be judged by the fact that *Life* and *Time* magazines ultimately called for his resignation.[51] *Time* pointed out, quite correctly, "If Adams applied his own rules, he could logically reach no other conclusion than that he should resign." However, this observation was preceded by *Time*'s predictable flight into fantasy. "If there was one Eisenhower accomplishment that Democrats and Republicans could agree on," said the magazine, "it was that a stern White House code—far tougher than the code of congressional politics that Harry Truman brought down the hill from the Senate—had erased the petty stains of mink coats, freezers and influence peddling." Apparently, the editors of *Time* had managed to erase completely from their minds the influence peddling charges which had previously been leveled against Richard Nixon, C. Wesley Roberts, Peter Strobel, Harold Talbott, Adolph Wenzell, Edward Mansure, Hugh Cross, Robert Ross, Richard Mack, and John Doerfer.

[47] *Newsweek*, June 30, 1958, p. 13.
[48] *Time*, June 23, 1958, p. 13.
[49] *New York Times*, June 19, 1958.
[50] *Time*, June 30, 1958, p. 12.
[51] "Adams and the Level of Principle," *Life*, June 23, 1958, p. 35. *Time*, June 23, 1958, p. 11.

In the letter accepting Adams' resignation, the President told his aide that he "deeply deplored the circumstances that have decided you to resign." But if he "deplored" the improprieties of his assistant, his letter, which was almost unbelievably laudatory under the circumstances, made no mention of it. "Your selfless and tireless devotion to the work of the White House and to me personally has been universally recognized," the President said. "Your total dedication to the nation's welfare has been of the highest order. Your performance has been brilliant; the public has been the beneficiary of your unselfish work." Almost as if to challenge the veracity of the Republican demands for Adams' ouster, Eisenhower assured his friend, "After six years of intimate association you have, as you have had throughout, my complete trust, confidence and respect." The resignation was accepted, but "with sadness."[52]

Shortly after his resignation, the White House social secretary told Adams that the President planned to honor him with a testimonial dinner. The dinner, she said, was to be followed by an evening of square dancing in the East Room of the White House. Why the President thought that his aide would enjoy an evening of gaiety, given the circumstances, is difficult to understand. Predictably, however, Adams opposed the plan. "I had no heart at that time for square dancing," he later wrote.[53] A few days later Eisenhower called his aide into his office and presented him with a sterling silver punch bowl. It was the gift the President had intended to present to Adams at the testimonial dinner. The inscription on the side of the huge bowl read, "To Sherman Adams, The Assistant to the President, 1953–1958. For tireless service to the public, brilliant performance of every duty and unsurpassed dedication to his country. From his devoted friend, Dwight D. Eisenhower."[54]

Even today it is unclear whether the President specifically requested Adams' resignation. Shortly after Adams made his radio and television statement, John L. Steele, chief of the Washington Bureau for *Time* and *Life* magazines, stated categorically that the President had dismissed his trusted aide. According to Steele's account, which has, incidentally, been widely accepted, Eisenhower decided to dismiss his assistant on August 28. It was on that date that National Chairman Meade Alcorn reported that his secret, closed-door survey had revealed that every single member of the Republican National Committee and Finance Committee favored Adams' ouster. Faced with this survey the President decided, "with the greatest reluctance," that his aide had to go. Describing the decision as the "hardest, most hurtful one" he had made as Presi-

[52] For the text of the President's letter to Adams, see *The New York Times*, September 23, 1958.

[53] Adams, *First-Hand Report*, p. 451.

[54] Dwight D. Eisenhower, *The White House Years: Waging Peace* (Garden City, New York: Doubleday and Company, Inc., 1965), p. 317.

dent, Eisenhower told Alcorn, "You've got to handle it. It's your job, the dirtiest job I could give you."[55]

Alcorn turned to this distasteful assignment on September 10, or some forty-eight hours after the Republican debacle in the Maine elections. Adams, who was vacationing at a remote fishing camp in New Brunswick, was asked to return at once to the nation's capital. When he returned to his White House office, the chairman told his friend and fellow Dartmouth graduate that the President had called for his resignation. Many of the party's more conservative benefactors, Adams was told, had refused to contribute as long as he remained. At that very moment, Alcorn pointed out, the House and Senate campaign chairmen Richard M. Simpson and Andrew F. Schoeppel were threatening to issue a public ultimatum to the President should Adams stay on as assistant. As Adams was a professional, it was obvious to him that no member of the team was worth such an open breach among Republicans. The case was closed. He agreed to submit his resignation.[56]

The accounts given by both Eisenhower and Adams in their separate memoirs differ fundamentally with the one given by Steele, however. In *First-Hand Report*, Adams states categorically, "The President did not ask me to resign and neither did Alcorn or the Vice President. That decision was left to me." Adams did concede, however, that both Alcorn and Gerald Morgan had told him that Eisenhower was "troubled" by the furor which the controversy had caused within the Republican ranks. As soon as he heard this, Adams wrote, he quickly decided to submit his resignation. "I would have done so long before then," he said, "if Eisenhower had not been so firmly opposed to my leaving his staff."[57] Eisenhower's recollection of the resignation, as set down in the second volume of his *The White House Years*, is in essential agreement with the one given by Adams. Eisenhower wrote that after the Maine elections, "I was convinced that there was nothing more that could be done to restore the Governor's former usefulness in the White House, and decided it would be best for him to resign, feeling sure that he would voluntarily conclude to do so."[58] According to Eisenhower, the following morning Adams called to say that he had decided to submit his resignation.

Nevertheless, the President's handling of the Adams affair must be regarded as a classic example of political ineptitude. The first indication that the Presidential Assistant had been guilty of indiscretions came in February, and by June anyone with the slightest degree of perceptivity could see that Adams had violated Eisen-

[55] John L. Steele, "How the Pros Shot Sherm Adams Down," *Life*, September 29, 1958, p. 28.
[56] *Ibid.*, p. 29.
[57] Adams, *First-Hand Report*, pp. 447–48.
[58] Eisenhower, *The White House Years: Waging Peace*, p. 316.

hower's proclaimed code of conduct. Yet, Adams was not dismissed. In fact, the President continued to insist that his aide had been guilty of but a slight imprudence and nothing more. Even the normally staid and conservative *New York Times* was moved to comment editorially shortly after Adams' departure that "both President Eisenhower and Mr. Adams ought to have recognized the impropriety of his position long ago; but through a curious form of astigmatism they do not seem to recognize it yet."[59]

In September, however, Eisenhower yielded to the demands of panic-stricken Republican candidates to oust Adams despite the fact that nothing of any real consequence had been disclosed between June and September to alter the essentials of the controversy. Thus, the President's belated decision to call for Adams' resignation made it appear that he had either yielded to an unholy pressure within his own party and dismissed an innocent man or had been willing, at least from June until September, to condone a double standard of conduct for his assistant. To many observers it appeared that the President had managed to dismiss his aide at precisely the wrong time for precisely the wrong reason. All in all, commented T.R.B. in *The New Republic,* it had been "a textbook illustration of how not to run politics."[60]

[59] *New York Times,* September 23, 1958.
[60] T.R.B., "Power in the Palace," *New Republic,* October 6, 1958, p. 2.

Chapter 15

HAIL TO THE CHIEF

Vice is a monster of so frightful mien
As to be hated, needs but to be seen;
Yet seen too often, familiar with her face,
We first endure, then pity, then embrace.

ALEXANDER POPE

IT SEEMS ONLY FAIR that President Eisenhower should shoulder
most of the responsibility for the moral deterioration of his Great
Crusade. Obviously, the style, the tone, indeed the very integrity
of an organization is shaped largely by its leader. It is shaped by
the caliber of his appointments; it is shaped by his specific direction of the organization; and it is shaped by his own personal behavior. Objectivity impels one to conclude that President Eisenhower failed—perhaps in differing degrees, but failed nonetheless—
to provide either the men, the direction, or the example so necessary
to establish that high degree of morality he sought for his Administration.

In the first place, the President exhibited an amazing propensity
to appoint men to high government positions who displayed a
poorly defined sense of public responsibility, men who exhibited an
almost uncanny inability to perceive the impropriety of activities
which ultimately led to their resignations. While most of these appointments were subject to Senate approval, it would seem unreal-
istic to expect this over-burdened body to have scrutinized President
Eisenhower's appointees more critically than it did those of previous
Presidents. Historically, the Senate has permitted the Chief Executive considerable freedom in choosing his subordinates, no matter
how ill-conceived their choices appeared to be. The *Congressional
Record* of June 16, 1958, reported, for example, that Senator John
F. Kennedy, hardly one to be accused of being an Eisenhower lackey,
had had 195,957 opportunities to oppose Eisenhower appointees
from 1953 through 1957. Yet, he failed to cast a single dissenting

vote in the period 1953 through 1956, and cast only three dissenting votes in 1957, when he opposed Jerome K. Kuykendall as chairman of the Federal Power Commission, Dr. Don Paarlberg as Assistant Secretary of Agriculture, and Scott McLeod as Ambassador to Ireland. And in these three instances, the men were approved by the Democrat-controlled Senate by overwhelming majorities.[1]

Some defenders argued that those who allegedly violated conflict of interest standards were guilty of nothing more than operating within the standards of ethics long accepted as proper by the American business community. It is correctly noted that the business community was not particularly incensed by these incidents of impropriety under President Eisenhower, although most failed to mention that this same group had not viewed the mink coat and deep freezer controversies under Truman with like equanimity. Clearly though, such a defense is vulnerable on at least two grounds. First, it is difficult to concede that the ethical standards governing American business had fallen so low as to regard such behavior from public officials as proper. Secondly, the view ignores the illustrious public service records of such former businessmen as David Lilienthal, Robert Lovett, Paul Hoffman, and Bernard Baruch, among others.

Even in the face of such defense, however, one retains a disquieting feeling about the business-oriented officials who served the Eisenhower Administration. The men who resigned under fire were not youngsters; they were middle-aged men, old enough and experienced enough to have developed some rather exacting standards for discerning right from wrong, propriety from impropriety, acceptable behavior from unacceptable. The record, however, made it all too clear that they had not. It was possible, of course, that these men had for so many years pursued and accumulated capital, or at least had been fascinated by and attracted to those who did, that their drive for materialistic acquisition had become a matter of habit, completely outside the framework of morality and ethics. Indeed, if one assumes that these men were neither scoundrels nor fools, and there is really little evidence to suggest that they were either, this may be the only plausible general explanation for their behavior.

In many respects, the attraction to wealth may have been the dominant motif of the Eisenhower Administration. Certainly, if a single interest governed America in recent times, this was it. Shortly after his appointment as Eisenhower's first Secretary of the Interior, Douglas McKay set the tone by remarking, "We're here in the saddle as an administration representing business and industry."[2] In a speech before the Joint Economic Committee, the

---

[1] U.S., *Congressional Record*, 85th Cong., 2d Sess., 1958, 104, Part 9, p. 11257.
[2] Quoted in Arthur Schlesinger, Jr., *Kennedy or Nixon: Does It Make Any Difference?* (New York: The Macmillan Company, 1960), p. 47.

President's chairman of the Council of Economic Advisers, Dr. Raymond J. Saulnier, went so far as to argue that "the ultimate purpose [of the American economy] is to produce more consumer goods. This is the goal. This is the object of everything that we are working at: to produce things for consumers."[3]

There were few scholars among the President's golfing, hunting, and bridge playing associates—few clergymen, few union leaders, and surprisingly few military men. Indeed, his social friends, like his political appointees, were drawn almost exclusively from the business community; they were invariably men who had met a payroll. Eisenhower's first Cabinet, which purportedly contained no less than nine millionaires, perhaps best exemplified the President's awe of the successful entrepreneur. The spectacle provoked Upton Sinclair to argue that such an attitude was not unusual with the "hillbilly," a term he used to denote all those raised of poor parents in the Southwest. "Eisenhower grew up to have a great awe of wealth and to think of a millionaire as the most wonderful of God's creations," Sinclair contended. "That is the dominating fact about his life—and about his administration."[4]

Nevertheless, Eisenhower might have established a rigorously ethical Administration if he had provided it with strong, bold leadership. Again, however, he failed. He failed simply because his deeds seldom matched his words. In part, the President's failure may be attributed to his obvious distaste for executive or administrative leadership. His disinterest was so pronounced as to provoke Clinton Rossiter, a noted authority on the American Presidency, to comment, "The plain truth is that Mr. Eisenhower was not especially interested in either the purposes or mechanics of most parts of the federal administration, and the first requisite of a successful administrator at the top of the pyramid is, surely, an unforced interest in what goes on below."[5]

It would seem no accident then that every conflict of interest case studied here was disclosed by either an enterprising reporter or a congressional committee. There was, in fact, little evidence to suggest that the investigatory apparatus of the executive branch was ever used to determine whether members of the "team" were complying with the leader's promise of the most exacting code of ethics ever invoked by a candidate for President. "If charges of corruption were ever made against anyone serving by your appointment, would you allow those charges to be stifled or buried? Would you wait eighteen months until someone forces the corruption into the open?" Eisenhower had asked a Miami audience in September, 1952. "You wouldn't wait eighteen minutes. Neither would I," he

[3] *Ibid.*, p. 48.

[4] Upton Sinclair, "Hillbilly Ike," *California Liberal*, January, 1960, p. 3.

[5] Clinton Rossiter, *The American Presidency* (New York: Harcourt, Brace and World, Inc., 1960), p. 166.

had answered.[6] In office, however, his performance belied his promise.

With all due charity, when the President faced the real, rather than the imagined, case of impropriety, he invariably operated under less than exacting standards. Indeed, it is no exaggeration to say that his reaction to the conflict of interest cases in his Administration ranged from neglect, through indifference, to outright applause for the alleged wrongdoers. Never did the President decry publicly the moral laxities of an appointee; never was an official publicly dismissed. Nixon had set the pattern in 1952. He was kept on the ticket, not because his actions were vindicated, but solely because he happened to be gifted in the field of theatrics. Observing Eisenhower's penchant for bold talk and meek action, James Reston quipped, "Both in golf and in politics, his back swing has always been better than his follow through."[7]

In the long run, however, Eisenhower's lack of administrative expertise was, perhaps, no more important in shaping the character of his Administration than was his failure to provide the official family with a personal example of irreproachable behavior. Despite the President's unsurpassed ability to moralize, the fact remains that during Eisenhower's Administration gifts poured into the White House and his Gettysburg farm—and were accepted—at rates which were unprecedented in the annals of American history.[8]

Clearly, gifts are not evils in and of themselves. The exchanging of gifts among nations and individuals is an established custom and is generally regarded as nothing more than a manifestation of one's friendship or respect for another. The United States itself gives gifts. And as Secretary of State John Foster Dulles properly observed, "If we thought all giving was an evil practice, then the first place to stop would be to stop ourselves."[9] The President may accept a gift from a foreign chief of state, not because of its inherent value, but because of the delicate questions of international relations involved. Few would charge, for example, that Presidents Jackson and Coolidge were motivated by a desire for personal gain when they accepted, respectively, a full-grown lion from Morocco and a huge hippopotamus from Liberia.[10]

The only restriction on the President's acceptance of such gifts, other than his own conscience, is the constitutional provision which states, "No person holding any office of profit or trust . . . shall, without the consent of the Congress, accept of any present, emolu-

[6] U.S., *Congressional Record*, 83d Cong., 1st Sess., 1953, 99, Part 3, p. 3095.
[7] Rossiter, *The American Presidency*, p. 163.
[8] "It's Christmas All the Time For U.S. Presidents," *U.S. News and World Report*, December 16, 1955, p. 39.
[9] "Once It Was Freezers and Mink Coats; Now—," *U.S. News and World Report*, November 8, 1957, p. 52.
[10] "It Is More Blessed," *Newsweek*, November 11, 1957, p. 45.

ment, office, or title, of any kind whatever, from any king, prince,
or foreign State."[11] An act of Congress, passed in 1881, provides
further that all such gifts be retained by the Department of State
until Congress specifically authorizes delivery.[12] An examination
of American history clearly reveals, however, that these restrictions
on gifts from foreign sources have not always been rigidly adhered
to. There are no restrictions at all on gifts from domestic sources.
Consequently, the standards governing presidential acceptance or
rejection of gifts have always been highly personalized and, as one
might expect, have varied from administration to administration.

However, the practice of the vast majority of Presidents, including Washington, Jefferson, John Quincy Adams, Polk, Andrew
Johnson, McKinley, Theodore Roosevelt, Wilson, Hoover, and
Kennedy, was to refuse all gifts which had a substantial value.
Gifts which had only a nominal value, e.g., books, canes, seeds,
socks, fruit, cigars, hats, etc., were generally accepted because they
could be regarded as mere tokens or symbols of respect or appreciation. The two most notable exceptions to this rule appear to be
Presidents Taft and Coolidge. On Taft's silver wedding anniversary
alone, for example, the President accepted gifts from over 300
donors. The list of the gifts, composed almost exclusively of pieces
of expensive silver, totaled some twenty-one typewritten pages.
Records indicate that Coolidge not only accepted most of the gifts
offered to him during his years in the White House but also, prudent
Yankee that he was, kept a careful record of all those received.
When he returned to his home in Vermont, most of the gifts went
with him.[13]

Still, the gifts accepted by Taft and Coolidge were insignificant
when compared with those received by President Eisenhower. According to a calculation made by *Newsweek* magazine less than
three years after his inauguration, the total value of gifts accepted
by the President had reached some $40,000.[14] By May, 1960,
columnist Drew Pearson asserted that the President had received
over $300,000 worth of machinery, livestock, and horticultural
goods for his Gettysburg farm alone.[15] Of course, the White House
never released any official figures on the value of these Presidential
gifts. Consequently, attempts to arrive at a total must be regarded
as estimates at best. Nonetheless, if either figure is approximately
correct, the extent of these Presidential gifts, which, incidentally,

[11] U.S., *Constitution*, Art. 1, sec. 9.
[12] 15 *U.S.C.* 115.
[13] U.S., *Congressional Record*, 85th Cong., 2d Sess., 1958, 104, Part 9, pp.
11254–55.
[14] "To The President With Very Best Wishes," *Newsweek*, December 12,
1955, p. 34.
[15] Drew Pearson, "The Washington Merry-Go-Round," *Benton* (Ill.) *Evening News*, May 23, 1960.

were not considered to be income and thus were tax free, was
certainly phenomenal. By any standard of conduct Eisenhower's
practice was questionable, while, by the standard he himself established in the campaign of 1952, his behavior was unpardonably
hypocritical. Surely, if Gresham's Law has validity in the field of
economics, it must have equal application in the field of morality.
Just as bad money tends to drive the good out of circulation, this
example of impropriety on the part of the President could do little
but lower the standards of conduct throughout the whole administrative structure.

Eisenhower failed to set any maximum whatsoever on the value
of a gift he might accept, although he made it a practice never to
accept money.[16] "I make this stipulation," he told reporters at a
press conference in August, 1957, "anything that is given me is
right out on the record. . . . I never accept gifts that I believe
have any [selfish] motive whatever behind them. . . . I merely try
to keep my relations with people on what I think is a friendly,
decent basis."[17] Slightly over two months later, the President remarked that in the last analysis "the problem should be decided
on the basis of good taste."[18] When one examines the White House
and Gettysburg gifts, assortments which included cattle, hogs, veni-
son, turkeys, chickens, hams, fish, lobsters, ducks, pheasants, cakes,
shoo-fly pies, peaches, strawberries, watermelons, and a half ton of
coffee from Emperor Haile Selassie of Ethiopia, one wonders in
what sense the words "good taste" had been used.

Indeed, about the only nonmonetary gifts reportedly rejected
by the President were a cat, a suit, and a deep freezer. Technically,
the cat, offered by the American Feline Society, was rejected by the
First Lady rather than by the President. It prompted one wit to
remark, "If they start accepting all kinds of cats and dogs, they
soon won't have room for the livestock." The suit, made by a leading manufacturer of summer clothing, was refused after Eisenhower
heard that the company planned to issue a news release and, thus,
"take the White House for a lot of free advertising."[19] The factors
which caused the President to reject the deep freezer are, of course,
too obvious to dwell upon at any length. Suffice it to say, however,
that no crusader worthy of his name would ever knowingly embrace the very symbol of decadence and corruption. However, an
examination of the rather formidable list of gifts which the President did accept for his Gettysburg holdings might cause one to
wonder if the farm's three deep freezers may not have constituted
one of Eisenhower's major financial outlays.[20]

[16] *Ibid.*
[17] *New York Times*, August 8, 1957.
[18] *Ibid.*, October 31, 1957.
[19] *U.S. News and World Report*, December 16, 1955, p. 41.
[20] Drew Pearson, "The Washington Merry-Go-Round," *Benton* (Ill.) *Evening News*, August 8, 1960. See also *ibid.*, February 23, 1961.

The farm land itself was almost completely landscaped with donations.[21] Included among these gifts were several hundred nut, apple, cherry, quince, and spruce trees and an almost countless variety of shrubs and bushes. In addition, the President accepted two complete flower gardens, a serpentine brick wall, an orchid-filled greenhouse, a $3,000 putting green with a $1,000 per year maintenance contract, and a thirty-foot flagpole. The President's renovated farm house also gained some lovely pieces via donations. Principal gifts from admiring individuals and organizations were a complete electric kitchen, twelve Chippendale chairs, a century-old fireplace with a marble mantlepiece, an antique sofa, a television set, a birch spice cupboard, 200 pieces of the finest sterling silver, twenty-six Royal Berlin porcelain plates heavily decorated with gold, and a silver bowl made by Paul Revere.

Most of the animals on the President's farm were also donated. Included among these gifts were several dozen registered Aberdeen Angus cattle, valued at up to $2,000 each, a number of prize Berkshire hogs, worth an estimated $500 each, a handsome quarter horse equipped with an expensive hand-tooled saddle, a black and white pony with wicker cart for the President's grandchildren, a variety of chickens, and some hunting dogs. The President did equally well in the area of farm machinery. A corn planter, a cultivator, a disk harrow, a side-delivery rake, and a $4,000 tractor were among the gifts to Eisenhower's burgeoning manor. The tractor, specially out-fitted with a cigarette lighter and FM radio, was one of the President's favorite gifts. When Eisenhower first saw the beautiful red and yellow machine he banged on the tire and exclaimed, "My golly this is lovely."[22] When the radio was turned on, however, the group in attendance was greeted by the raucous voice of a pitch-man who advised his listeners to "pick your suit right off the rack and save yourself some jack."[23] The crassness of the radio appeal seemed, somehow, not inappropriate under the circumstances.

Once the tractor had been carefully examined the happy President turned to his visitors saying, "Now let me show you something." The thing he wanted to show his guests proved to be yet another gift. Sitting in the open pasture was a jeep-styled Crosley golfmobile with a special fringed canopy on top. Of special interest, however, was the "Kattle-Kaller" which was mounted on the left-hand side of the steering column and which, when activated, made a

[21] The list of gifts accepted by President Eisenhower was compiled from the following sources: U.S., *Congressional Record*, 85th Cong., 2d Sess., 1958, 104, Part 9, pp. 11246–57; Drew Pearson, "The Washington Merry-Go-Round," *Harrisburg* (Ill.) *Daily Register*, October 20, 1955 and June 23, 1958; Drew Pearson, "The Washington Merry-Go-Round," *Benton* (Ill.) *Evening News*, February 23, 1961; *Newsweek*, December 12, 1955, pp. 34–35; "The First President Got the First Present," *U.S. News and World Report*, June 27, 1958, pp. 41–43.

[22] *Newsweek*, December 12, 1955, p. 35.

[23] Eric Sevareid, "Progress Is Getting out of Hand," *New Republic*, December 19, 1955, p. 5.

sound which was described by one reporter as a "melancholy moo-oo"[24] and by another as "like a bull."[25] But at any rate, CBS reporter Eric Sevareid announced, with an assumed seriousness, that when the President's secret service chauffeur pressed the Kat-tle-Kaller, the whole herd of Black Angus heifers galloped madly toward the tiny runabout, and two of the more aggressive ones actually tried to climb the fence separating the party from the cattle. The spectators were saved, Sevareid said, only because the fence happened to be constructed of chain links rather than the more traditional barbed wire.[26] One wonders if it were a gift, too. Of the performance, the President beamed, "They'll do it every time."[27]

Eisenhower justified his acceptance of these Gettysburg gifts on the theory that the people "want to build that up as a good looking place some day to be sort of a public property."[28] It was painfully obvious, moreover, that the news media accepted the President's explanation. The few segments of the American press which devoted some space to these presidential gifts, *U.S. News and World Report* being the most striking example, tended to treat the President's acceptance of them as perfectly proper. Their reaction was much like that of a White House official who told newsmen that the President could properly accept a gift valued at a thousand dollars, while a lower ranking official might properly be condemned for accepting as little as a twenty-five dollar ham, simply because "the office of the President is too big to influence by any gift."[29] Such a view caused one to wonder, of course, whether the office had, by some strange alchemy, grown since Truman was President.

The one real exception to the general journalistic apathy was, once again, columnist Drew Pearson, who seemed singularly bent upon maintaining his reputation as the nation's leading muckraker. For many Republicans, including Eisenhower himself, who was reported to have become livid upon reading some of the columns by the caustic journalist, Pearson seemed singularly bent upon maintaining his Truman-bestowed title of the "Washington S.O.B." Ignoring the question as to whether Pearson was, or was not, an S.O.B.—perhaps great journalists have to be S.O.B.s in the figurative sense—there is little doubt that in devoting his attention to this extremely touchy subject Pearson was following in the very best tradition of such muckraking journalists as Lincoln Steffens, Upton Sinclair, Mark Sullivan, and Ray Stannard Baker.

Pearson's most sensitive revelations concerned the rather strange manner in which the President's Gettysburg farm was

---

[24] *Newsweek,* December 12, 1955, p. 35.
[25] Sevareid, *New Republic,* December 19, 1955, p. 5.
[26] *Ibid.*
[27] *Newsweek,* December 12, 1955, p. 35.
[28] *New York Times,* August 8, 1957.
[29] *U.S. News and World Report,* December 16, 1955, p. 41.

financed during his years in the White House.[30]   In conjunction
with a reporter for the *York* (Pa.) *Gazette,* Arthur Geiselman, Pearson discovered that the farm was actually "leased" to three wealthy
oilmen: W. G. "Billy" Byars, an independent oil operator from
Texas; W. Alton Jones, president of Cities Service; and George E.
Allen, the President's Gettysburg neighbor and a director of nearly
two dozen corporations.   During the Eisenhower Presidency all of
the farm's expenses, including those for a great variety of permanent improvements, were paid for with checks drawn on a joint
account established by Byars and Allen in the Gettysburg National
Bank.   Although Jones's name never appeared on the joint account,
Pearson obtained correspondence which indicated that he always
paid an equal third of the farm expenses—which were, if one is to
accept Pearson's figures, nothing short of phenomenal.   The columnist estimated that the group sustained a net loss of a full half-
million dollars in the Gettysburg venture.

The fact that these three tycoons did not realize a profit was
not, in itself, particularly unusual.   What was unusual was the fact
that there was no evidence that the triumvirate ever made any serious attempt to make the venture pay.   Anybody interested in making money, for example, would hardly have been expected to spend
some $30,000 for a single "stall barn."   Yet, Victor Re, the con-
tractor who built the structure, freely admitted that he had been
paid that amount with a check from the Byars-Allen account.   When
questioned further about the seemingly exorbitant expenditures,
however, he told Pearson, "I ought not to be talking about other
people's business."[31]   Pearson discovered, moreover, that George
Allen claimed tax deductions each year for the "huge" losses he
suffered at Gettysburg.   When two tax agents questioned the industrialist about the deductions Allen told them, "This is the President's farm.   Question me about anything else in my tax returns.
But don't ask me to talk about the President's farm."[32]

No discussion of the Truman Administration would ever be
considered complete without some reference to the celebrated mink
coat scandal.   It seems only proper, therefore, to conclude this investigation of certain aspects of the Eisenhower Administration with
a reference to Mrs. Eisenhower's not so famous beaver coat.   The
story began when Maine trapper Jasper Haynes prevailed upon
Senator Margaret Chase Smith to ask the First Lady if she would
accept a beaver coat from the Maine trappers associations.   He was
worried, he said, because "ladies just weren't wearing beaver coats

[30] The Pearson columns which dealt with the financing of the Eisenhower
farm during his Presidency include: Drew Pearson, "The Washington Merry-
Go-Round," *The Benton* (Ill.) *Evening News,* January 13, 1961; *ibid.,* January
14, 1961; *ibid.,* February 23, 1961.
[31] *Ibid.,* January 13, 1961.
[32] *Ibid.,* February 23, 1961.

[at present]." Unfortunately, at least for Haynes and his fellow
Maine trappers, if not for the beavers, the initial offer was declined.
But then Jasper Haynes had a vision. "Last March I had a dream,"
he exclaimed. "I could see Mrs. Eisenhower very clearly. I heard
her say, 'I have reversed my decision. I will accept the coat.' "[33]

Solely on the basis of this dream, apparently, Haynes made
another appeal to Mrs. Eisenhower, which incidentally was in the
form of a personal letter written on Maine birch-bark, and begged
the First Lady to reconsider. Following this second plea, Mrs.
Eisenhower agreed to accept the "makings" of a coat, which in this
case proved to be seventeen prime beaver pelts, and later paid
$385 to have them made up into a three-quarter length garment.
An almost euphoric Haynes told reporters at the official unveiling
that such a coat would have retailed for at least $1,800. It was iron-
ic that the unveiling came in the same week that the State Department demoted deputy chief of protocol Victor Purse for allow-
ing his wife to accept an Oldsmobile convertible from King Saud
of Arabia. Purse had been guilty, according to the State Department, of "bad judgment."[34] When questioned about the Purse controversy at his press conference that week, Eisenhower said, "I know
that many members of this government have been offered automo-
biles, and I hear that the State Department is now wrestling with
one. Well, they will have to wrestle with it. I don't know exactly
what it is."[35] From the President's diction, one might conclude that
the automobile in question was a Stutz Bearcat rather than an
Oldsmobile.

Perhaps this comment is the key to an understanding of the
President's Great Crusade. For in the last analysis, Eisenhower did
not know exactly what public morality was either. Of course he
uttered the right words. Indeed, throughout his Administration he
remained dogged in his resolve to fight corruption and pontifical
in his public denunciations of it. Unfortunately, however, he
seemed almost completely oblivious to the numerous instances of
impropriety within his own official family. Acts, which if performed
by the Democrats would have produced the most sanctimonious
moral indignation in the Eisenhower camp, were accepted with
complacency so long as they did little or no damage to the Republican party or to the President's personal image. Nobody was ever
discharged, at least publicly, and even the resignations were invariably determined by popular reaction rather than moral principle.

Of course, the adulatory press continued to perpetuate the
myth that Eisenhower was the keeper of the nation's conscience
throughout his Administration, but a careful examination of the

---

[33] "Mamie and the Fur Trade," *Time*, November 11, 1957, p. 26.
[34] *New York Times*, October 29, 1957.
[35] *Ibid.*, October 31, 1957.

President's own flabby standards of propriety, and of his handling of the many conflict of interest cases during his eight years in office, indicated all too clearly that he had, at best, only a superficial understanding of the basic ingredients of public morality. The depth of his thinking on the problem can fairly well be judged by a remark he made on a visit to Washington's Mt. Vernon home in 1958. When the President came upon a ceremonial sword which had been given to the first President he turned to an aide and said, "Do you suppose they investigated him for getting that?"[36]

[36] *U.S. News and World Report,* June 27, 1958, p. 41.

Chapter 16

IT DIDN'T END WITH IKE

The next President himself must set the moral tone—and I refer not to his language but to his actions in office. For the Presidency, as Franklin Roosevelt observed, "is pre-eminently a place of moral leadership"—and I intend to restore that kind of leadership and atmosphere beginning in 1961.

JOHN F. KENNEDY

DESPITE the fact that Presidents Kennedy and Johnson issued the most exacting of codes governing conflict of interest,[1] each was forced to accept the resignation of a high administrative official following charges of improper conduct. Fred Korth, President Kennedy's Secretary of the Navy, resigned after it was revealed that he had used official Navy Department stationery, as well as the

---

[1] Exec. Order No. 10939, 26 *Fed. Reg.* 3951 (1961). On April 26, 1961, President Kennedy issued a most restrictive order concerning conflict of interest. Prepared by the United States Civil Service Commission and entitled "Employee Responsibilities and Conduct," it was circulated to all department and agency heads. A cover letter written by Frederick G. Dutton, Special Assistant to President Kennedy, stated, "Each department and agency head will be responsible to bring the proper minimum standards of conduct to the attention of all its employees." The code prohibited the disclosure of "official information"; prohibited the use of such information for private gain; prohibited all outside employment, including teaching, lecturing, and writing, if it "might reasonably result in a conflict of interest or an apparent conflict of interest"; prohibited the acceptance of gifts which might reasonably be interpreted as affecting one's impartiality; and prohibited the use of federal property for anything other than "officially approved activities." Civil Service Commission 5 *C.F.R.* 1001 (1961). See also *The New York Times*, July 27, 1961. Less than three weeks after President Johnson's Assistant Secretary of Commerce, Herbert W. Klotz, was forced to resign over a conflict of interest controversy, the Chief Executive broke new ground in the field by requiring that most top government officials file complete financial statements. Exec. Order No. 11222, 30 *Fed. Reg.* 6469 (1965). In a special statement, the President declared, "We cannot tolerate conflicts of interest or favoritism—or even conduct which gives the appearance that such actions are occurring—and it is our intention to see that this does not take place in the Federal Government." Charles Mohr, "Johnson Orders Top Aides To File Finance Reports," *New York Times*, May 10, 1965.

department's yacht *Sequoia*, in conducting private business. One letter, addressed to an officer of the Fort Worth, Texas, Continental National Bank, which Korth formerly headed and in which he still owned stock, stated, "I am . . . planning on September 20 to have a little party aboard the *Sequoia*, primarily for my Texas friends. . . . I am just wondering whether you . . . have some extra good customers that it would be nice to have." One of the persons who enjoyed this bit of Texas-in-Washington hospitality on the *Sequoia*, public relations man Phil Reagan, ultimately deposited $50,000 in the Continental Bank, where he said it would stay "until hell freezes over."[2]

A second and simultaneous controversy involving Secretary Korth concerned his connection with the highly controversial TFX aircraft contract which had been awarded to General Dynamics Corporation, located, coincidentally, in Fort Worth. Senator John McClellan's Permanent Subcommittee on Investigations, which conducted extensive hearings in 1963 and 1964 into the awarding of the TFX contract, raised the question of conflict of interest after it discovered that Korth had not disqualified himself from the contractual negotiations even though General Dynamics was located in his home community and Continental Bank had been one of twenty participants in a $200,000,000 loan to General Dynamics.[3] It was further revealed by the McClellan subcommittee that General Dynamic's bid on the Air Force-Navy fighter had been approximately $130,000,000 higher than one submitted by Boeing Aircraft, located in Belleview, Washington.[4]

Korth, whose lack of perception surely ranked with that of certain officials in the Eisenhower Administration, apparently saw nothing irregular in either his role in the TFX dispute or the letters concerning Continental National Bank. With some emotion, for example, he told Senator Karl Mundt, a member of the McClellan subcommittee, "I resent, sir, even your asking me what safe-

[2] "Turbulent Wake," *Newsweek*, November 4, 1963, p. 27. See also George C. Wilson, "Senate Probers Scrutinize Korth Letters," *Aviation Week and Space Technology*, October 28, 1963, pp. 22–24.

[3] U.S., Congress, Senate, Permanent Subcommittee on Investigations of the Committee on Government Operations, *Hearings, TFX Contract Investigation,* Part 7, 88th Cong., 1st Sess., 1963, pp. 1881–83. An investigation conducted by the Department of Justice later revealed that the amount of capital supplied by Continental Bank amounted to less than one percent of the total loan and concluded that no federal statute had been violated. Tom Wicker, "Korth Reported Asked To Resign for 'Indiscretion,' " *New York Times,* October 14, 1963. In an editorial of October 16, 1963, *The New York Times* termed Secretary Korth's testimony "less than distinguished" and stated, "Because of his association with a bank in Fort Worth, which participated in loans to the General Dynamics Convair plant in the same city, Mr. Korth should have disqualified himself from any participation in the award of a contract." *New York Times,* October 16, 1963.

[4] Senate Permanent Subcommittee on Investigations, *TFX Hearings,* Part 7, 1963, pp. 1850–51.

guards I might have taken to be an honest man [in the TFX nego-
tiations]. . . . I repeat that I believe that I am a man of integrity.
If you find or this committee finds that I am not, certainly you
should so recommend to the President and I will promptly hand in
my resignation."[5] And even after admitting to reporters that his
letters indicated that he had retained "an interest in the welfare of
the [Continental] bank" he heatedly denied that any "of these instances in any way involved my official responsibilities" and added,
"I deeply resent any insinuation that these few trivial incidents and
communications raise a question concerning my character."[6]

Still, the circumstances surrounding the abrupt resignation, or
dismissal, of Secretary Korth remained muddled at best. The ven-
erable columnist Arthur Krock of *The New York Times* asserted
categorically that as soon as President Kennedy heard of his Secretary's indiscretions, he sent word to him that a resignation was in
order.[7] The evidence suggests that this may well have been the
case. However, the Administration appeared extremely reluctant
to discuss the details of the case with newsmen, although one
spokesman did offer the opinion that Korth would "fit better" in
private life than in government service. Still the Secretary's insistence that he had resigned "so that I may return to private business and attend to my private affairs" was never publically rejected
by the Administration.[8] Then, too, though President Kennedy accepted the Secretary's resignation with unusual speed and omitted
his customary regrets, he nonetheless thanked Korth warmly for
"all you have done to advance our national defense."[9]

Thus, President Kennedy would hardly qualify for a chapter
in *Profiles in Courage* as a result of his public stance in the Korth
case.[10] It was hardly edifying, for example, for the Administration
to say simply that the official had done nothing illegal. Few people

[5] *Ibid.*, p. 1881.

[6] "The Administration: Anchors Aweigh," *Time*, October 25, 1963, p. 25.

[7] Arthur Krock, "The Korth Case," *New York Times*, November 3, 1963.

[8] Tom Wicker, "Korth Quits Post as Head of Navy," *New York Times*,
October 15, 1963. See also "The Pentagon: With Uncommon Speed," *Newsweek*, October 28, 1963, p. 22.

[9] Wicker, *New York Times*, October 15, 1963. In his press conference of
October 31, 1963, President Kennedy told reporters that although he "had no
evidence that Mr. Korth acted in any way improper in the TFX matter," he
pointed out that that had "nothing to do with any opinion I may have about
whether Mr. Korth might have written more letters and been busier than he
should have been in one way or another." *New York Times*, November 1, 1963.

[10] Following the Korth resignation, Republican Congressman H. R. Gross of
Iowa asked on the floor of Congress, "What has happened to the Kennedy *Profiles in Courage?* What has happened with respect to his bold and reassuring
words as spoken when he was a candidate for the Presidency; when, for political
purposes, he was pointing a finger at the Eisenhower Administration and the
Sherman Adams-Goldfine episode?" U.S., *Congressional Record*, 88th Cong.,
1st Sess., 1963, 109, Part 16, p. 21033.

had contended that Korth was a crook or a scoundrel—that he had broken either a Federal law or an administrative regulation. What the Secretary had displayed, however, was something decidedly less than the exacting code of ethical behavior that candidate Kennedy had promised the American public. Legality aside, it was behavior, as James Reston perceived, which was "morally insensitive and stupid."[11] Finally, it was behavior which clearly has come to be regarded as unacceptable by contemporary standards.

President Johnson's single conflict of interest dispute involved Assistant Secretary of Commerce Herbert W. Klotz. It stemmed from a suit filed by the Securities and Exchange Commission against the Texas Gulf Sulphur Company and twelve of its officers, directors, and employees for making illegal use of inside information for personal gain.[12] Specifically, the SEC accused the officers of purchasing, or taking options to purchase, over 45,000 shares of Texas Gulf stock while at the same time withholding or giving misleading information to the general public concerning the company's discovery of a two-billion dollar zinc, copper, and silver deposit near Timmins, Ontario. After a core sample of November, 1963, indicated the possibility of a metal bonanza the company had, for example, moved its drilling rig, planted the drill site with trees, and left a worthless core sample behind. Moreover, after *The New York Times* of April 11, 1965, reported on the "sensational" copper strike near Timmins, a Texas Gulf press release termed the report "unreliable" and maintained, "Any statement as to the

[11] James Reston, "Who Will Dare Investigate The Investigators?" *New York Times,* November 1, 1963.

[12] On August 19, 1966, the Federal District Court for the Southern District of New York dismissed the complaint against the company and ten of the officials. Two of the defendants, engineer Richard H. Clayton and secretary David M. Crawford, were found to have violated Section 10 (b) of the Securities and Exchange Act of 1934 and Rule 10b-5 of the Securities and Exchange Commission. Securities and Exchange Commission v. Texas Gulf Sulfur Company, 258 F. Supp. 262 (S.D. New York 1966). Section 10 (b) of the Securities and Exchange Act provides, "To use or employ, in connection with the purchase or sale of any security registered on a national securities exchange or any security not so registered, any manipulative or deceptive device or contrivance in contravention of such rules and regulations as the Commission may prescribe as necessary or appropriate in the public interest or for the protection of investors." 15 *U.S.C.* 78. Rule 10b-5 of the Securities and Exchange Commission provides, "It shall be unlawful for any person, directly or indirectly, by the use of any means or instrumentality of interstate commerce, or of the mails, or of any facility of any national securities exchange, (1) to employ any device, scheme, or artifice to defraud, (2) to make any untrue statement of a material fact or to omit to state a material fact necessary in order to make the statements made, in the light of the circumstances under which they were made, not misleading, or (3) to engage in any act, practice, or course of business which operates or would operate as a fraud or deceit upon any person, in connection with the purchase or sale of any security." 17 *C.F.R.* 240 (1951).

size and grade of ore would be premature and probably misleading."[13]

Assistant Secretary Klotz, who was not one of the defendants
in the case and whose name was not mentioned until page fourteen
of the SEC complaint, was listed as one of the ten persons who
benefited as a result of tips from insiders.[14] Specifically, Klotz received his tip on the Gulf Sulfur stock from Miss Nancy Atkinson,
described by *Newsweek* as "a vivacious thirty-four year old divor-
cee," who formerly worked in the Department of Commerce.[15] Miss
Atkinson had, in turn, received her tip from Kenneth Darke, one
of the Texas Gulf geologists who had participated in the Canadian
explorations and who was a "long time family friend" of Miss
Atkinson.[16] Although Klotz readily admitted that Miss Atkinson
had mentioned to him that the company's prospects looked "very
good," he insisted that she had given him no "specific information"
on the ore discovery. After watching the market for a time, however, the assistant secretary acted on the tip and took out an option
to buy 2000 shares of Texas Sulfur stock.[17]

Klotz estimated that he cleared $14,600 on his 2000 shares of
stock, but this proved an extremely deceptive figure inasmuch as
the assistant secretary had calculated it on the basis of the stock's
increase in value from the time he purchased the options—when the
stock sold for $29.70 per share—until the day of the announcement
of the ore discovery on April 16, 1964, when the stock jumped to
$37.00 per share. Following the company's press release, the stock
very quickly went to slightly over $70.00 per share.[18] Thus, as

[13] *New York Times*, April 11, 1964. See also "Wall Street: A Sulphurous
Scandal," *Newsweek*, May 3, 1965, p. 69; "Wall Street: On the Inside Track,"
Time, April 30, 1965, p. 96. On April 16, 1964, the officials of Texas Gulf Sul-
fur announced to their stockholders, meeting at the plush Houston Club in
Houston, Texas, that a major ore deposit had been discovered in Timmins,
Ontario. *New York Times*, April 17, 1964. For an interesting analysis of the
controversy see "Texas Gulf Suit Opens New Door for SEC," *Business Week*,
April 24, 1968, pp. 24–25. Chris Welles, "Bonanza Trouble," *Life*, August 6,
1965, pp. 29–30, 32, 34, 37.
[14] Eileen Shanahan, "SEC Insider Suit Names Texas Gulf Aides," *New York
Times*, April 20, 1965. In the SEC complaint the secretary was identified only
as Herbert W. Klotz, a resident of McLean, Virginia. Department of Commerce
officials later confirmed the fact that the man mentioned in the complaint was
the Assistant Secretary of Commerce. Eileen Shanahan, "Aide Resigns in Wake
of Suit by SEC," *New York Times*, April 23, 1965. According to at least one reporter, Louis M. Kohlmeier of *The Wall Street Journal*, the members of the
commission had been concerned about the propriety of listing the ten names
inasmuch as none had been charged with violating Federal law. Indeed, Mr.
Kohlmeier reported that following the assistant secretary's resignation there
was "a resurgence of feeling inside the SEC that Mr. Klotz shouldn't have been
named in the complaint against Texas Gulf." Louis M. Kohlmeier, "The Klotz
Affair: Impact on Capital," *Wall Street Journal*, April 27, 1965.
[15] *Newsweek*, May 3, 1965, p. 69.
[16] Eileen Shanahan, "U.S. Official in Texas Gulf Deal Denies He Had
Specific Details," *New York Times*, April 21, 1965.
[17] *Ibid.*, p. 63.
[18] *Ibid.*, pp. 63, 65.

generous as the Klotz profit appeared to be, it was but a small portion of the return he ultimately derived from his investment. Indeed, the assistant secretary himself appeared somewhat taken aback by his windfall. He told one *Newsweek* reporter, "You know how it is, I took a flyer and was amazed to find myself the beneficiary of such a big rise."[19] He insisted, however, he had done no wrong because the purchase of the private stock was in no way connected with his official responsibilities in the Department of Commerce. "In my official capacity with the Department of Commerce I have never had nor could be expected to have any dealings with the Texas Gulf Sulfur Company or its officials," he said.[20] "I got a stock tip pure and simple like you'd hear in a barbershop."[21]

The specific circumstances surrounding the Klotz dismissal, if indeed it was a dismissal, remained as unclear as those in the Korth case. One fact, however, was perfectly clear. Seventy-two hours after the Securities and Exchange Commission filed its suit in the District Court, Herbert W. Klotz was no longer a public employee. It is also true that virtually all of the news media assumed, and in many instances stated categorically, that the resignation had been demanded by President Johnson himself. Indeed, *The New York Times* reported that the President had "berated" one or more members of the commission over the telephone for not having kept him fully informed about possible indiscretions by members of his Administration. The implication seemed clear that, had the President known of Klotz's stock market transactions, he would have removed him at an earlier date.[22]

Still, like President Kennedy in the Korth case, President Johnson's words failed to match his deeds. First of all, Secretary of Commerce John T. Connor, rather than the White House, announced Klotz's resignation. This was, according to *The New York Times,* an "unusual procedure" inasmuch as Klotz was a member of the President's subcabinet. Moreover, the terse note by Secretary Connor to the gathered newsmen stated simply that "Assistant Secretary Herbert W. Klotz has submitted his resignation and . . . it has been accepted by the President."[23] Following this announce-

[19] *Newsweek,* May 3, 1965, p. 70.

[20] Shanahan, *New York Times,* April 21, 1965.

[21] *Time,* April 30, 1965, p. 96.

[22] Shanahan, *New York Times,* April 23, 1965. The President, according to some reports, called SEC Chairman Manuel F. Cohen, who was home recuperating from a recent heart attack. There was some confusion, however, as to whether the President actually "berated" the commissioner or whether he simply requested additional information on the case. Some people, notably Congressman J. Arthur Younger of California and reporter Louis M. Kohlmeier of *The Wall Street Journal,* questioned the propriety of the President calling a member of a supposedly independent regulatory commission in any case. U.S., *Congressional Record,* 89th Cong., 1st Sess., 1965, 109, Part 7, p. 9174. See also Kohlmeier, *Wall Street Journal,* April 27, 1965.

[23] Shanahan, *New York Times,* April 23, 1965.

ment, the White House appeared to be "at pains" to disassociate itself from the whole affair. Presidential Press Secretary George Reedy, for example, told newsmen that although neither the President nor any of his aides had asked for the assistant secretary's resignation, he "did not know" whether Secretary Connor had done so.[24]

The exchange of letters between President Johnson and Klotz was similar to those exchanged between President Kennedy and Secretary Korth. Klotz, who continued to maintain "that my conscience is clear and I am satisfied that I have not violated the public trust," told the President that he was submitting his resignation solely because "the variety of interpretations of my involvement [in the SEC case] has made it obvious to me that I must fight the battle of the innuendoes and under all circumstances avoid any possible embarrassment to you and the Federal Government." In accepting the resignation, the President told Klotz that Secretary Connor had "spoken warmly of your contributions" and added his own personal appreciation "for the fine work you have performed."[25]

In examining the Korth and Klotz cases, it is striking how much these two men behaved as the public officials who were forced to leave the Eisenhower Administration. In view of the publicity given those prior controversies, it is somewhat surprising that even so few as two high officials were unable to discern the difference between acceptable and unacceptable behavior for the contemporary public official. However, given the rather stern ethical standards expressed by Presidential candidates Kennedy and Johnson, it may be even more surprising that these Democratic Presidents behaved much like their Republican predecessor when faced with actual examples of misconduct in their official families. Certainly the posture of both Kennedy and Johnson indicated the wisdom, once again, of Arthur Krock's dictum, "The stern ethical attitude of Presidential candidates is prone to undergo a softening process when they enter the White House."[26]

Still, a measure of satisfaction can be derived from the fact that both the Kennedy and Johnson Administrations were relatively free of a phenomenon which had plagued both the Truman and Eisenhower Administrations. Moreover, an examination of the past eight years reveals, beyond doubt, that the overwhelming majority of public officials have learned the story of Caesar's wife, that they know perfectly well that their behavior must be free of even

[24] Charles Mohr, "Johnson Accepts Klotz Resignation, Praises His Work," *New York Times*, April 24, 1965. Given the nature of the President's personality, it would appear highly unlikely that any cabinet officer would take it upon himself to dismiss a member of the subcabinet.
[25] *Ibid.*
[26] Krock, *New York Times*, November 3, 1963.

the suspicion of guilt—that for the contemporary public official at least, the *appearance* of things is tantamount to the *reality* of things. When it was revealed that Secretaries Korth and Klotz had failed to comprehend this elementary fact, there was no outcry from their fellow Democrats or from their fellow public officials. There was no protest that these two public spirited servants had been abused. On the contrary, their behavior was generally regarded for what it was—foolish, unethical, and unacceptable. It has not been many years since the cliché, "steal a bottle of milk and go to jail; steal a railroad and go to Washington," was a popular dictum. Today, it seems clear that people who steal railroads do not go to Washington. It appears equally clear, moreover, that public servants today who so much as accept a railroad ticket from a questionable source cannot even stay in Washington, at least in government service. And that, by any definition, is progress.

BIBLIOGRAPHY

GOVERNMENT PUBLICATIONS

Code of Federal Regulations.
Congressional Record.
Decisions of the Comptroller General of the United States.
Federal Register.
Federal Trade Commission Decisions.
General Statutes of Kansas.
Kansas Senate Journal.
Official Opinions of the Attorneys General of the United States.
United States Code.
U. S. Congress, House. Antitrust Subcommittee of the Committee on the Judiciary. *Hearings, Activities of Peter Strobel.* 84th Cong., 1st Sess. Washington: Government Printing Office, 1955.
U. S. Congress, House. Antitrust Subcommittee of the Committee on the Judiciary. *Report Pursuant to H. Res. 22.* 84th Cong., 1st Sess. Washington: Government Printing Office, 1956.
U. S. Congress, House. Committee on Government Operations. *Availability of Information From Federal Departments and Agencies.* House Report No. 2947. 84th Cong., 2d Sess. Washington: Government Printing Office, 1956.
U. S. Congress, House. Committee on Government Operations. *Inquiry Into the Expansion and Operation by General Services Administration of the Government Nickel Plant at Nicaro, Cuba.* House Report No. 2390. 84th Cong., 2d Sess. Washington: Government Printing Office, 1956.
U. S. Congress, House. Committee on Government Operations. *Military Clothing Procurement.* House Report No. 1168. 85th Cong., 1st Sess. Washington: Government Printing Office, 1957.

U. S. Congress, House. Select Committee on Expenditures in the War Department. *Expenditures in the War Department–Aviation.* Report No. 637. 66th Cong., 2d Sess. Washington: Government Printing Office, 1920.

U. S. Congress, House. Special Government Activities Subcommittee of the Committee on Government Operations. *Hearings, Inquiry Into the Expansion and Operation By General Services Administration of the Government Nickel Plant at Nicaro, Cuba.* 84th Cong., 2d Sess. Washington: Government Printing Office, 1956.

U.S. Congress, House. Special Subcommittee on Legislative Oversight. *Hearings, Investigation of Regulatory Commissions and Agencies.* Parts 1–13. 85th Cong., 2d Sess. Washington: Government Printing Office, 1958.

U. S. Congress, House. Special Subcommtitee on Legislative Oversight. *Hearings, Responsibilities of Broadcasting Licensees and Station Personnel.* Part 1. 86th Cong., 2d Sess. Washington: Government Printing Office, 1960.

U. S. Congress, House. Special Subcommittee on Legislative Oversight. *Independent Regulatory Commissions.* Report No. 2711. 85th Cong., 2d Sess. Washington: Government Printing Office, 1958.

U. S. Congress, House. Subcommittee of the Committee on Armed Services. *Report and Hearings, Raylaine Worsteds, Inc., Case Before Armed Services Board of Contract Appeals,* No. 1842. 85th Cong., 2d Sess. Washington: Government Printing Office, 1958.

U. S. Congress, House. Subcommittee of the Committee on Expenditures in the Executive Departments. *Hearings, Inquiry Into the Procurement of Automotive Spare Parts by the United States Government.* 82d Cong., 1st Sess. Washington: Government Printing Office, 1951.

U. S. Congress, House. Subcommittee of the Committee on Government Operations. *Hearings, Military Clothing Procurement.* 85th Cong., 1st Sess. Washington: Government Printing Office, 1957.

U. S. Congress, Senate. *Administrative Procedures in Government Agencies.* The Attorney General's Report of the Committee on Administrative Procedures. 77th Cong., 1st Sess. Senate Doc. 8. Washington: Government Printing Office, 1941.

U. S. Congress, Senate. Committee on Armed Services. *Hearings, Nomination of Harold E. Talbott, To Be Secretary of the Air Force.* Part 4. 83d Cong., 1st Sess. Washington: Government Printing Office, 1953.

U. S. Congress, Senate. Committee on Interstate and Foreign Commerce. *Hearings, Nomination of John C. Doerfer To Be a Member of the F.C.C.* 83d Cong., 1st Sess. Washington: Government Printing Office, 1953.

U. S. Congress, Senate. Committee on Interstate and Foreign Commerce. *Hearings, Nomination of John C. Doerfer to F.C.C.* 83d Cong., 2d Sess. Washington: Government Printing Office, 1954.

U. S. Congress, Senate-House. Joint Committee on Atomic Energy. *Hearings, Utility Contract Between Atomic Energy Commission and Mississippi Valley Generating Company.* 83d Cong., 2d Sess. Washington: Government Printing Office, 1954.

U. S. Congress, Senate-House. Joint Committee on Atomic Energy. *Hear-*

ings, S. 3323 and H.R. 8862, To Amend the Atomic Energy Act of 1946. Parts 1 and 2. 83d Cong., 2d Sess. Washington: Government Printing Office, 1954.

U. S. Congress, Senate. Permanent Subcommittee on Investigations of the Committee on Government Operations. *American Lithofold Corp., William M. Boyle, Jr., Guy George Gabrielson.* Report No. 1142. 82d Cong., 2d Sess. Washington: Government Printing Office, 1952.

U. S. Congress, Senate. Permanent Subcommittee on Investigations of the Committee on Government Operations. *Hearings, Harold E. Talbott—Secretary of the Air Force.* 84th Cong., 1st Sess. Washington: Government Printing Office, 1955.

U. S. Congress, Senate. Permanent Subcommittee on Investigations of the Committee on Government Operations. *Hearings, Hugh W. Cross—Chairman of the Interstate Commerce Commission.* 84th Cong., 2d Sess. Washington: Government Printing Office, 1955.

U. S. Congress, Senate. Permanent Subcommittee on Investigations of the Committee on Government Operations. *Hearings, TFX Contract Investigation.* Parts 1–10. 88th Cong., 1st Sess. Washington: Government Printing Office, 1963–64.

U. S. Congress, Senate. Permanent Subcommittee on Investigations of the Committee on Government Operations. *Textile Procurement in the Military Services.* Report No. 1166. 85th Cong., 1st Sess. Washington: Government Printing Office, 1957.

U. S. Congress, Senate. Report of the Subcommittee of the Committee on Labor and Public Welfare. *Ethical Standards in Government.* 82d Cong., 1st Sess. Washington: Government Printing Office, 1951.

U. S. Congress, Senate. Subcommittee of the Committee on Military Affairs. *Aircraft Production in the United States.* Report No. 555. 65th Cong., 2d Sess. Washington: Government Printing Office, 1918.

U. S. Congress, Senate. Subcommittee on Antitrust and Monopoly of the Committee on the Judiciary. *Hearings, Power Policy: Dixon-Yates Contract.* Parts 1 and 2. 83d Cong., 2d Sess. Washington: Government Printing Office, 1954.

U. S. Congress, Senate. Subcommittee on Antitrust and Monopoly of the Committee on the Judiciary. *Hearings, Power Policy: Dixon-Yates Contract.* 84th Cong., 1st Sess. Washington: Government Printing Office, 1955.

U. S. Congress, Senate. Subcommittee on Antitrust and Monopoly of the Committee on the Judiciary. *Power Policy: Dixon-Yates Contract.* Staff Report Pursuant to S. Res. 61 as Extended by S. Res. 170. 84th Cong., 2d Sess. Washington: Government Printing Office, 1956.

U. S. Congress, Senate. Subcommittee To Study Senate Concurrent Resolution 21 of the Committee on Labor and Public Welfare. *Hearings, Establishment of a Commission on Ethics in Government.* 82d Cong., 1st Sess. Washington: Government Printing Office, 1951.

United States Constitution.

United States Statutes at Large.

TABLE OF CASES

Ames v. Board of Education, 97 N.J. Eq. 60 (1925).
Dayton Airplane Company v. United States, 21 Fed. 2n 675 (1922).

Harrison v. Elizabeth, 70 N.J.L. 591 (1904).
Humphrey's Executor v. United States, 295 U.S. 602 (1935).
Lopez v. United States, 373 U.S. 427 (1963).
McElhinney v. Superior, 37 Neb. 744 (1891).
Mississippi Valley Generating Company v. United States, 147 Ct. Cl. 1
    (1959).
Nuckols v. Lyle, 8 Idaho 589 (1902).
On Lee v. United States, 43 U.S. 747 (1952).
Rankin v. United States, 98 Ct. Cl. 357 (1943).
Securities and Exchange Commission v. Texas Gulf Sulfur Company, 258
    F. Supp. 262 (S.D. New York 1966).
Sturr v. Borough of Elmer, 75 N.J.L. 443 (1907).
United States v. Mississippi Valley Generating Company, 364 U.S. 520
    (1961).
Wiener v. United States, 357 U.S. 349 (1958).
Woodward v. Wakefield, 236 Mich. 417 (1926).

ARTICLES

"The ABC's of Dixon-Yates." *U.S. News and World Report,* November
    19, 1954: 27–29.
"The Accuser." *Newsweek,* February 24, 1958: 25–26.
"Accuser Accused." *Newsweek,* February 17, 1958: 30.
"The Acquittal." *Time,* October 6, 1952: 21–22.
"Adams and the Level of Principle." *Life,* June 23, 1958: 35.
"The Adams Case." *Newsweek,* June 23, 1958: 23–26.
"The Administration: Anchors Aweigh." *Time,* October 25, 1963: 25.
"The Administration: More Imprudence?" *Newsweek,* August 18, 1958:
    26–27.
"The Administration: Pants Too Long?" *Time,* January 21, 1957: 14.
"The Administration." *Time,* June 30, 1958: 9–13.
"The Affair Nixon." *Commonweal,* October 3, 1952: 620–21.
"Air Secretary Quarles: He Can Do Anything." *Newsweek,* August 22,
    1955: 20.
"Answering Back." *Newsweek,* October 13, 1952: 33.
Begeman, Jean. "Nixon: How the Press Suppressed the News." *New
    Republic,* October 6, 1952: 11–13.
"Behind Nixon's Speech." *Newsweek,* October 6, 1952: 24–25.
"Behind the Scenes: Ike and the Talbott Affair." *Newsweek,* August 8,
    1955: 20.
Bendiner, Robert. "The FCC—Who Will Regulate the Regulators?" *Re-
    porter,* September 19, 1957: 26–30.
"Case of Nerves." *Broadcasting—Telecasting,* December 2, 1957: 106.
Cater, Douglas. "The ABC of Dixon-Yates, or, How To Get Less for
    More." *Reporter,* October 21, 1954: 13–16.
Clapp, Gordon R. "Dixon-Yates Deal." *Nation,* October 2, 1954: 286–87.
"A Conflict of Interest." *Commonweal,* January 25, 1957: 422.
"Conflict of Interest." *Time,* November 14, 1955: 106.
"The Corruption Issue: A Pandora's Box." *Time,* September 24, 1956:
    14–15.
"Curtain for Mr. Roberts." *Time,* April 6, 1953: 30.
"Cyclone Over Kansas." *Newsweek,* February 23, 1953: 29.

Davis, Kenneth S. "Chairman Roberts Leaves the Crusade." *New Repub-
lic,* April 6, 1953: 7–8.
———. "The Press and Wesley Roberts." *New Republic,* March 23, 1953:
9–12.
"The Day It Got Hot at Burning Tree." *New Republic,* July 11, 1955: 3.
"The Defense of Checkers." *Commonweal,* October 10, 1952: 3–4.
"Dimout." *Newsweek,* July 11, 1955: 27.
"Dirty Business." *New Republic,* March 3, 1958: 3–5.
"Dixon-Yates Push." *Newsweek,* June 27, 1955: 24.
"The Dixon-Yates Row Was a TVA Diversion." *Saturday Evening Post,*
December 11, 1954: 10.
"Doerfer's Resignation." *New Republic,* March 21, 1960: 6.
"Doggone Gifted." *New Republic,* October 13, 1952: 2.
"Ed and Mr. Mansure." *Time,* February 20, 1956: 16.
"The End of Dixon-Yates?" *Time,* July 11, 1955: 15–16.
"The End of the Talbott Story." *U.S. News and World Report,* August
12, 1955: 72.
"Exit Adams." *Time,* September 29, 1958: 12–13.
"Exit Under Fire." *Newsweek,* February 25, 1957: 38.
"Extra! Extra!" *New Republic,* March 30, 1953: 6.
"The Failure To Lead on Moral Issues." *Democratic Digest,* April, 1960:
8.
Fairfield, William S. "Dr. Schwartz Goes to Washington." *Reporter,*
March 20, 1958: 24–28.
"Favors Were a Mistake." *Business Week,* June 21, 1958: 34, 36.
"The First President Got the First Present." *U.S. News and World Report,*
June 27, 1958: 41–43.
"Front-Page Name." *Newsweek,* August 1, 1955: 74.
Furlong, William Barry. "The Senate's Wizard of Ooze: Dirksen of Illi-
nois." *Harpers,* December, 1959: 45.
Goodman, Walter. "About Face on Dixon-Yates." *New Republic,* July 18,
1955: 6–8.
———. "The Innocence of the Executive-on-Loan." *New Republic,*
September 19, 1955: 9.
"The Great Free Lunch Inquiry." *Broadcasting—Telecasting,* October 14,
1957: 130.
"Hail and Fancy Farewell." *Time,* August 22, 1955: 18–19.
Halsey, Margaret. "Beware the Tender Trap." *New Republic,* January 13,
1958: 7–9.
Hard, William. "Washington's Big Brawl: Dixon-Yates." *Reader's Digest,*
April, 1955: 17–22.
"Hear No Evil, See No Evil, Speak No Evil." *New Republic,* September
13, 1954: 3–4.
"Ike's Dilemma." *Newsweek,* September 29, 1952: 23–25.
"Ike Should Cancel Dixon-Yates Contract." *Time,* November 22, 1954: 39.
"Investigations: You Are To Be Pitied." *Time,* March 10, 1958: 16.
"An Issue of Principle." *Nation,* October 4, 1952: 287–89.
"It Is More Blessed." *Newsweek,* November 11, 1957: 40–45.
"It's Christmas All the Time For U.S. Presidents." *U.S. News and World
Report,* December 16, 1955: 39–41.

Jaffe, Louis L. "The Scandal in TV Licensing." *Harpers,* September, 1957: 77–79, 82, 84.

Johnsen, Katherine. "Information Shroud Irks House Unit." *Aviation Week,* November 19, 1956: 30–31.

———. "Moss Probe Would Abolish OSI, Says Ross Confused in His Job." *Aviation Week,* July 30, 1956: 30–31.

Johnson, Gerald W. "Morals for Gentlemen." *New Republic,* August 15, 1955: 16.

"Just Plain Dick." *Variety,* October 1, 1952: 101.

Kenworthy, E. W. "Dixon-Yates: The Riddle of a Self-Inflicted Wound." *Reporter,* January 26, 1956: 19–25.

Knebel, Fletcher. "Ike's Cronies." *Look,* June 1, 1954: 57–61.

——— and Wilson, Jack. "The Scandalous Years." *Look,* May 22, 1951: 31–37.

"The Little Mansures." *Fortune,* April, 1956: 108.

"The Lost Rule." *Nation,* February 22, 1958: 149.

"Lo, the Investigator." *Time,* February 24, 1958: 14–15.

"Mack's Exit Just Starts the Story." *Business Week,* March 8, 1958: 28–29.

"Mamie and the Fur Trade." *Time,* November 11, 1957: 26.

May, Roland W. "The FCC Inquiry." *Nation,* February 15, 1958: 138–40.

McGill, Ralph. "There Was a One-Party Press in the Talbott Scandal." *Democratic Digest,* October, 1955: 16–17.

McMillin, Miles. "Congress and the FCC Shenanigans." *Progressive,* April, 1958: 12–15.

"Meet Dixon and Yates." *Life,* November 8, 1954: 34–35.

"The Mess Is in Us." *Christian Century,* October 8, 1952: 1149–51.

"Mitchell's Charges." *America,* September 4, 1954: 530.

"More Furor Over Influence: What Adams Case Stirred Up." *U.S. News and World Report,* July 4, 1958: 49–54.

"The Nation." *Time,* June 23, 1958: 11–13.

Nixon, Richard. "My Side of the Story." *Vital Speeches,* October 15, 1952: 11–15.

"Not Much News in Los Angeles." *New Republic,* September 29, 1952: 8.

"Off to a Fast Start." *New Republic,* November 15, 1954: 3.

"Once It Was Freezers and Mink Coats; Now—." *U.S. News and World Report,* November 8, 1957: 50–53.

"The Ordeal of Sherman Adams." *Newsweek,* July 21, 1958: 17–19.

"Our Archaic Laws on Conflict of Interest." *New Republic,* September 12, 1955: 8.

"Oversight?" *Newsweek,* February 3, 1958: 22, 27.

"The Pentagon: With Uncommon Speed." *Newsweek,* October 28, 1963: 22.

"The President." *Facts on File Yearbook,* March 10, 1960: 87–88.

"The President: 'I Will Decide.'" *U.S. News and World Report,* August 5, 1955: 99.

"Remarks of General Eisenhower at Wheeling, W. Va." *U.S. News and World Report,* October 3, 1952: 72.

"Remarks of Senator Nixon at Wheeling, W. Va." *U.S. News and World Report,* October 3, 1952: 72, 74.

"The Reporter's Notes." *Reporter,* February 20, 1958: 2, 4.

"The Reporter's Notes." *Reporter,* July 10, 1958: 3.

"Republicans." *Time,* September 29, 1952: 11–13.

"Return Engagement." *Reporter,* August 11, 1955: 4.

"Richard Nixon's Secret Income." *New Republic,* September 29, 1952: 1–11, 17.

Rogers, Lindsay. "Professor-at-Large." *Reporter,* April 16, 1959: 42–44.

Sevareid, Eric. "Progress Is Getting Out of Hand." *New Republic,* December 19, 1955: 5.

"The Shape of Things." *Nation,* October 11, 1952: 313.

Sinclair, Upton. "Hillbilly Ike." *California Liberal,* January, 1960: 3.

"Sir Mordred." *New Republic,* September 29, 1952: 5–6.

"Sluice and Bobble." *Time,* June 27, 1955: 15–16.

"Smeared and Cleared." *Fortune,* June, 1956: 49.

Solow, Herbert. "GSA: Washington's Most Durable Mess." *Fortune,* August, 1955: 76–77, 182, 185–86, 188.

———. "The Struggle for Nicaro." *Fortune,* April, 1952: 97–98, 220, 222, 224.

———. "Who's Going To Clean up Nicaro?" *Fortune,* June, 1953: 108, 246, 248–49.

"Star Crossed." *Time,* December 5, 1955: 23–24.

Steele, John L. "How the Pros Shot Sherm Adams Down." *Life,* September 29, 1958: 28.

"Step Down." *Newsweek,* March 10, 1958: 37–38.

"Storm in Kansas." *Time,* March 30, 1953: 18.

"Stormy Weather." *Newsweek,* March 21, 1960: 41–42.

Straight, Michael. "Dear Stub . . . Signed Dwight." *New Republic,* December 27, 1954: 13–15.

———. "More Light on Dixon-Yates." *New Republic,* October 18, 1954: 6–11.

———. "New Light on Dixon-Yates." *New Republic,* October 11, 1954: 8–10.

Strout, Richard L. "Tom Stokes and Sherman Adams." *New Republic,* July 7, 1958: 10–12.

"Sunset Cruise." *Time,* March 21, 1960: 15.

"Talbott Business Connection Questioned." *Aviation Week,* July 25, 1955: 13–14.

"Talbott's Mulligan Stew." *Life,* August 1, 1955: 75.

"The Teapot (Dome?) Tempest." *Nation,* June 28, 1958: 573.

"Texas Gulf Suit Opens New Door for SEC." *Business Week,* April 24, 1965: 24–25.

"Time Bomb." *Time,* October 6, 1952: 70, 73.

"To the President With Very Best Wishes." *Newsweek,* December 12, 1955: 34–35.

T.R.B. "Consider the Facts." *New Republic,* June 30, 1958: 2.

———. "Correspondence." *New Republic,* April 7, 1958: 24.

———. "Innocence Abroad." *New Republic,* June 23, 1958: 2.

———. "Power in the Palace." *New Republic,* October 6, 1958: 2.

———. "Washington Wire." *New Republic,* December 19, 1955: 2.

———. "Washington Wire." *New Republic,* February 24, 1958: 2.

———. "Washington Wire." *New Republic,* March 10, 1958: 2.

"Turbulent Wake." *Newsweek,* November 4, 1963: 27.

"Two Men in the White House: The Heat's On." *Newsweek*, June 30, 1958: 15–19.
"Uncle Sam's Landlord." *Time*, June 28, 1954: 18.
"The Unknockables." *Esquire*, June, 1966: 84–85.
"The Unlovable Counsel." *Time*, February 17, 1958: 26.
"Wall Street: A Sulphurous Scandal." *Newsweek*, May 3, 1965: 69–70.
"Wall Street: On the Inside Track." *Time*, April 30, 1965: 96, 98.
"Washington Front." *America*, August 6, 1955: 445.
Welles, Chris. "Bonanza Trouble." *Life*, August 6, 1965: 29–34.
"What Senator Nixon Said." *U.S. News and World Report*, October 3, 1952: 61.
"Why Government Jobs Go Begging." *Business Week*, August 10, 1957: 156.
"Why Men Hate To Leave Home." *Business Week*, August 10, 1959: 36.
Wilson, George C. "McClellan To Press Korth Conflict Probe." *Aviation Week and Space Technology*, October 21, 1963: 26–27.
———. "Senate Probes Scrutinize Korth Letters." *Aviation Week and Space Technology*, October 28, 1963: 22–24.
"A Wise Decision." *Newsweek*, April 6, 1953: 28.

BOOKS

Abels, Jules. *The Truman Scandals*. Chicago: Henry Regnery Company, 1956.
Adams, Sherman. *First-Hand Report: The Story of the Eisenhower Administration*. New York: Harper and Brothers, 1961.
The American College Dictionary. New York: Random House, 1962.
The Association of the Bar of the City of New York. *Conflict of Interest and Federal Service*. Cambridge: Harvard University Press, 1960.
Benham, Sir Gurney. *Benham's Book of Quotations*. London: George G. Harrap and Company, Ltd., 1948.
Bolles, Blair. *How To Get Rich in Washington*. New York: W. W. Norton and Co., Inc., 1952.
Corwin, Edward S. *The President: Office and Power*. New York: New York University Press, 1957.
Costello, William. *The Facts About Nixon: An Unauthorized Biography*. New York: The Viking Press, 1960.
Eisenhower, Dwight D. *Crusade in Europe*. Garden City, New York: Doubleday and Company, Inc., 1948.
———. *The White House Years: Mandate for Change, 1953–1956*. Garden City, New York: Doubleday and Company, Inc., 1963.
———. *The White House Years: Waging Peace*. Garden City, New York: Doubleday and Company, Inc., 1965.
Hughes, Emmet John. *The Ordeal of Power: A Political Memoir of the Eisenhower Years*. New York: Atheneum, 1963.
Kant, Immanuel. *Fundamental Principles of the Metaphysic of Morals*. New York: The Library of Liberal Arts, 1949.
Manning, Bayless. *Federal Conflict of Interest Law*. Cambridge: Harvard University Press, 1964.
Mazo, Earl. *Richard Nixon: A Political and Personal Portrait*. New York: Harper and Brothers, 1959.

Miller, William Lee. *Piety Along the Potomac.* Boston: Houghton Mifflin Company, 1964.

Nixon, Richard. *Six Crises.* New York: Pocket Books, Inc., 1962.

Rossiter, Clinton. *The American Presidency.* New York: Harcourt, Brace and World, Inc., 1960.

Schlesinger, Arthur, Jr. *Kennedy or Nixon: Does It Make Any Difference?* New York: The Macmillan Company, 1960.

Schwartz, Bernard. *The Professor and the Commissions.* New York: Alfred A. Knopf, 1959.

Steinberg, Alfred. *The Man From Missouri.* New York: G. P. Putnam's Sons, 1962.

Tocqueville, Alexis de. *Democracy in America.* New York: J. & H. G. Langley, 1843.

NEWSPAPERS

The Benton (Ill.) *Evening News.*
Chicago Daily Tribune.
Daily Egyptian [Southern Illinois University].
The Harrisburg (Ill.) *Daily Register.*
Kansas City Star.
New York Herald Tribune.
The New York Times.
New York World Telegram and Sun.
St. Louis Post-Dispatch.
The Tulsa Tribune.
Wall Street Journal.
The Washington Post.
The Washington Star.

INDEX

Adams, John Quincy, 207
Adams, Sherman: defended by Eisenhower, 11, 12, 14, 16, 19, 189, 190; contact with CAB, 12, 13; letters to Murray Chotiner, 12, 13, 14; gifts from Goldfine, 15, 16, 17, 20, 23, 24; defended by Hagerty, 16, 19, 20, 23; letter to Harris subcommittee, 16, 20; contact with FTC and SEC, 16, 17, 18, 21, 22, 23, 24, 25; personality, 18, 19, 198, 199; compared to Truman cases, 19, 24; political reaction, 21, 189, 190, 195–202 *passim;* testifies before Harris subcommittee, 22, 23, 24, 25; Dixon-Yates case, 74, 74*n;* Talbott case, 83; Cross case, 112, 113; Mansure case, 116, 120, 121; newspaper coverage, 190, 199; Raylaine case, 190, 191, 192; Armed Services Subcommittee report, 192; testimony of John Fox, 193, 194; television appearance, 195, 196; resigns, 195; defends action, 196; resignation accepted, 200; President's gift to Adams, 200; mentioned, 187, 216*n*
Alcorn, Meade, 171, 200, 201
Allen, George E., 134, 211
Allen, Thomas H., 69
America, 88
Americans for Democratic Action, 52
Ames v. Board of Education, 141
Ancient Order of United Workmen, 42–50 *passim*
Andar Incorporated, 167, 168, 169
Anderson, Clinton, 70
Anderson, Jack, 151, 152, 194
Anderson, Robert, 163, 164, 165, 166
Anderson, Webster, 144
Appalachian Company, 136

Armstrong, J. Sinclair, 74
Army-McCarthy hearings, 160
Arn, Edward, 44, 45, 46, 49
Arrowsmith, Marvin, 58
Atkinson, Nancy, 218
Atomic Energy Act of 1946, 57
Atomic Energy Commission, 55–60 *passim,* 70, 71, 74, 75
Augean Stables, 197
Austin, Rosewell M., 191
Avco Manufacturing Corporation, 80, 81

Baker, George, 151, 162
Baker, Newton, 86
Baker, Ray Stannard, 210
Baldwin-Lima-Hamilton Corporation, 80
Balmer, William, 116, 118, 124, 125
Balmer and Moore, 119, 124
Barber, Earl, 152
Bard, Robert C., 191
Bare, Robert O., 141, 142, 143, 144
Bartlett, Charles, 76, 78
Bartley, Robert T., 146
Baruch, Bernard, 204
Begeman, Jean, 29
Bender, George H., 81, 104
Bennett, David, 7
Bennett, Edgar, 42, 43, 47, 48
Bennett, John B., 182
Bergerman, Milton, 135
Blair, William, 154, 186
Boeing Aircraft, 215
Bolling Air Force Base, 84
Boston Port Development Corporation, 18, 193
Boyd, McDill, 46

DATE DUE

DEMCO 38-297